KEYNES ON POPULATION

Keynes on
Population

JOHN TOYE

OXFORD
UNIVERSITY PRESS

OXFORD

UNIVERSITY PRESS

Great Clarendon Street, Oxford OX2 6DP

Oxford University Press is a department of the University of Oxford.
It furthers the University's objective of excellence in research, scholarship,
and education by publishing worldwide in

Oxford New York

Athens Auckland Bangkok Bogotá Buenos Aires Calcutta
Cape Town Chennai Dar es Salaam Delhi Florence Hong Kong Istanbul
Karachi Kuala Lumpur Madrid Melbourne Mexico City Mumbai
Nairobi Paris São Paulo Singapore Taipei Tokyo Toronto Warsaw

and associated companies in Berlin Ibadan

Oxford is a registered trade mark of Oxford University Press
in the UK and certain other countries

Published in the United States
by Oxford University Press Inc., New York

British Library Cataloguing in Publication Data

Data available

Library of Congress Cataloging in Publication Data
Toye, J. F. J.
Keynes on population / John Toye.
p. cm.
Includes bibliographical references.
1. Keynes, John Maynard, 1883–1946—Views on population.
2. Population—Economic aspects. I. Title.
HB103.K47 T69 2000   304.6—dc21   00-022358
ISBN 0–19–829362–3

1 3 5 7 9 10 8 6 4 2

Typeset by Best-set Typesetter Ltd., Hong Kong
T.J. International Ltd, Padstow, Cornwall

To Professor Sir Hans Singer

for his inspiration

Preface and Acknowledgements

My research into John Maynard Keynes's opinions on population and economic development has been something of a labour of love. Like love, it has brought me frustration, surprises, hours of silent puzzlement, silly misunderstandings, and moments of unexpected delight. Many people thought that my time and energies would have been much better channelled in quite different directions. I persisted, some might say stubbornly, but in truth sometimes against my own better judgement. Now the time has come to allow others to inspect the fruit of this strange passion for an episode in the history of economic ideas.

Many people have assisted me in the task of preparing Keynes's manuscript on 'Population' for publication. The Provost and Scholars of King's College, Cambridge, the owners of the copyright, gave permission for its use. The Modern Archivist, Jacqueline Cox, helped and advised me in many ways, including sending me a copy of her excellent account of the history of Keynes's papers.

Richard Toye has been a tower of strength throughout. He provided me with copies of important archive documents and a variety of valuable references, as a by-product of his own research. He also read through the penultimate draft in its entirety, advising me on problems of shape and structure. For this assistance, and for his constant interest and encouragement, I am greatly indebted to him. Donald Winch read an early draft of Chapters 1 to 4, and made some very astute criticisms, shared his scholarship with me, and gave me invaluable guidance at a vital stage in the research process. Special thanks are also owed to Diane Frazer-Smith, who amazingly identified the name 'Haffkine' for me in the manuscript of 'Population' on the basis of her school days in India, and who provided much valuable secretarial assistance in the first stages of research and writing. The Institute of Development Studies generously permitted me sabbatical leave in 1997 during which the bulk of the writing was done.

I have received valuable advice on useful references and/or copies of relevant material from Anne Booth, Robert Griffith-Jones, Matthew Lockwood, Murray Milgate, Brian Reddaway, Hans Singer, Tony Thirlwall, Tom Tomlinson, Janet Toye, and Nicholas von Tunzelmann. One of the pleasantest aspects of the writing of this book has been the stimulating conversations I have had about it with Kaushik Basu, Michael Dale, Tim Dyson, James Galbraith, Geoff Harcourt, Heather Joshi, Amartya Sen, Sheila Smith, and Adrian Wood.

My first published attempt to grapple with this subject was an article in the *Cambridge Journal of Economics*, vol. 21, no. 1. It greatly benefited from the comments of two anonymous referees. I am grateful to the publishers of the article, Oxford University Press, for permission to draw on some of its contents for the purposes of this book.

Quotations from Keynes's writings are of three kinds. Extracts from the *Collected Writings* are indicated in the text by the letters *CW*, followed by volume and page numbers. Quotations that are not in the *Collected Writings*, but are to be found in the Keynes Papers in the King's College Library Modern Archive, are indicated by the relevant Archive classification number. This is sufficient for identification and retrieval. Finally, some Keynes letters in the Stopes Collection of the British Museum have been identified by the BM classification code.

Archive material from the Beveridge Papers, in the Library of the London School of Economics and Political Science, is indicated by the letters BEV, followed by the relevant classification number.

Contents

Contents

Contents

Introduction

This is a book, one more book in the great torrent of books, about John Maynard Keynes, the world-famous economist and one of the most talented people of his generation. J. M. Keynes was born in Cambridge in 1883, the eldest child of John Neville Keynes, a Cambridge University Lecturer in economics and, later, its senior administrative officer, and his wife, Florence Ada Keynes, who herself became in middle life the Mayor of Cambridge. He was educated first at preparatory school in Cambridge and then at England's most famous public school, Eton College, where he did well and was a popular pupil. In 1902, he entered King's College, Cambridge as an undergraduate. He read Mathematics and took a first-class degree in 1905, although without being at the top of the list.

During this period, he was much influenced by being a member of the society known as the Apostles. Some say that he adopted their view that the pursuit of truth is the supreme object of life. He also established lifelong relationships with, among others, Lytton Strachey, Leonard Woolf, Clive Bell, and the two Stephen sisters, Vanessa and Virginia, all of whom later formed the core of the artistic community known as the Bloomsbury Group.

Keynes was originally a mathematician and a philosopher, but after graduation he took up the study of economics under the guidance of the leading English economist of the day, Alfred Marshall. He decided against taking the Economics Tripos, preferring to do the Civil Service entrance examination. Coming second on the list, he missed a post at the Treasury, and instead served as a Clerk in the India Office from 1906 to 1908. He found the work undemanding, but had time to read extensively about the administrative mechanisms by which the British government controlled the activities of the imperial government of India. He also took the opportunity to work on his *Treatise on Probability*, which was submitted for a Prize Fellowship at King's, failing in 1908, but succeeding the following year. He had already decided to resign from the India Office and return to Cambridge to lecture on economics. The brief India Office experience moulded his outlook in various ways.

The five years until 1914 were Keynes's initiation into the life of a Cambridge don. They were filled with the writing of lectures, the supervision of students, the assumption of the editorship of the *Economic Journal*, external examining, and enthusiastic participation in the lively social life of a university town. In 1912–13, he wrote and had published his first book on economics, *Indian Currency and Finance*. In this, he combined institutional knowledge gained at the India Office with a clear grasp of monetary theory to advocate a gold exchange standard for India. The book won him a seat on a Royal Commission investigating this subject, whose report endorsed his own arguments. Success indeed for a young man of thirty! This was the point in Keynes's life and career that he wrote the lecture on 'Population' which is reproduced in this volume.

Soon after the outbreak of the First World War, Keynes joined the Treasury as a temporary civil servant. In this capacity, he dealt with loans to Britain's allies, and with the control of foreign exchange expenditure, winning official recognition of his financial skills. At the end of the war, he went as the Chancellor of the Exchequer's deputy to the Paris Peace Conference, where he was engaged on the question of German war reparations. He formed the view that the Allied attempts to exact huge sums from Germany were wicked and misguided, so he resigned from the Treasury in June 1919 and then wrote a passionate indictment of the Paris peace terms in *The Economic Consequences of the Peace*.

It was this book, with its eloquent idealism and its critical portraits of the leading Allied statesmen, that put him on the world stage.

For the next two decades, Keynes returned to academic life in Cambridge. However, he combined this with an enormous range of other interests, including economic journalism, business, public affairs, the arts, and eventually farming. Despite all these additional activities, he planned and wrote a number of books on monetary economics, including *A Treatise on Money*, and contributed to the public debate on the causes of and possible cures for Britain's high unemployment. Both of these strands were interwoven in his greatest intellectual achievement, *The General Theory of Employment, Money and Interest*, published in 1936. It is on this book, above all else, that his enduring fame rests.

Its revolutionary contribution to economics was the virtual creation of the subject that is now called macroeconomics. Beginning from Marshall's version of the quantity theory of money, Keynes and his collaborators developed the concept of a monetary production economy. In such an economy, money itself is treated as one asset among others, and one that has a non-neutral impact on the process of capital accumulation. He showed that, under these assumptions, it was possible for involuntary unemployment to occur as a result of a lack of effective aggregate demand. This contradicted the prevailing view that involuntary unemployment would be eliminated by downward price adjustment in the labour market.

The final phase of his life (1937–46) was overshadowed by ill-health and the pressures of the Second World War. In 1940, he returned to the Treasury in an advisory role. He worked on problems of domestic war finance and the design of new international financial institutions, including the International Monetary Fund and the World Bank. Their purpose was to replace the international economic anarchy of the inter-war years with something more rational and conducive to peace. He did not live to see the results. He died prematurely, exhausted by the labour of securing for Britain a large post-war loan from the United States.

Such, in brief compass, was Keynes's life. Sketching it out may serve two purposes. Some readers will be newcomers to Keynes's story, and will need to be introduced first of all to its main outlines, even in such a summary manner as the above. Many others will be very familiar with it, and for them it is placed first for another reason. It is there to give the right perspective to what follows. Keynes's high achievements should never be forgotten. At all times, they should be kept in the forefront of our minds. He scaled great heights both in economic theory and in economic policy, and also by bringing theory and policy more closely together. For this, he will always deserve the admiration and gratitude of posterity. It is important to say this here, because this book's purpose is not to recount once again the details of his great triumphs. They can easily be found elsewhere, especially in two recent substantial and excellent biographies (Skidelsky, 1983, 1992; Moggridge, 1992).

In contrast, this book shows another aspect of Keynes, one that redounds less to his glory. The telling of this other story is not intended to make it *the* story about him. There is no intention, even if it were possible, to deny what already stands to his eternal credit, or to snatch away the laurels long since won. What follows is one extra strand in the whole story of Keynes's personality and thought, and one that has been little remarked on. That is the justification for adding one small book to the great library of books on Keynes, namely, that it says something additional, and something not altogether familiar, even to those who have studied Keynes with great care.

My first attempt to tackle the subject of Keynes and population, made in an article published in 1997, caused a passing storm. The article received extensive national newspaper coverage, not only in Britain, but also, to my knowledge, in the US, India, Italy, and Austria. The news was that I had said that Keynes was racially prejudiced. The newspaper comment on this was mixed, but

generally critical. On the one hand, there was outrage that I
dared to say such a thing about a cultural icon like Keynes. It was
taken as a kind of secular blasphemy. On the other hand, there
were elaborate expressions of indifference. Everybody knew this
already, and, even if they did not, it was hardly a surprise since
in those days everybody who was anybody was racially prejudiced. I mention these reactions so that readers can consider
them as they read Keynes's own words, and my commentary on
them.

In the journalistic imagination, my article became an attempt
to destroy Keynes's reputation. To the contrary, far from being
an enemy of his reputation, I have in the past publicly defended
it. My long-standing interest in Keynes was revived when he
became the object of strident criticism by monetarist economists
in the 1970s. There was then a concerted, and none too subtle,
campaign to overthrow his posthumous influence. The main
thrust was to demolish his macroeconomics. Harry Johnson also
led a diversionary skirmish in the area of development economics, complaining bitterly of Keynes's malign influence over the
economic policies of governments in developing countries. Since
it was not clear to me how Keynesian policies could be applied
to development strategies, except as austerity policies to permit
capital accumulation, Johnson's accusations seemed well off
target and more the product of bile than clear reasoning, and
therefore in need of some correction. In making these correc-
tions in chapter 2 of my *Dilemmas of Development* (Toye, 1993), I
became a defender of Keynes's reputation, at least to the extent
of maintaining that he had done no harm to poor countries'
prospects of economic development. To the suggestion that
Keynes had deluded the leaders of newly independent countries
with his 'collectivist' thinking, I replied that Keynes had in the
1920s provided an excellent early critique of Soviet economic
policies and planning and sustained it in the 1930s, despite his
own movement in favour of more protection and more state
control of investment in the mixed economy. His advocacy of

multilateral trade and payments in the 1940s was also generally helpful to the prospects of world development.

I then embarked on a broader and more comprehensive study on Keynes's views on the political economy of development. The purpose of my research, desultory at first but more systematic once I had more time available for it, was to go beyond existing treatments, and then to show how his thoughts on development could be brought to bear on the interpretation of his life and thought as a whole.

On the latter point, I have reached two firm, if negative, conclusions. The first is that little validity attaches to the claim that

it is possible to draw from the writings of John Maynard Keynes, without artificiality, a logically coherent and embracing structure of ideas, based upon a single vision, which permeated all aspects of his thought and which, except for one major and identifiable change, was constant through time. (Fitzgibbons, 1988: 1)

There is an artificiality at the very heart of the method by which such constancy conclusions are advanced. The reader is drawn into assuming what has to be proved, and quotations are treated as if they were indeed no more than individual coloured threads in a single tapestry of thought. The specific contexts which give the quotations their original meaning are allowed to fall out of sight, and, lacking contexts, words can be selected and woven into a tapestry of vision that shows a single pattern. My story of Keynes and population has an entirely different thrust. Its theme is change, not constancy, and the abandoning of intellectual positions under the impact both of momentous events, particularly the First World War, and defeat in debate by a man of lesser genius.

The second negative conclusion is to find against the Whig interpretation of Keynes as an economist, one that sees *The General Theory* as the *telos* of his professional endeavours and interprets everything he did before that either as an anticipatory step, or else as irrelevant. Keynes himself gave more than a little colour to this interpretation, and has been followed in it by many subsequent commentators. I want to follow the path less travelled, to tell the story of the brilliant young economist who committed himself to a nineteenth-century framework of economic thought, and stayed with it for nearly twenty years, despite his inability to make anything out of it, and despite the scepticism from colleagues that it brought him.

In this publication, I concentrate attention on Keynes's views on population and the terms of trade, and their relation both to each other and to economic development. His changing views on population have been a neglected topic in the literature, because they fit so ill with the Whig interpretation. Since his death, only Rostow (1960/1953: 184–93) and Petersen (1964: 46–71) have attempted surveys of Keynes on population. However, scholarly as they were, both Rostow's and Petersen's surveys have now become outdated. Through the great efforts of archivists, editors, and biographers, much more material on Keynes has become available to researchers. On the subject of population, too, the old account needs to be brought up to date with the help of new documents. The most important of these are Keynes's unpublished lectures of 1912 and his 1914 manuscript entitled 'Population'. Both Rostow's and Petersen's surveys strongly suggest that these authors were unaware of their existence. Their availability allows us now to make a much richer and more coherent exploration of the content of Keynes's early neo-Malthusianism.

The existence in the King's College Modern Archive of a manuscript of a lecture written by Keynes on 'Population' is not especially widely known. Technically, it was first published on microfilm in 1993. It has not been available before now in book form. The absence of this lecture from *The Collected Writings of John Maynard Keynes* seemed to me to be unfortunate, and possibly one cause of the general lack of interest in, and misconceptions about, the questions that interested me. As far as I could see, but contrary to received opinion, this manuscript was the source of a number of Keynes's later writings on the subject of population, writings which could not be fully understood without an appreciation of its contents. In Chapter 2 I have set out the reasons why I believe this manuscript merits publication alongside the *Collected Writings* and the text of 'Population' itself is presented as an appendix to that chapter. I am reasonably confident that I have now established the correct reading of the manuscript, although the possibility of remaining errors cannot be wholly excluded.

Since the manuscript itself has no footnotes, there are a number of quotations for which the source has to be verified, and a large number of textual references which need to be clarified for the modern reader. The latter are unusually wide-ranging. They include references or allusions to eighteenth-century writings on social utopias and population, to the attitudes of nineteenth-century economists to contraception, to anti-neo-Malthusian writings in Europe in the early twentieth century, and to pre-1914 social conditions in India, Egypt, and China. This diversity, itself a reflection of Keynes's very broad intellectual reach, posed a problem. Full explanations presented in note form would have greatly over-burdened the original text. So, as an alternative, I decided to produce, in Chapter 3, my own commentary on 'Population' that tries to elucidate all those matters which would otherwise have been the subject of lengthy notes. By highlighting phrases from the manuscript in bold type, the text in Chapter 2 has been cross-referenced with the commentary in Chapter 3. Shorter notes have been placed at the end of the appendix to Chapter 2.

Chapter 5 locates 'Population' within the context of Keynes's championship of neo-Malthusianism, his part in the campaign for legalized birth control, his ultimate recantation of neo-Malthusian population doctrines, and the link between Malthusian and Keynesian doctrines of deficient demand. In particular, the text of 'Population' is there related to his 1933 essay on Malthus, to chapter 2 of *The Economic Consequences of the Peace*, his 1923–4 debate with Beveridge, and his unsatisfactory relationship with Marie Stopes. I use the hitherto unpublished letters exchanged between Keynes and Marie Stopes to shed light on the nature of Keynes's political involvement with the various pro-birth-control campaigns of the 1920s. Understanding this political dimension of his population work gives an important clue to explaining the phases of his subsequent recantation of neo-Malthusianism. This aspect is also absent from Petersen's survey, which treats the whole matter as if it were one purely of academic discourse on the problem of optimum population. Such an approach misses the great shift in Keynes's perspective, from academic discourse to activist persuasion, that resulted from his experience of the First World War (O'Donnell, 1992: 770). How and why he finally abandoned his former views on population in the 1930s is also documented and explained. The controversy around whether Malthus in some way anticipated the *General Theory* is also considered.

Chapter 6 brings the story to a convenient conclusion by considering two episodes from the 1940s. Partly from a mistaken view of the speed of population decline and partly from the exigencies of the politics of war finance, Keynes finally moved into the pro-natalist orbit. He embraced the policy of universal family allowances after many years of opposing it. The argument, at least as old as Malthus, that pauperism would be encouraged, if social security systems took cognizance of family size proved to be no obstacle to his conversion. Thus his neo-Malthusianism became not only intellectually, but also practically, defunct.

The other episode of the 1940s is the demolition of the doctrine of the tendency for the terms of trade of manufactures to decline. It was certainly still alive in the thinking of such important junior members of Keynes's circle as Joan Robinson, Brian Reddaway, and James Meade in the first half of the decade. The basic framework of thinking that was inherited, through Keynes, from the nineteenth century had been challenged only rarely.

This was despite the fact that statistical attempts to verify it had been of the most casual kind. Soon after Keynes's death, confidence in this part of his intellectual edifice rapidly evaporated, as the new doctrine of the secular decline of the terms of trade of agriculture was propounded. It is to one of the two authors of this novel doctrine, Hans Singer, in gratitude for his inspiration and friendship, that this book is dedicated.

Such is the plan of this book. The bare outline cannot convey the range and interest of Keynes's discussions in 'Population', and the illumination that it brings not only to Keynes's other writings on the subject and on economics more generally, but also to current development thinking. Keynes also raises questions that have been or remain highly sensitive: sexuality in his time, and what I shall refer to as 'race discourse' in our own. One of the aspects of 'Population' that dismays me is the extent to which the young Keynes took a ruthless Social Darwinist line towards the populations of India, Egypt, and China, in clear distinction to the policies of education and economic improvement that he advocated for the British working class. To me, these contrasting attitudes can be explained only by imputing to Keynes a mind tainted by racial discrimination. To what extent was this merely a reflection of the outlook of his age, rather than something important in his own character?

That Keynes was not alone in his racial prejudices is quite true, as is made clear in Chapter 4. With the ebb of Christian belief and the advance of the would-be science of evolutionary biology, the opportunities for heavy prejudices to skate along on a thin layer of science were manifold, and frequently taken, not least by those writers who thought themselves to be in the very vanguard of social progress. Yet at all times, not excluding Edwardian England, there have been others who can spot a racial stereotype before it hits them in the face, and who have understood that discrimination on the basis of such stereotypes may be the source of a self-reinforcing spiral of mutual destruction. That Keynes was not of this party detracts, in my opinion, from his status as an intellectual hero and wise guardian of his age. There was some clay in the feet, after all.

What to do with this melancholy information? Some have cheerfully advised me to let sleeping dogs lie. In many ways, I was tempted to do just that. It would have been pleasanter for everyone, especially me, to have forgotten the whole enterprise and carried on as before, with Keynes's status as a cultural icon unchallenged. Does it matter who we regard as our heroes and heroines, provided that the virtues which we attribute to them, albeit mythically, are admirable? Some would say not.

It is possible to argue, on the other hand, that to stay silent would be to invest our knowledge of the presence of clay with too great a significance. Keynes's mature achievements are what they are. Why continue to deny that there were also blemishes? Let us ask what would have been Keynes's own wishes in the matter. He did not, like Cromwell, actually ask to be painted 'warts and all'. However, he did himself seem to feel it something of a personal obligation to tell the truth about the character of other people, as he saw it. Perhaps more importantly, in an early paper on 'Truth', he also wrote:

We cannot establish truth's paramount importance, and yet only by admitting it can we avoid chaos . . . It is impossible to know what ought to be omitted unless nothing is omitted. (quoted in Fitzgibbons, 1988: 61)

Would not that have been Keynes's own reply to any who might seek to 'protect' his reputation by discouraging the publication of an enquiry such as the one that follows?

I

Population and the Terms of Trade
from Malthus to Keynes

I. INTRODUCTION: THE CLASSICAL POLITICAL
ECONOMY MODEL

Today, diminishing returns to a fixed factor is seen to be a completely general result, which applies just as surely when capital is constant and combined with additional units of land and labour, as when land is constant and combined with additional units of capital and labour. By contrast, in the nineteenth century, land was taken to be the only factor of production whose supply was fixed, and this supposition was what justified the long-held distinction between agriculture (and mining) on the one hand and manufacturing industry on the other. This distinction led the great economic thinkers of that age to develop a problematic which included the expectation of declining terms of trade for industry. It was supposed that the price of agricultural (and mining) products would rise relative to the price of industrial products, as the unit costs of the former increased relative to the unit costs of the latter. This simple expectation is what I shall refer to here as the Cambridge doctrine of the terms of trade.[1]

Before examining how J. M. Keynes attempted to revive this doctrine, the historical background of the population/terms of trade nexus needs to be surveyed. It is illustrated by selections from the writings of Malthus, Ricardo, Torrens, John Stuart Mill, W. S. Jevons, and Alfred Marshall. This review suggests that the basic framework of ideas about the economics of agriculture and industry remained remarkably unchanged throughout the nineteenth century. However, the detailed manner of its treatment, including the degree of anxiety expressed by individual economists about the consequences of population growth, did vary quite considerably. Further, and without being too mechanical about it, one can suggest that these variations were much influenced by the ways in which the actual economic relations between England (or Europe) and America developed through the course of the century.

In the economic literature of the time, discussions of this relationship are often conducted in terms of a dualism of types of economy. On the one hand, certain economies are classified as 'old countries'. This type is defined by the available agricultural land being long settled, and population and capital stock being closely adjusted to the stock of natural resources. Other economies are classified as 'new countries', defined by the opposite, namely, that the process of agricultural settlement is incomplete, and capital is less than would be optimal given the available natural resources. The geographically vague terms 'Europe' and 'America' were often used to exemplify this dualism in a stylized way. British economists often substituted 'England' for 'Europe'.[2] The use of the term 'America' came after mid-century to encompass other lands of white settlement, such as Australia, New Zealand, and South Africa. At the same time, a separate literature, which is not discussed further in this book, grew up on the economics of the British Empire. This focused squarely on the new areas of British white settlement, and the issues of tariff reform and imperial confederation (Wood, 1983a).

In nineteenth-century English political economy, at least from the time of Malthus, the belief that ultimately the terms of trade of industrial manufactures relative to agricultural produce would decline was inextricably linked to the analysis of the sustainability of population growth. The link between the two was the doctrine of the tendency to diminishing returns in agriculture, while industry was subject to increasing returns. Throughout the century it was generally believed that agriculture (and mining) was essentially different from all other kinds of economic activity because both extension of the cultivated (or mined) area and the more intense cultivation (or deeper mining) of an existing unit of land were operations in which, *ceteris paribus*, increasing applications of labour and capital would necessarily produce diminishing returns. Agricultural (and mining) technology could improve, and any such improvements had the effect of offsetting cost increases due to diminishing returns. Industrial operations were believed, by contrast, to have no tendency at all to diminishing returns. Even in the absence of technical progress, it was said, scale expansion of manufacturing brought increasing returns. The critical point here is not so much the confusion of returns to a fixed factor with returns to scale, but the belief that the supply of land was absolutely fixed, at least in 'old countries', whereas the supply of population and capital were infinitely expandable.

Any economy whose main economic sectors operated under these different laws of returns was believed to face potentially serious welfare problems when the growth of its population was rapid. This was because the increment to population would be accommodated mainly by the expansion of employment in manufacturing. Thus, it would be vulnerable to a subsistence crisis when the price of basic needs, such as food and fuel, inevitably rose in terms of the price of manufactures. In that event, one of two things could happen. One was that the standard of living for the mass of the people would fail to rise above the existing very low subsistence level, and the excess population would fall prey to the positive checks of famine and disease. The other was that, if the effect of these positive checks were to be eased by the import of cheap food from abroad, or by emigration, these expedients could be only temporary. Ultimately, a crisis of immiserization was unavoidable. In short, economic growth based on the continuous expansion of manufacturing relative to agriculture and mining would prove to be unsustainable.

II. MALTHUS

Malthus put the doctrine of diminishing returns in agriculture as follows:

Man is necessarily confined in room. When acre has been added to acre till all the fertile land is occupied, the yearly increase in food must depend upon the amelioration of the land already in possession. This is a stream which, from the nature of all soils, instead of increasing, must be gradually diminishing . . . (Malthus, 1989/1803: i. 13)

By 1803, Malthus had raised the question of the balance between the agricultural and industrial sectors, suggesting that the latter had become disproportionately large. His fear that structural change in favour of the industrial sector was becoming unsustainable became one of the dominant themes of nineteenth-century political economy, and, as will be shown, lasted (at least in Cambridge) far into the twentieth century. In Malthus, the main concern was that population was growing so fast that the supply of the means of subsistence would not be able to keep pace, so intensifying existing positive checks to population growth. At the same time, however, Malthus did also recognize that the 'luxuries' that manufacturing industry produced could, if the poorest people developed a taste for them, be an incentive for prudential restraint of fertility and a strengthening of preventive checks at the expense of positive checks (Winch, 1996: 272–3). Thus, the growth-limiting effect of diminishing returns in agriculture could be moderated not only by improved methods of cultivation, but also by increasing the share of manufactured goods in the consumption basket of the mass of the people.

The idea of a balance between the two sectors of the national economy led Malthus to support the Corn Laws in order to protect agriculture. Others disputed Malthus's case for the need of a balance between agriculture and industry within the confines of the national economy. Why not, they asked, break the constraint on the supply of the means of subsistence by importing food, and then use the food to expand the population working in the manufacturing sector and reap the benefits of a consequent increase in the international division and specialization of labour? Why could not Britain enrich itself by importing more food and exporting more manufactures?

To this line of argument, Malthus offered the following reply:

It has been suggested . . . that Europe ought to grow its corn in America, and devote itself solely to manufactures and commerce, as the best sort of division of labour of the globe. But even on the extravagant supposition that the natural course of things might lead to such a division of labour for a time, and that by such means Europe could raise a population greater than its lands could possibly support, the consequences ought justly to be dreaded. It is an unquestionable truth that it must answer to every territorial state, in its natural progress to wealth, to manufacture for itself, unless the countries from which it had purchased its manufactures possess some advantages peculiar to them besides capital and skill. But when on this principle America began to withdraw its corn from Europe, and the agricultural exertions of Europe were inadequate to make up the deficiency, it would certainly be felt that the temporary advantages of a greater degree of wealth and population . . . had been very dearly purchased by a long period of retrograde movements and misery. (Malthus, 1989/1803: ii. 64–5)

Malthus is here asserting that ultimately the external terms of trade must turn against manufactures, so that countries which make themselves wholly dependent on production and export of manufactures will be more adversely affected by 'retrograde movements and misery' than those that retain, even by artificial means such as tariff protection, their own agricultural sector.

The import of food financed by the proceeds of the exports of manufactures was not the only possible method of sustaining a growing population in the face of diminishing returns to agriculture. Malthus also considered whether encouraging the out-migration of part of the population was an adequate remedy to the problem of redundant population. He argued that the conditions of survival in uncultivated parts of the globe were so arduous that those who had an incentive to emigrate would have great difficulty in settling there, and that inertia was such that even good opportunities (such as in America) might not be taken up. For these reasons he concluded that emigration was at best 'a very weak palliative' for over-population (ibid. i. 340–7). It did not, in his opinion, provide a satisfactory escape route from the dilemma of the disproportion between population and means of subsistence that he was presenting, any more than did a policy of increased reliance on imported food.

III. RICARDO AND TORRENS

Ricardo refined the doctrine of diminishing returns to agricultural investment. He argued that the extension of the cultivated area always required a move on to inferior soils, because the most fertile land would always be farmed first. Although labour productivity on the most fertile land might rise as a result of improvements in cultivation, any such rise was expected to be more than counter-balanced by the fall in output per worker occasioned by the move to ever more marginal soils.

Nevertheless, on the question of whether a policy of freely importing foreign corn was desirable under such circumstances, Ricardo took a position totally opposed to that of Malthus, although he shared the underlying analysis of diminishing returns in agriculture. He strongly supported the abolition of the Corn Laws that Malthus defended.[3] His optimism about the prosperity that Britain could achieve by reliance on imported food was quite remarkable in its day:

A rise in real wages is necessarily followed by a real fall in profits, and, therefore, when the land of a country is brought to the highest state of cultivation,—when more labour employed on it will not yield in return more food than what is necessary to support the labourer so employed, that country is come to the limit of its increase both of capital and population.

The richest country in Europe is yet far distant from that degree of improvement, but if any had arrived at it, by the aid of foreign commerce, even such a country could go on for an indefinite time increasing in wealth and population, for the only obstacle to this increase would be the scarcity, and consequent high value, of food and other raw produce. Let them be supplied from abroad in exchange for manufactured goods, and it is difficult to say where the limit is at which you would cease to accumulate wealth and to derive profit from its employment. (quoted in Eltis, 1984: 230)

The logical limit, given the model, is reached after world-wide diminishing returns have brought the entire globe to 'the highest state of cultivation', as Ricardo defined it. But, unlike Malthus, Mill, and Marshall, and oddly, given his own highly self-consistent method of economic thinking, Ricardo neglects to explore further this possibility. This is presumably because he considers that the decline in the international terms of trade of manufactures is too distant to be worth discussing.

For this reason, I would be inclined to give Ricardo an exceptional status. He was the least concerned about limits to growth among all those economists who believed that growth in already developed countries would, sooner or later, succumb to some kind of obstacle, or come up against some kind of ceiling.[4] Far from there being unanimity on this issue from Ricardo to Keynes, the latter, as we shall see, believed much more than the former that there was something problematic about the extent to which Britain relied on imported food.

Robert Torrens was the classical economist to whom W. W. Rostow traced the roots of the Keynes–Beveridge debate (Rostow 1960/1953: 185–6). In support of that derivation, Rostow quotes the following passages from Torrens's *Essay on the Production of Wealth* (1821). Torrens did not rely for his proof solely on the existence of diminishing returns in agriculture. He also believed that the scope for technical progress was greater in manufacturing than in agriculture. He argued that

even if the effective powers of appropriative and agricultural industry were to undergo no diminution, still, in the progress of wealth and population, the exchangeable value of wrought goods, as compared with raw produce, would gradually fall . . . every improvement in manufacturing industry, which enables material to be wrought up with the expenditure of a less quantity of subsistence, must . . . reduce the exchangeable value of manufactured goods, as compared with fruits of the soil . . . (ibid. 185 n. 2)

He extended this idea to international transactions by considering trade between an old and a new country, again in the context of population growth:

Now, as new countries advance in population, the cultivation of inferior soils must increase the cost of raising raw produce, and the division of labour reduce the expense of working it up. Hence, in all new settlements, the increasing value of raw produce must gradually check its exportation, and the falling value of wrought goods progressively prevent their importation . . . (ibid. 186 n. 2 cont.)

However, Torrens thought, like Ricardo, that 'centuries must roll away' before these problems would affect England's exchange of cheap manufactures for America's cheap food.

IV. JOHN STUART MILL

John Stuart Mill was more firmly in the tradition of Malthus on the issue of changing terms of trade. When, in his *Principles of Political Economy*, he came to discuss Malthus's principle of population, he acknowledged that Malthus had failed to consider the additional volume of subsistence goods which each increment to population makes possible. However, relying on the law that 'the produce of the land increases, *ceteris paribus*, in a diminished ratio', which he regarded as 'the most important proposition in political economy' (quoted in Hollander, 1985: i. 212), he also pointed out that 'It is vain to say that all mouths which the increase of mankind calls into existence bring their hands with them. The new mouths require as much food as the old ones, and the hands do not produce as much' (Mill, 1904/1848: 118). Thus Mill endorsed the idea of an optimum size of population. The progress of improvement in the agricultural sector could increase the size of the optimum, but if population surpasses the optimum that is validated by the state of agricultural technology, its reduction would raise the average level of welfare.

Mill also taught that, when population growth exceeds the current optimum, the terms of trade of manufactures against raw produce deteriorate. In book IV, chapter ii, Mill identified this as a corollary to his proposition that returns in agriculture tended to diminish:

The tendency, then, being to a perpetual increase in the productive power of labour in manufactures, while in agriculture and mining there is a conflict between two tendencies, the one towards an increase in productive power, the other towards a diminution of it, the cost of production being lessened by every improvement in the processes, and augmented by every addition to population; it follows that the exchange values of manufactured articles compared with the products of agriculture and of mines, have, as population and industry advance, a certain and decided tendency to fall. (ibid. 426)

This was true despite the fact that manufactures depend on raw materials that originate in the agricultural and mining sectors, both of which he took to be subject to the law of diminishing returns. The share of such raw materials in the total costs of manufactures was so small that the upward cost pressures of the law of diminishing returns would be 'much over-balanced by the diminution continually taking place in all the other elements; to which diminution it is impossible at present to assign any limit' (ibid.).

Following Malthus, Mill then examined two expedients by which a country might hope to mitigate the inability of its land to meet additional demands generated by population growth except on ever more onerous terms—food imports and emigration. He argued that the tendency of the exchange value of industrial products to fall affects not merely a country's internal terms of trade between industry and agriculture, but also the international exchange values of the products of industry and agriculture, where the existence of trade allows countries to specialize in one category of products or the other:

The law . . . of diminishing return to industry, whenever population makes a more rapid progress than improvement, is not solely applicable to countries which are fed from their own soil, but in substance applies just as much to those that are willing to draw their food from any accessible quarter that can afford it cheapest. (ibid. 121)

Mill does not warn against dependence on imported food as fiercely as Malthus had done. This may have been because he was writing in peacetime rather than during a war; or because he foresaw very great immediate (albeit still temporary) benefits that could be had if imported American maize replaced domestically grown wheat as the staple food of the poor; or for both reasons. He thought that imported food could create a breathing space from population pressure on the industrial terms of trade for 'some generations'.

On the expedient of emigration, Mill was also somewhat more sanguine than Malthus. Under certain conditions of proximity of the land to be colonized and willingness on the part of people to migrate, 'this remedy is completely effectual'. However, reality did not fulfil all the desired conditions, and so

it still remains to be shown by experience whether a permanent stream of emigration can be kept up, sufficient to take off, as in America, all that portion of the annual increase (when proceeding at its greatest rapidity) which being in excess of the progress made during the same short period in the arts of life, tends to render living more difficult for the averagely situated individual in the community. And unless this can be done, emigration cannot, even in an economical point of view, dispense with the necessity of checks to population. (ibid. 122)

Mill had been impressed by the extraordinary migration from Ireland after the great famine of the 1840s, but wanted to keep an open mind about whether this method of lightening population pressure could be routinely effective when some of the new settlements were as distant from Britain as Australia and New Zealand. He suspected that this kind of long-distance migration might be rather less effective in this regard than the existence of an open frontier of uncultivated land in the American West. In this, he represented an intermediate position between Malthus's 'weak palliative' position a generation before and Alfred Marshall's unclouded optimism about Anglo-Saxon imperialism a generation later.

V. W. S. JEVONS

The views of W. S. Jevons are worthy of mention not because of their conformity to the classical political economy model of population growth and the terms of trade, but because of their contrast with it. From his standpoint of the early 1860s, Jevons accorded an unusually positive role both to emigration and to continued growth of population at home. He saw emigration, domestic population growth, and the extensive importation into Britain of food and raw materials as three aspects of the operation of a benign colonial system:

Modern Britain does not and could not stand alone. It is united on the one hand to ancient agricultural Britain, and on the other hand to the modern agricultural nations of our stock, which are growing in several continents. Of the same language and manners, and bound together in the same real interests of trade, Britain and her colonial offspring must be regarded for the present as a single whole (Jevons, 1965/1906: 219–20)

Population and the Terms of Trade

According to Jevons, the vigorous growth of population size at home created a strong demand for imports of food and raw materials. The strength of this demand raised wages in the white settler colonies to a level that made emigration positively attractive to young people. Jevons insisted that the emigration of his day was caused by 'external allurements', and not by internal pressure (ibid.).[5] The migrants were then able to expand the supply of primary commodity exports, and Britain was able to employ a growing domestic population in manufacturing for domestic consumption and export at rising levels of income.

Jevons waxed lyrical about the 'union of happy conditions' that were the consequences of this system for Britain. However, more ominously, he recognized that the combination of growing population, capital accumulation, and rising income per head was one that 'hardly any country before enjoyed'. He swiftly added that no country could expect to enjoy it for long. His reason for saying so was his belief that, if other checks did not operate first, Britain's happy conditions would end as fast as its commercial reserves of coal were exhausted.

For the present our cheap supplies of coal, and our skill in its employment, and the freedom of our commerce with other wider lands, render us independent of the limited agricultural area of these islands, and apparently take us out of the scope of Malthus's doctrine . . . We are like settlers spreading in a rich new country of which the boundaries are yet unknown and unfelt.

In the increasing depth and difficulty of coal mining we shall meet that vague but inevitable limit which will stop our progress. We shall begin, as it were, to discover the further shore of our Black Indies. The wave of population will break upon that shore, and roll back upon itself.

. . . A farm, however far pushed, will under proper cultivation continue to yield forever a constant crop. But in a mine there is no reproduction, the produce once pushed to the utmost will soon begin to fail and sink towards zero. *So far, then, as our wealth and progress depend upon the superior command of coal we must not only cease to progress as before— we must begin a retrograde career.* (ibid. 200–1; emphasis in original)

Jevons's argument starts from the point that Mill recognized, namely that manufactures depend on raw materials that originate in the agricultural and mining sectors and that are subject to diminishing returns. Whereas Mill dismissed this effect as overbalanced by reductions in the other components of manufacturing costs, Jevons makes it the whole engine of his future scenario. He is unique among the political economists considered here in effectively denying the significance of the fact that the manufacturing sector has increasing returns. Because manufacturing is so very heavily dependent on the consumption of coal, and (he seems to believe) coal cannot be imported cheaply from abroad, a Malthusian check to population growth will operate, and immiserization will set in, with added impact because coal is an exhaustible resource. Because of his belief that diminishing returns influence *both* sectors, he is also the odd man out in being the only one of the economists considered here not to predict an ultimate deterioration of the terms of trade of manufactures *vis-à-vis* agricultural products.

VI. ALFRED MARSHALL

Marshall gave his account of the law of diminishing returns in a lecture in 1885 entitled 'The Pressure of Population on the Means of Subsistence':

The law as it stands is incontrovertible . . . The law acts with different force as to different things . . . (mines have a law for themselves). But it does not follow from this law that an increase in population would increase the pressure on the means of subsistence.

For man wants not only raw but manufactured commodities: and in producing these the organisation that is rendered possible by numbers cheapens production, so that it would be possible for the growth of population (the capital per head being constant) to increase the means of supporting life in some directions as much as it diminishes it in others. (Marshall, 1975/1867–90: ii. 389)

Having thus opened up this possible method of escape from population pressure, albeit without Malthus's refinement of manufactures consumption being a disincentive to large families, Marshall was quick to deny its relevance to the economic circumstances of England:

I don't deny that that may possibly be the result in some places where the cost of raw material is a small part of the whole cost of living. But in such a country as England where sufficient raw produce can be got only by importing from a distance; where the cost of raw produce consumed by the working classes is a very large part of their cost of living; there I think it is certainly not so. (ibid.)

Thus Marshall confirmed the view expressed in his earlier paper on 'The Future of the Working Classes' (1873) that the rapid increase in population in Britain was producing a 'competition for food [which] dogs the heels of progress, and perpetually hinders it' (Pigou, 1925: 117). At that time Marshall thought that the only solution for this was a social compact of parents from all classes to increase their investment in the education of each child. General acceptance of a social obligation to raise educational standards would increase the cost of child-rearing, which under a budget constraint would reduce the number of births per family.

By 1885, however, Marshall had opted for another solution, emigration. His lecture notes include, after a statement of the disadvantages of very rapid population growth, the parenthetical remark '(But for all that, in the interest of the world, I do not want the increase of English population to be slower than it is.)'. His reason for this is given in one of the lecture's conclusions:

Since the whole English people, except the residuum, is a long way above the average of the world, it is scarcely possible to suppose any curtailment of English population which would not lower the average quality of the inhabitants of the world, their average wealth and average well-being. (Marshall, 1975 / 1867–90: 390, 393)

At some date in the 1870s, then, Marshall ceased to be a Malthusian in the sense of an advocate of birth limitation for economic reasons. He seems to have become convinced that the continuous emigration of people of Anglo-Saxon stock was not only fully feasible, but represented one of the best hopes for the future progress of the world. By 1879, he was already engaged in 'race discourse'. In *The Economics of Industry* he wrote:

There can be no doubt that this extension of the English race has been a benefit to the world. A check to the growth of population would do great harm if it affected only the more intelligent races, and particularly the more intelligent classes of those races . . . if Englishmen multiply less rapidly than the Chinese, this spiritless race will overrun portions of the earth that otherwise would have been peopled by English vigour. (ibid. 387)

Once the *Principles of Economics* was published in 1890, Marshall was able to look back with satisfaction on the lifting of the food supply constraint, and the rising standard of living which the progressive cheapening of food imports had permitted. Ricardo's prophecy of material progress without discernible limit seemed to have been fulfilled. One long quotation must suffice to encapsulate Marshall's 1890 view:

if it were true that the real wages of labour were forced down by the difficulty of obtaining food, as was in fact the case in England a hundred years ago; then indeed the working classes might relieve themselves from the pressure of Diminishing Return by reducing their numbers. But they cannot do so now, because there is no such pressure. The opening of England's ports, in 1846, was one among many causes of the development of railways connecting the vast agricultural lands of North and South America and Australia with the sea. Wheat grown under the most advantageous circumstances is brought to the English working man in sufficient quantities for his family at a total cost equal to but a small part of his wages. An increase in numbers gives many new opportunities for increased efficiency of labour and capital. . . . Of course the Englishman is not unaffected by the law of diminishing return . . . [but the] cost [of his food] to him, being now governed by the supplies which come from new countries, would not be greatly affected by a diminution or an increase in the population of this country. *If he can make his labour more efficient in producing things which can be exchanged for imported food, then he will get his food at less real cost to himself, whether the population of England grows fast or not.* (Marshall, 1920/1890: 576; emphasis added)

And yet, by 1907, Marshall had become markedly more circumspect. In the *Principles*, Marshall included a calculation from which he concluded that 'the pressure of population on the means of subsistence may be held in check for about two hundred years, but not longer' (ibid. 150 n. 1). In his article on 'Social Possibilities of Economic Chivalry', the estimate was drastically reduced. Having reproduced the gist of the long quotation set out above, he added the following qualification:

But the world is really a very small place, and there is not room in it for the opening up of rich new resources during many decades at as rapid a rate as has prevailed during the last three or four. When new countries begin to need most of their own food and other raw produce, improvements in transport will count for little. From that time onwards the pressure of the Law of Diminishing Return can be opposed only by further improvements in production; and improvements in production must themselves gradually show a diminishing return. Great, therefore, as has been the rate of social progress of Britain during the last generation, we may not be contented with it. There is an urgent duty on us to make even more rapid advance during this age of economic grace, for it may run out before the end of the century. (Pigou, 1925: 326)

Victorian triumphalism was thus to some extent superseded by Edwardian anxiety, and Malthus's unquestionable truth that one day America would withdraw its corn from Europe was reintroduced into the debate as the basis for that anxiety. Even so, and after his bets had been thoroughly hedged in the Malthusian direction, Marshall was still expecting his age of economic grace to extend as far as the end of the twentieth century. Not so Keynes.

VII. KEYNES'S 1912 LECTURES
ON POPULATION

Keynes pursued many and varied intellectual interests; one of them was the population question. In comparison with monetary economics, population questions remained always in the second rank of his intellectual interests. He never wrote a book on demography. Nevertheless, from the earliest years of his academic life, he repeatedly discussed population issues in his books and academic papers as well as in his journalism. He continued to write on population matters intermittently throughout his career, up to and including his Galton Lecture in 1937, after which illness and then wartime duties supervened.

From the beginning, he did not shy away from public polemics on issues related to the quality of population. The first illustration of this was his vigorous support of Marshall in a public debate in 1910–11 with Karl Pearson, Professor of Eugenics at London University. The topic was whether physical degeneration in children was purely hereditary (as Pearson held), or could also be caused by negative environmental influences, such as parental alcoholism—the position that Marshall and Keynes defended. The ground of dispute was the methodological adequacy of a study by Pearson and his junior colleague Ethel Elderton. Keynes did not prompt Marshall's critique of this but quickly engaged himself in support of Marshall, focusing on the inadequacy of the data (especially wage data) to bear out Pearson's statistical inferences (PP/45/316/4/162, 166, and 169). In this debate, Keynes confined himself to criticizing a statistical method: he did not elaborate any positive views of his own on population, although his sympathy for the view that environmental influence did affect child welfare is obvious enough.

Soon after, however, Keynes revealed himself as much more of a neo-Malthusian and a Social Darwinist than Marshall ever was, even in his later years. The next protracted statement of

Keynes's views on population questions is to be found in his unpublished lecture notes of 1912, which are reproduced as an appendix to this chapter. He lectured to Cambridge undergraduates on the Principles of Economics in the years 1910/11 to 1913/14 (Moggridge, 1992: 188). In a surviving version of his 1912 lecture notes on the supply of labour, twelve pages are devoted to the growth of population (UA/6/9/15–27; O'Donnell, 1992: 779 and n. 12). For Keynes, population issues lay squarely under the rubric of economics, and he followed Marshall's *Principles of Economics* in discussing population in relation to the supply of labour as part of the treatment of the factors of production.

The 1912 lecture notes fall neatly into two halves. The first half follows closely the arguments of a then-recent *Economic Journal* article on Malthus and population by Lujo Brentano (1910). Starting with the barest summary of Malthus's conclusion that population will always press on the limits of available means of subsistence, Keynes finds in Brentano's statistics of declines in the marriage rate and in the number of children per marriage evidence to confirm the proposition, that, contrary to Malthus, 'fertility does diminish as prosperity increases'. He concludes the first half of his lectures on the growth of population with an uncompromising rejection of the relevance of the Malthusian problem to 'civilised countries':

The particular difficulties therefore which Malthus foresaw no longer face us. In civilised countries the automatic increase in population does *not* put a perpetual barrier against the permanent improvement of the working classes. (UA/6/9/22; emphasis in original)

In other words, the population problem as conceived by Malthus and some of the other English classical political economists had been solved (Robbins, 1978: 73–82). The second half of the lecture notes accordingly move on to a variety of post-Malthusian dilemmas.

Following Marshall, Keynes puts these new dilemmas explicitly in a post-Darwinian frame: 'If Malthusian ideas originally stimulated Darwinian ideas, the latter now lead us to modify the former' (UA/6/9/22). The suspension of the Malthusian law of population for certain classes of society, or portions of the world, implied, for Keynes, that natural selection would work perversely: 'There is a marked process of selection at work in favour of the elements that we regard as least good', because 'the poorest and least intelligent part of the population . . . reproduces itself most rapidly' (ibid.). Thus he states the problem of adverse natural selection, which will be the subject of extensive discussion in Chapter 4.

The supposed perverse operation of natural selection was something to which Keynes had no easy answer, but he continued to explore its implications. He distinguished between its manifestation within a given civilized country, where he thought that it might be solved in time by the growth of prosperity and education, and its manifestation between countries, the civilized and the rest, where he thought the matter was in the hands of forces which could not be controlled, only observed and described. One of these forces was 'the primitive instinct for the preservation of one's own race, whatever it may be', an instinct to which the leaders of the civilized countries were perhaps blinded by their own cosmopolitan attitudes. Keynes made a personal declaration at this point in his lecture:

My own sympathies are with the cosmopolitans, but it is necessary for a cosmopolitan never to forget the struggle for the survival of races and classes which the progress of civilisation has done very little to weaken. (UA/6/9/24)

The implication of never forgetting racial and class struggles was the need to ensure that the balance between the plenty of the prosperous and the civilized and the power and numbers of the rest was maintained in favour of the former.

Contrary to Marshall, Keynes believed that England was once again on the verge of overpopulation. He stated that 'the point has probably been reached already and will certainly be reached soon when any increase in population must diminish the average level of prosperity' (ibid.). Thus a choice would arise between a world with fewer, richer people and a world with more but poorer people. Which was better? Keynes was puzzled, but inclined 'with some compromise, to prefer a high level to numbers'. He did not, however, expect the actual size of world population to be determined by such ethical discussions. Rather, he supposed that question would 'in fact be answered on irrational and unethical grounds almost wholly' (UA/6/9/25–6).

Keynes believed that the evidence of incipient overpopulation was to be found in statistics of the unit values of manufactured exports relative to the unit values of food imports. Moreover, he thought that he had found such evidence, and that the trend in the exchange ratios of manufactures against raw produce had some years previously passed a turning point and begun to decline.

In the final paragraphs of his lecture notes, where he turned to the issue of the terms of trade, he was neither summarizing the research of others, nor thinking aloud about the intractable puzzle of the *summum bonum* that others had posed before. Rather, his notes begin to convey a strong sense of his own personal involvement and contribution:

I believe myself that we are perhaps now at the moment of turning in the ratios of exchange between manufactures and raw produce. The return to a given amount of capital and labour may still be increasing, but this movement of relative advantage is probably in favour of the agricultural countries and the rentowner [?] . . .

My own investigations, (the details of which I have no time to enter into here) lead me to believe that in the case of U.S.A. a given amount of raw products will purchase 15% to 20% more of the services of manufactures than they would 15 years ago, and that the turning point may possibly have occurred some time in the '90s. (UA/6/9/27).

What do we know of Keynes's own investigations into this matter? Very little, except that he published a two-page review of the Board of Trade's annual return of UK import and export statistics (1900–11) in the *Economic Journal* for December 1912 (*CW*, xi. 219–21). In this review he abstracted two tables in the return from which the price deflators of UK imports and exports between 1900 and 1911 could be estimated. Export prices were shown to be steady, while import prices had risen. Keynes concluded:

The deterioration—from the point of view of this country—shown above is due, of course, to the operation of the law of diminishing return for raw products which, after a temporary lull, has been setting in sharply in quite recent years. There is now again a steady tendency for a given unit of manufactured product to purchase year by year a diminishing quantity of raw product. The comparative advantage in trade is moving sharply against industrial countries. (ibid. 221)

In a footnote to clarify the span of the temporary lull, Keynes cites Bowley (1903: 628) to the effect that export prices fell relative to those of net imports from 1873 to 1889, but rose from 1890 to 1900. He notes that 'it is the abnormal tendency prevailing during the 'nineties which has since come to an end' (ibid.).

Bowley had described his numbers as the 'ratio of export index to import index'. This is potentially confusing. In fact, a rising ratio indicates a rise in the import price index faster than that in the export price index, and a falling ratio indicates the opposite. His ratios are set out in Table 1. It was the rise of this ratio in the years 1900-2, plus the 1912 Board of Trade tables showing that the prices of manufactured exports had risen more slowly from 1900 than the prices of imports of food and raw materials, that Keynes put together, and from which he deduced the existence of a 'turning point' in 1900. His defence of this particular deduction was to be a recurring professional preoccupation for him for more than another decade.

Table 1. Bowley's ratios of export index to
import index, 1873–1902 (1873 = 100)

1873	100	1883	118	1893	105
1874	103	1884	115	1994	102
1875	107	1885	114	1895	102
1876	110	1886	113	1896	102
1877	118	1887	111	1897	103
1878	114	1888	113	1898	103
1879	116	1889	112	1899	99
1880	119	1890	104	1900	94
1881	123	1891	105	1901	95
1882	118	1892	106	1902	100

VIII. CONCLUSION

The idea that the law of diminishing returns applied uniquely to
land, and that investment in agriculture and industry operated
under quite distinct laws of physical returns, was a powerful
and persistent one. In Victorian Britain, rapid economic growth,
accommodating unprecedented population growth and a simultaneous rise in the standard of living, was an immense novelty.
The question of the sustainability of these phenomena could
hardly be avoided. What were the limits to growth? The theory
of diminishing returns to land gave nineteenth-century English
economists a framework within which they provided their individual answers to this question. As has been shown, the answers
were quite diverse. Most of them believed that the economic
growth and structural changes that they witnessed were not
indefinitely sustainable, and would either come to a halt, or
go into reverse sooner or later. Only Ricardo had visions of
indefinite progress, and he was not self-consistent. The main
difference of opinion among economists of growth was about
whether the halt or reversal would begin sooner or later. As the
century progressed, the view increasingly gained ground that
importing American food and encouraging large-scale emigra-

tion would successfully delay the operation of the food supply constraint.

Since this type of economic discourse was still current at the start of the twentieth century, it is not altogether surprising that Keynes entered into it, following tradition by linking the question of optimal population to movements in the terms of trade of industrial produce relative to agricultural produce. What is more surprising is that he embraced the gloomiest end of the spectrum of debate, seeing the limits to growth as binding in the immediate future, while Marshall's nearly simultaneous prediction was of another century of growth. Neither Keynes's formative intellectual milieu, the much-discussed 'presuppositions of Harvey Road', nor his personal temperament, which was outgoing and optimistic, do much to explain the pessimism of his economic outlook at this date. This therefore remains something of an unsolved puzzle, given the difficulty of finding much validation of his pessimism in the empirical data that he examined. Whatever the reason, economic pessimism had gripped him, and he remained in its grip through the composition of his 1914 lecture on 'Population', through the Great War and its aftermath, and until the very end of the 1920s.

NOTES

1. The justification for this usage is that the doctrine originated with Malthus, and continued to flourish among Cambridge economists after being abandoned by others.
2. Those who made this substitution were not, however, really intending to exclude Wales, Scotland, and Ireland from the scope of their analysis.
3. For an illuminating technical discussion of why Ricardo believed that diminishing returns in agriculture, combined with *constant* returns in manufacturing, justified the abolition of the Corn Laws, see Evans (1989: 61–8).

4. This view, however, goes somewhat counter to that expressed by Hans Singer (1975: 1–2).
5. Jevons had himself emigrated from Britain to Australia in 1854 and remained there until 1859, in order to make money for himself (Wood, 1983a: 102).

Appendix: Extract from Keynes's
Lecture Notes of 1912

Principles of Economics, Vol. 2 [Catalogue reference UA/6/9/16–27]

The Supply of Labour

(1) Growth of population
(2) Length of working life
(3) Length of working day
(4) Efficiency of labour

[UA/6/19/16]

12th March 1912

Growth of Population

Subject comes into importance with writings of Malthus, fellow of
Jesus, the first of the Cambridge economists, inspirer of Darwin.

• All nations of which we have historical knowledge so prolific that
  their growth is only kept in check by a scarcity of the necessities of
  life or some violent cause.
• On account of the law of diminishing returns, there is no prospect
  that the yield to labour of the necessaries of life can possibly
  increase so fast as population tends to increase.
• (Arithmetical and geometrical ratios not to be interpreted literally)
• There is no reason to suppose that either of these conclusions will
  not be equally applicable to the future.

The final conclusion is, therefore, one of extreme pessimism. There
seems no means by which the working class can permanently raise
themselves from a condition of misery. Malthus could only suggest
the universal practice of continence and late marriage.

[UA/6/9/17]

The pessimism of Malthus and the urgency of his problem has been
withdrawn from influence over our own generation on account of
the extraordinary circumstances, which he could not have foreseen, in

which new countries and the means of transport have temporarily suspended the law of diminishing returns.

But this can only be temporary, and if his first generalisation is true, his final conclusion must ultimately be fulfilled.

The course of events since he wrote seems to have borne out his first contention. Whether we consider Europe or the new world, wherever economic pressure has been removed population has expanded accordingly.

When he wrote the population of England and Wales was about 9m.; it has increased fourfold to 36m. i.e. fourfold in four generations; from the Norman Conquest until the time of the Stuarts the population of England had varied from 2 to 4m.

In the same period the increase in U.S.A. has been from 5m. to 92m. i.e. it has about doubled every generation.

[UA/6/9/18]

If the population of the world were to increase as fast as that of Europe has done during the last 25 years, we should at the end of 1000 years be standing shoulder to shoulder. And if we were to take the American rate. . . .

But when we look into the matter more closely there seems some reason for doubting the validity of applying to the future Malthus's generalisation.

Firstly, the birth rate has not consistently advanced, as according to Malthus it should, when economic pressure is removed. On the whole it has *declined*; and a fall in the death rate has had a good deal to do with the increase of population—and this is a factor which cannot possibly continue much further.

Also the more we see of human beings in the mass in conditions somewhat removed from those of extreme economic pressure, the more doubtful does Malthus's psychological assumption seem as to the unlimited propensity of the human race to propagate.

Population and the Terms of Trade

[UA/6/9/19]

The most striking criticism of the applicability of Malthus's psychological assumptions to present and future conditions is that of Professor Brentano. Malthus, it is true, admitted the possible influence of the raising of the standard of life: but Brentano goes much further.

(1) When the low stage of civilisation has been passed at which sexual desire acts with the same elementary force as among animals, both the marriage rate and the birth rate largely depend upon the economic advantageousness of marriage and children.

Change which takes place when a large family, instead of being an advantage, began to occasion expenses. In last 25 years a decline in the marriage rate is in G.B., Russia, Hungary, Italy, U.S.A., Australia, Chile [?]. In Germany from 1881–1900 an increase in large towns.

(2) Explanations:

(a) In upper classes length of preparation for career postpones marriage. On the other hand factory workers find it easier to make a home than agricultural labourers. Hence rise in Germany. England already industrialised.

(b) In upper class increasing expense of social requirements. This has always acted in families with entailed estates.

[UA/6/9/20]

(c) Altered position of women.
Greater demands from marriage.

These are explanations of decline of marriage rate

(3) Now for birth rate

'All European, Australian, and the majority of American states, whether their marriage-rate has risen or fallen, have experienced a decline in their birth rate during the past thirty years.'
Due to decline in number of births per marriage.

In France, birth rate has declined from 39 in reign of Louis XVI to 23. The more prosperous the district, the lower the birth rate.
In England 200,000 more children would have been born in 1901 if the birth rate had been the same as in 1861.

Decline affects skilled artisans as well as propertied classes. 'Maternity' payments by Hearts of Oak Society have declined in every consecutive period of five years since 1871.

Whether deliberately or not, there seems no reason to doubt that fertility does diminish as prosperity increases.

In Holland and Germany fertility has been correlated with low rents; in Italy with illiteracy.

[UA/6/9/21]

The decline in Australia has been faster than in any European country.

The fertility of the Whites in New England is only half as great as in most European countries.

Differences of creed, race, occupation or domicile, which are advanced to account for differences in the rate of fertility appear on closer inspection to reduce themselves to differences and changes in material prosperity.

The evidence shows that the decrease is due primarily to the disinclination, not to the inability, to bear children.

(1) Competition of other pleasures
(2) Disinclination of women to spend their whole life in childbed
(3) The man's consideration for the health of his wife
(4) Greater delicacy of feeling towards children
(5) Economic disadvantages of having children
(6) Possibility of effective influence of these motives by the use of preventive checks.

Authorities: Marshall Prin [?] chap. 4
         Brentano The Doctrine of Malthus
         Econ JI Sept. 1910
         Cannan Theories of Production and Distribution chap. V

[UA/6/9/22]

The particular difficulties therefore which Malthus foresaw no longer face us. In civilised countries the automatic increase in population does *not* put a perpetual barrier against the permanent improvement of the working class.

But we are now aware of a new problem, hardly less serious.

If Malthusian ideas originally stimulated Darwinian ideas, the latter now lead us to modify the former. There is a marked process of selection at work in favour of the elements which we regard as least good. In a given country it is the poorest and least intelligent part of the population which reproduces itself most rapidly; and it is in the most civilised countries that the birth rate is falling off fastest.

Example of Cambridge.

We are faced by a dilemma.

The Malthusian Law of Population, when it is in operation, maintains the lower classes of the population in a condition of perpetual misery. But it is an engine of evolutionary progress, and those classes of society, or portions of the world, for which its operation is suspended, are liable to be overwhelmed by the rest.

[UA/6/9/23]

Example of Greece and Rome.

Brentano:—'The increase of the white population of USA depends today on the continual immigration from Europe; if this were to cease, the North American Republic would, in view of the great fertility of the negro, become black in quite a short, predeterminable time.'

We seem to be in this matter in the hands of forces which we cannot control. We can only observe and describe them.

The problem within a civilised country may possibly be solved in time by the growth of prosperity and education. The struggle between different races and countries is, at the present time as it has been at other times, confusedly reflected in national prejudices and policy—alien acts, military strength, imperialism. Yellow peril, South African, Australian and American feeling against coloured immigration. In these forms the primitive instinct for the preservation of one's own race, whatever it may be, now shows itself.

On the other hand we have policies and sympathies dictated by leaders who have freed themselves from or are less susceptible to this primitive instinct.

They feel sympathy with the aspirations of others and very alien races; they are pleased by the existence of varied civilisations and would assist weaker nationalities; they are less convinced than the former that their own race contains within itself all that there is in the world most desirable; they are open to the charge of being cosmopolitan; and they are occupied by the task of improving the moral and material conditions of their own and other races, possibly blind to the wholly irrational but immensely powerful struggle for survival, through the mere force of the instinct of population.

My own sympathies are with the cosmopolitans, but it is necessary for a cosmopolitan never to forget the struggle for the survival of races and classes which the progress of civilisation has done very little to weaken.

[UA/6/9/25]

This is one of the features of the problem of population, and is likely to be, perhaps within our lifetimes, more important than it is now. It depends upon the antithesis between plenty [?] on this our side and power and numbers on the other from the racial point of view.

But there is another arising out of the same antithesis between plenty and numbers from the ethical and political point of view. The point has probably been reached already and will certainly be reached soon when any increase in population must certainly diminish the average level of prosperity.

Is it better to have 100 people well off or 1000 people somewhat less well off. The more one reflects on this problem the more puzzling it seems. I incline, with some compromise, to prefer a high level to numbers. Does the goodness of the world depend upon the number of people in it, or does it wholly depend on the general level of goodness and well-being of those there are regardless of their number.

[UA/6/9/26]

Yet some day the world will have to determine what is the fit and desirable number of inhabitants for it.

I suppose the question will in fact be answered on irrational and unethical grounds almost wholly.

[UA/6/9/27]

While, however, the problem of population as it faces us in the future has a somewhat different form from that in which it presented itself to Malthus, we must not be altogether oblivious of Malthusian considerations. In spite of the decline of the birthrate in certain countries, the population of the world is still increasing fast.

I believe myself that we are perhaps now at the moment of turning in the ratios of exchange between manufacturers and raw produce. The return to a given amount of capital and labour may be still increasing, but this movement of relative advantage is probably in favour of the agricultural countries and of the rentowner [?]

Example of India:

My own investigations, (the details of which I have no time to enter into here) lead me to believe that in the case of U.S.A. a given amount of raw products will purchase 15% to 20% more of the services of manufacturers than they would 15 years ago, and the turning point may possibly have occurred some time in the 90's.

2

Keynes's Manuscript on 'Population'

I. INTRODUCTION

Keynes's manuscript on 'Population', the basis of a lecture he delivered on 2 May 1914, was not finally published in any form until 1993, and then only as one small part of the archive of Keynes's papers that was made available by King's College, Cambridge in a commercial microfilm version. The cost of this version places it beyond the reach of all except very well-endowed university libraries. Thus, despite the microfilm publication, 'Population' remains a relatively unknown piece of Keynes's writing, even to the academic world. Now a hard copy edition of it is published for the first time in the Appendix to this chapter.

The manuscript on 'Population' was not included in the Royal Economic Society's thirty-volume edition of Keynes's *Collected Writings*. Why not? At first glance, it might seem that the omission was not deliberate, but rather a result of an editorial oversight. When volume X of the *Collected Writings*, the *Essays in Biography*, was published in 1972, the editorial note at the beginning of the essay on Malthus stated: 'The earliest version of this essay that survives among Keynes's papers dates from 1922' (*CW*, x. 71). This statement shows that in 1972 the editors simply did not know of the existence of 'Population'. For it is manifest to the reader of 'Population' that this is the earliest known version of Keynes's essay on Malthus. Some scholarly confusion remains about the date of the earliest version of the 1933 Malthus essay (see, for example, Cox, 1995: 167; Winch, 1996: 26n. 58; and

Waterman, 1998: 297–8). A reading of 'Population' itself should make everything quite clear.

Accordingly, the final volume of the *Collected Writings*, which was published in 1989, provided a correction to the original editorial note of 1972. This begins, in the revised form:

> The earliest surviving form of this essay is the paper Keynes gave in May 1914 to The Political Philosophy and Science Club at New College, Oxford, entitled 'Is the problem of population a pressing and important one now?' In 1922 Keynes expanded the material on Malthus and read the paper on various occasions to his Monday evening Political Economy Club in Cambridge, and, on 2 April 1924, to the London Political Economy Club. (*CW*, xxx. 164)

The inference to be derived from this correction must be that it was at some time between 1972 and 1989 when the existence of 'Population' came to the editors' attention. Exactly when this discovery occurred, and in what circumstances, I do not know. However, after the discovery had been made, the editors did *not* then choose to publish it among the various Omissions from the previous volumes that were printed in volume XXX. Therefore, an editorial oversight is not the explanation for the exclusion of 'Population', even though when the edition was planned, this manuscript's existence was unknown to the editors.

The exclusion of 'Population' from the edition was a matter of editorial policy. The *Collected Writings* have a 'General Introduction' which appears at the front of each volume. This states the editors' intentions for the whole series. It classifies Keynes's writings into five categories. They are: his published books; his own collections of articles and pamphlets; his published but uncollected writings; a few hitherto unpublished writings; and his correspondence with economists and those concerned with public affairs. The editors also say that the series will attempt to publish a complete record of Keynes's serious writing as an economist. Specifically, their intention was 'to publish almost completely the whole of the first four categories'. 'Almost completely' means that 'the only exceptions are a few syndicated articles where Keynes wrote almost the same material for publication in different newspapers or in different countries, with minor or unimportant variations'.

The editors mention their concern to respect Keynes's intentions with regard to the public presentation of his writings. What were his intentions? Did Keynes himself perhaps later disown the views expressed in 'Population'? Is there any evidence for this? Hardly so, for he was glad enough to see it again (or possibly a later variant of it) when it turned up unexpectedly one day in 1930. He wrote to his wife Lydia on 10 October 1930: 'I have found my long lost article on Malthus! The bed maker turned it up dusting' (Cox, 1995: 167, citing PP/45/190). It is true that in his 1941 will, he asked his executors to destroy the greater part of his economic and personal papers. However, no one ever seems to have taken that request seriously and, in any case, he left no instructions about the disposal of individual papers (Cox, 1995: 164–5).

The explanation for the absence of 'Population' is much more straightforward than this. One should recall that the statement of editorial policy was made before the existence of 'Population', the various early philosophical papers, and a cache of supplementary papers on the *General Theory* was known. In the course of preparing the edition, the hitherto unpublished writings turned out to be much more numerous than just the few that were originally known about. It thus became impractical to adhere to the policy of publishing almost completely the whole of the first four categories of writing, including the previously unpublished writings. So, the editors decided that 'omissions [of unpublished material] that came to light after the publication of the relevant volumes' would simply be left as omissions (Moggridge, personal communication, 1997). They made an exception to this rule for those materials concerning *The General Theory* that were discovered in the famous laundry-basket, but not for any other unpublished material that had resurfaced after the relevant volume had appeared.

One sympathizes with the difficulty of editors who discover much extra material late in the course of bringing out their edition. At the same time, the editorial choice made in these difficult circumstances has had the odd consequence that, except on the subject of the creation and criticism of *The General Theory*, it is possible for trivial items to be included in the edition simply because they were published by Keynes, while more important unpublished material that was discovered at a late date has been left out. Hence, taking the example of population, in the *Collected Writings* can be found the preface to the 1922 Cambridge Economic Handbook on *Population*, although this is a much less substantial piece than the 1914 Oxford lecture on the identical subject, which itself is not to be found. Again, simply because it was in a published book, an exceptionally bland single-paragraph message, sent by Keynes to the American Birth Control Conference of November 1923, is there in the Omissions (*CW*, xxx: 7), while 'Population' is not. Therefore, as things stand at present, it is possible to come away from a reading of the *Collected Writings* with a significant underestimate of what constitutes Keynes's 'serious economic writing' on the subject of population. Since a fuller treatment was accorded to material surrounding *The General Theory*, it is inevitable also that the balance between that and other economic topics in the edition stands in need of some redressing.

There is, therefore, work for successors of the editors of the *Collected Writings* to do. It is now time to make 'Population' more generally available, so that readers may judge for themselves its intrinsic importance and its place in the whole sweep of Keynes's thought. The fact that some of its contents, most especially its 'race discourse', diminishes his reputation for wisdom and compassion, at least in my opinion, should not become a reason for continuing to neglect a part of the historical truth about Keynes.

There is no analogy between the 'minor and unimportant variations' involved in the syndication of newspaper articles and the differences between the published Malthus essay of 1933 and the lecture from which this had originated some twenty years earlier. One major difference is that the treatment of Malthus on population is much fuller in the 1914 lecture. Another is that the earlier version goes on to discuss India, Egypt, and China's populations in a way that is not paralleled in any other writing by Keynes. Any reader can now compare the two texts, and if this is done it will be seen immediately that, while 'Population' is indeed the first known version of the 1933 essay, the differences between the documents are major and substantial.

II. SUMMARY OF THE ARGUMENT OF 'POPULATION'

Keynes's 1914 lecture on 'Population' is by no means simply an expansion of the material in the 1912 lecture notes. Virtually all of the ideas in the latter reappear in 'Population', with a greater or lesser emphasis. However, important new themes are added. Indeed, the whole of the first twenty folios is new material. An initial short biographical sketch of Malthus and his father extends itself, as Keynes warms to his task, to an evaluation of the originality and influence of the *Essay on the Principle of Population* in its own time, and of those elements which remained relevant in 1914. Before he reached his main theme, and as a prologue that grew beyond a mere introduction, he produced what became the first draft of the essay on Malthus, not finally published until 1933. As Keynes himself acknowledges, it was only on Fo. 21.3 of 'Population' that he 'reached at last what was, when I sat down to write, to have been the central topic' of the paper, namely the thesis that the world of his day was overpopulated.

In advancing this thesis in the remainder of the lecture, Keynes begins to reformulate some of the material in the 1912 lecture notes. His analysis is in two parts, of the West and of the East. The situation of the West has become bleaker because of the alleged 1900 turning point in the terms of trade, indicating that the period in which Malthusian mechanisms had been held in abeyance was coming to an end. The story of the East is that these mechanisms have never been in abeyance. The cases of India, Egypt, and China are then introduced to illustrate this, and to suggest that the effects of colonial governments' measures to raise the standard of living are doomed to fail because of relentless population increase under the sanction of popular religion. In these circumstances, and given the existence of a world market for food, Keynes argued that there was a collective-action problem of insufficient incentive for any single country to try to curb its population growth. Rather, public opinion was rallying to a patriotic pro-natalism that would, he believed, tend to reduce the average standard of living.

Keynes wanted to turn the tide of public opinion against pro-natalism. In the period of temporary abeyance of Malthusian mechanisms in the West, he saw the falling birth rate as the result of favourable developments, the reduced desire and reduced opportunity (within marriage) for procreation and the increased ability by means of artificial checks to avoid undesired children. He saw the need, in the straitening (as he thought) economic conditions of the West, to spread the use of artificial checks from the upper and middle to the working classes. He therefore vigorously denounced the superstition and obscurantism of those pro-natalists who opposed such a diffusion of contraception, and even open public discussion of the issue.

He added an argument that would appeal to those who worried about the perverse operation of natural selection. To oppose the diffusion of contraception was to refuse to do something that would reduce that perverse effect. At a time when the quality of the population, as well as its quantity, was a matter of public discourse, to say that the policy one advocated would reduce the proportion of the population born to the poorest, the

49

least intelligent, the least virtuous, and the least prudent (and Keynes did say all of these things of the working class) was regarded as a very powerful argument.

In his 1912 lecture notes, Keynes observed that perverse natural selection operated between countries, as well as between classes: 'It is in the most civilised countries that the birth rate is falling off fastest' (UA/6/9/22). Here, the diffusion of artificial checks would be impossible: 'I do not see what hope there is for much improvement, moral or material, for the races of India and China, so long as the popular religions of these countries attach so great an importance to early marriage and numerous off-spring' (Fo. 35). For Keynes, it was a matter of finding appropriate defences against 'the fecundity of the East'. In this context, it was harder to press the argument for more widespread contraception at home against the pro-natalists' call for a levelling up in fertility between classes. He was sensitive to the charge that he was advocating 'race suicide', and had to cast around for reasons why that was not what his position entailed. He admitted the existence of dilemmas, but put his trust in draconian measures of immigration control and restrictive intervention in the international food trade to turn the trick for 'the most civilised nations'.

III. 'POPULATION': A READER'S GUIDE

A typeset reproduction of the manuscript on 'Population' is set out in the Appendix to this chapter. The extant version is evidently incomplete and is unfinished in the sense that it is not a fair copy of a final version of a lecture. Keynes numbered each Folio. However, although the manuscript starts with Fo. 1 and ends with Fo. 39, it lacks Fos. 2, 3, 5, and 8–12 and has four additional sheets, Fos. 21.1, 21.2, 21.3, and 26.1. It thus has thirty-five Folios. It is not, *pace* Skidelsky (1992: 429), 'a thirty-nine page manuscript'. The Appendix reproduces the original Foliation.

After the final Folio I have reproduced the scribbled pencil notes that Keynes made, after delivering his lecture, on the back of his manuscript.

The date of composition of 'Population' is not entirely clear. On the one hand it could have been a set of notes cobbled together immediately before the lecture. This is the impression given by Fo. 31, where Keynes begins a sentence with the words 'Even today, Saturday May 2 . . .' But there is other internal evidence which suggests, although it does not conclusively prove, that part of the draft was written in the previous year, 1913, and then laid aside. On Fo. 27 Keynes originally wrote: 'When I was in Egypt this year', but subsequently corrected 'this' in pencil to 'last'.[1] While it is possible that Keynes could simply have been mistaken about how long ago he had been in Egypt, this explanation seems less plausible than supposing that at least a part of the manuscript dates from 1913. What if anything would follow, if this were true? Only that we would see 'Population' not just as an occasional offering, prompted by the need to give a guest lecture, but as something begun under the recent impress of his Egyptian experience and which blocks out themes which will continue to resonate, though with gradually decreasing vibrancy, in his subsequent work.

Because the manuscript is not a final fair copy, phrases are often crossed out, presumably as Keynes changed his mind in the process of composition about what he wanted to say, and the way he wanted to say it. The crossed-out phrases are reproduced as they appear in the manuscript. Many of the replacements show quite trivial verbal changes, but one on Fo. 36 is of special significance. It shows that Keynes originally wrote a shorter and more moderate conclusion to his lecture, but then deleted this in favour of a more elaborate and more provocative statement.

Keynes did not make any use of numbered footnotes in his text, although he did make the occasional note in the margin. All the note cues that appear in the text are editorial; they are keyed to the editorial notes at the end of the text. The notes are designed to provide very brief guidance on the people or subjects to whom Keynes refers. For some of his references, however, clarification cannot be provided so briefly. To solve this problem, a commentary on the text is provided in Chapter 3. There, phrases from the text are printed in bold type. Around them, the commentary is structured. A cross-reference is given to the place in the manuscript where the phrase appears. This seemed to be the least clumsy way of solving the problem of annotation.

The reader will notice that Fo. 13 of the manuscript begins in mid-sentence, indicating that a previous page or pages, presumably Fos. 8–12, are missing. This is the only obvious instance of a break in the text. Fortunately, it is not at all difficult to supply some idea of the contents of the missing pages. The final version of the essay on Malthus provides us with the necessary clue. In the 1933 version, between the reference to 'a letter written by his father to Robert Malthus on his election to a fellowship' and the number '250,000', we find a clear connecting passage (*CW*, x: 82–4). This passage is likely to be a refined and polished version of what was said in the missing pages of the manuscript of 'Population'. I have therefore taken the liberty of inserting this passage as an interpolation in the extant text, so that the reader can appreciate the continuity that very probably characterized the original argument. This single large editorial interpolation is to be distinguished from the interpolations that Keynes made in his own text.

NOTE

1. Keynes visited Sir Robert Furness in Egypt in March and April 1913, travelling to Cairo, Luxor, and Alexandria.

Appendix: 'Population'

[Fo. 1]

Robert Malthus, the first of the Cambridge economists, ~~after being a pupil for two or three years of Gilbert Wakefield,~~ came up to Jesus in 1784.[1] ~~After reading history, poetry, and modern languages and~~ He is said to have been fond of cricket and skating, obtained prizes for Latin and English Declamations, graduated as ninth wrangler in 1788 ~~(the year in which Gunning was fifth)~~ and was admitted Fellow of Jesus in 1793.[2] He resided irregularly up to his marriage in 1804, and had the pleasure of signing an order to cut Coleridge off the kitchens for non-payment of his college bill, an indignity not unavenged afterwards by various members of the Lake School ~~afterwards~~.[3] The grandfather or great-grandfather, in his intellectual associations, of some of our own [?], Malthus was an original member of that Political Economy Club whose ~~meetings~~ dinners still enliven the first Wednesday of every month, and of the Royal Statistical Society whose teas depress the first Tuesday.[4] ~~twin engagements which one member of the Erasmus sometimes finds an enemy of his perfect faithfulness to it.~~

[Fo. 4]

In later life Malthus engaged in ~~that celebrated~~ the controversy with Ricardo,[5] out of which was hatched the Ricardian law of Rent; and the loss of his fellowship through marriage was the occasion of his becoming the first occupant of the first chair of Political Economy established in this country, the Professorship of History and Political Economy in the East-India College at Haileybury. ~~Insert p.5~~

~~But it was in early life, while he was still a fellow of Jesus, that the brilliant generalisation occurred to him which has perpetuated his name. The story of its origin is well known. Daniel Malthus, his father, 'had been a friend and executor of Rousseau';—indeed he had applied to his son's education some 'peculiar opinions perhaps derived from the *Emile*';—and he followed the school of human progress and perfectibility of which William Godwin was~~

What we know of Malthus's father Daniel must be added to these ~~scanty~~ few details relating to Jesus and Haileybury, to complete a picture of ease, reflection, and gentleness. Daniel Malthus had been a friend and correspondent of Rousseau, and, it is alleged, one of his executors.[6] He spent his life at the Rookery, 'a small but beautiful estate' between Guildford and Dorking, and is described as 'a gentleman of good family and independent fortune attached to a country life, but much occupied in classical and philosophic pursuits, and with a strong bias towards foreign literature'. Diffidence ~~and~~ or idleness ~~perhaps~~, had prevented his ~~ever~~ bringing his ~~great~~ powers to fruition; he was ~~keenly~~ conscious of this; and anxious that his son should not suffer a like fate. He spent, therefore, peculiar pains on his son's education, choosing for one of his instructors ~~'men of no common mind', including for some time~~ Gilbert Wakefield, and kept him under his own immediate supervision, until the time came for him to go to Wakefield's college Jesus;—a course of action commented on thus by Malthus's biographer Otter[7]—'From some peculiar

opinions which his father seems to have entertained respecting education, he was never sent to any public school; and in this respect, is one, amongst many other remarkable instances in the present time, of men who have risen into eminence under the disadvantage of an irregular and desultory education'.

A few letters, which have been preserved, written by Daniel Malthus to his son, when the latter was an undergraduate at Jesus, present the father's character in a strong and amiable light. I will quote from a letter written by his father to Robert Malthus on his election to a fellowship:—

[editorial interpolation of *CW*, x. 82–4]

I heartily congratulate you upon your success; it gives me a sort of pleasure which arises from my own regrets. The things which I have missed in life, I should the more sensibly wish for you.

Keynes's Manuscript on 'Population'

Alas! my dear Bob, I have no right to talk to you of idleness, but when I wrote that letter to you with which you were displeased, I was deeply impressed with my own broken purposes and imperfect pursuits; I thought I foresaw in you, from the memory of my own youth, the same tendency to lose the steps you had gained, with the same disposition to self-reproach, and I wished to make my unfortunate experience of some use to you. It was, indeed, but little that you wanted it, which made me the more eager to give it you, and I wrote to you with more tenderness of heart than I would in general pretend to, and committed myself in a certain manner which made your answer a rough disappointment to me, and it drove me back into myself. You have, as you say, worn out that impression, and you have a good right to have done it; for I have seen in you the most unexceptionable character, the sweetest manners, the most sensible and the kindest conduct, always above *throwing little stones into my garden*, which you know I don't easily forgive, and uniformly making everybody easy and amused about you. Nothing can have been wanting to what, if I were the most fretful and fastidious, I could have required in a companion; and nothing even to my wishes for your happiness, but where they were either whimsical, or unreasonable, or most likely mistaken. I have often been on the point of taking hold of your hand and bursting into tears at the time that I was refusing you my affections: my approbation I was precipitate to give you.

Write to me, if I could do anything about your church, and you want any thing to be done for you, such as I am, believe me, dear Bob, yours most affectionately,

DANIEL MALTHUS

Malthus's first essay in authorship, *The Crisis, a View of the Recent Interesting State of Great Britain by a Friend to the Constitution*, written in 1796, in his thirtieth year, in criticism of Pitt's administration, failed to find a publisher. Extracts quoted by Otter and by Empson indicate that his interest was already aroused in the social problems of political economy, and even in the question of population itself:

On the subject of population [he wrote] I cannot agree with Archdeacon Paley, who says, that the quantity of happiness in any country is best measured by the number of people. Increasing population is the most certain possible sign of the happiness and prosperity of a state; but the actual population may be only a sign of the happiness that is past.

In 1798, when Malthus was thirty-two years old, there was published anonymously *An Essay on the Principle of Population, as it affects the future improvement of Society: with remarks on the speculations of Mr Godwin, M. Condorcet, and other writers.*

It was in conversation with Daniel Malthus that there occurred to Robert Malthus the generalization which has made him famous. The story is well known on the authority of Bishop Otter who had it from Malthus himself. In 1793 Godwin's *Political Justice* had appeared. In frequent discussion the father defended, and the son attacked, the doctrine of a future age of perfect equality and happiness.

And when the question had been often the subject of animated discussion between them, and the son had rested his cause, principally upon the obstacles which the tendency of population, to increase faster than the means of subsistence, would always throw in the way; he was desired to put down in writing, for maturer consideration, the substance of his argument, the consequence of which was the Essay on Population. Whether the father was converted or not we do not know, but certain it is that he was strongly impressed with the importance of the views and the ingenuity of the argument contained in the MS., and recommended his son to submit his labours to the public.

The first edition, an octavo volume of about 50,000 words, is an almost completely different, and for posterity a superior book, to the second edition of five years later in quarto, which by the fifth edition had swollen to some 250,000 words in three volumes.

[Fo. 13]

250,000 by an elaboration of proof and historical research, without any substantial improvement in the author's clear and striking statement of the fundamental principles involved. ~~The first edition is not really the worse~~ Just as the fruitfulness and originality of Cambridge is largely preserved by the deficiencies of the University library, so the first edition of this book is not really the worse from having been written, as Malthus explains in the preface to the second edition, 'on the impulse of the occasion, and from the few materials which were then within my reach in a country situation'.

Insert
from p.14

Malthus's Essay is a very great book. The author was deeply conscious of the bigness of the ideas he was elaborating. It is no case of a man of second-rate powers hitting, more by good fortune than desert, on an unexpectedly important generalisation. ~~It may be worth while, perhaps, for me to quote his own introductory sentences. What I am quoting is the high-spirited rhetoric of a young man writing in the last years of~~ Indeed his leading idea had been largely anticipated in a clumsier way by other eighteenth century writers without attracting attention.

[Fo. 14]

Insert
p.13

The high-spirited rhetoric of a young man writing in the last years of the Directory[8] disappears from the late editions, which are quieter, more businesslike, more strictly attentive to the duties of ~~the~~ a scientific ~~great academic~~ pioneer in the study of sociological history. ~~He has become, later on, more interested in a history of the checks to population at all stages of Human Society from China to Peru, than in the impossibility and in the illimitable possibilities of the coming epoch.~~

This is how he begins:—
~~(pp 1-5, 10-11, 13, 14-17)~~
        II 15–17

whose store of facts and range of illustration had been immensely extended by a tour in 1799 'through Sweden, Norway, Finland, and a part of Russia, these being the only countries at the time open to English travellers' and another in France and Switzerland during the short peace of 1802.

[Fo. 15]

~~These quotations are sufficient for my present purpose. Malthus's reminiscences of the Mathematical Tripos led him to speak in a more~~

~~expert way than he ought of population increasing in a geometrical ratio and of subsistence increasing in an arithmetical ratio; nor did he see explicitly in what way his generalisation depends on the tendency towards diminishing returns in agriculture. But his main thesis is simple, clear, and irrefutable.~~

The book can claim a place amongst those which have had ~~the~~ a very great~~est~~ influence on the progress of thought. It is, tremendously, in the English tradition of humane science—in that tradition of Scotch and English thought, in which there has been, I think, a quite extraordinary continuity of *feeling*, if I may so express it, from the eighteenth century to the present time,—the tradition which is suggested, not to mention contemporaries, by the names of Locke, Hume, Adam Smith, Darwin and Mill,—~~I had almost added Wordsworth and Miss Austen~~—a tradition pre-eminently marked by a certain noble

[Fo. 16]

clarity, by ~~a passionate yet self-restrained~~ a love of truth ~~passionate but allied to self-restraint~~, by a sanity, free from sentiment or metaphysic, and by an immense disinterestedness and public spirit. There is a continuity in these writings, not only of feeling, but of actual matter. It is in this company, although not quite in the first rank of it, that Malthus belongs.

The direct influence of Malthus's book is easily pointed out. He was proudest himself of having converted Pitt[9] and Paley.[10] Pitt attended Commem. at Trinity on the 16th December, 1801. At a supper at Jesus Lodge he met Dr. Malthus and, Bishop Otter records, 'was induced to unbend in a very easy conversation respecting Sir Sidney Smith, the massacre at Jaffa, the Pasha of Acre, Clarke,[11] Carlisle, etc'. A year before Pitt, in dropping his new Poor Bill, had stated in the House of Comm. that he did so in deference to the objections of 'those

[Fo. 17]

whose opinions he was bound to respect', meaning, it is said, Bentham and Malthus.

The book, as is well known, had a part in the mental development of Darwin, who ~~writes~~ tells in his Autobiography how happening to read 'Malthus on Population' for amusement he came upon the idea which was the starting point of his theory. [:—'In October 1838, I happened to read for amusement "Malthus on Population", and being well prepared to appreciate the struggle for existence which everywhere goes on from long-continued observation of the habits of animals and plants, it at once struck me that under these circumstances favourable variations would tend to be preserved, and unfavourable ones to be destroyed. The result of this would be the formation of new species. Here then I had at last got a theory by which to work. . . .']

[Fo. 18]

The doctrine of population had a profound effect on the economic writers of the first half of the nineteenth century. It hung over them like a cloud; it involved them in a dogmatic pessimism out of which no ultimate escape seemed possible. Nations might become populous and empires powerful, but for the great mass of the subjects there was *never* to be any escape from a miserable condition.

'The Vicar of Wakefield 'was ever of opinion that the honest man who married and
(Cannan[12])
brought up a large family did more service than he who continued single and only talked of population'. Adam Smith said 'the most decisive mark of the prosperity of any country is the increase of the number of its inhabitants'. Paley As late as 1796, Pitt thought that a man had 'enriched his country' by producing a number of children, even if the whole family were paupers. Paley argued that 'the decay of population is the greatest evil a state can suffer; and the improvement of it the

[Fo. 19]

object which ought in all countries to be aimed at, in preference to every other political purpose whatsoever'. Then came Malthus. The increasing population of a state may be the *result* of its prosperity. But it is a *cause* of its distress. 'The actual population may be only a sign of the happiness that is past.' And under this influence the Classical Economists lived, and, as prophets of pessimism, were hated.

Nevertheless, as an American economist[13] has lately put it, it was Malthus who brought in the era of democratic philanthropy. 'Before Malthus this criterion was the prosperity of the sovereign and of the ruling classes; thereafter it becomes the welfare of the increasing masses . . . Malthus set before the eyes of men a new picture of the humble unit of population. ~~Instead of the man with the hoe, patient taxpayer and soldier of the king, frugal workman . . . contributing to swell the rents of landlords~~

[Fo. 20]

~~and the profits of employers, Malthus helped the world to see the human individual, striving to maintain a family and to win the joys of life, but finding the very number of his fellows an obstacle in the way towards these ends.~~ Before Malthus population was a question either of political or of commercial economy; with him it began to be a question of social economy.'

[Fo. 21]

But in the last half of the 19th century an extraordinary thing happened. Malthus was forgotten or disbelieved. The cloud was lifted, the Classical Economists dethroned; and the opinions of Paley and the Vicar of Wakefield gradually reasserted themselves,—until, at the present day, so far as one can judge from the utterances of English bishops, French politicians, and German economists, public opinion does not differ very much from what it was in 1790. In ~~all the~~ the three principal states of Europe an enormous literature is growing up, to demonstrate and lament the fall of the birthrate, and to call on all patriotic citizens to ~~propagate~~ procreate.

[Fo. 21.1]

There is of course a good deal in Malthus's book which subsequent writers have rightly discarded. His reminiscences of the Mathematical Tripos led him to use the analogy of geometrical and arithmetical ratio to describe the rates of growth of population and subsistence in a manner for which there was no just foundation. Nor did he see explicitly in what way his generalisation depended on the tendency towards diminishing returns in agriculture. Most important of all, experience has disproved his supposition that any increase in economic well-being tends to bring about a corresponding increase in the rate of propagation. For a failure to anticipate the great increase in the sources of food supply which have actually occurred he can scarcely be blamed.

But his main thesis is simple, clear, and irrefutable. There is a limit to the available supply of subsistence of quite a different kind from any limit that there may be to the tendency of the human race to propagate. In general the rate of propagation has actually been so great that equilibrium has only been brought about by the influence of various kinds of checks, most of them destructive of happiness. From such

[Fo. 21.2]

considerations two principal conclusions emerge,—first, the point with which Malthus was most immediately concerned, that all political projectors and setters forth of a Utopia have here presented to them a problem which they often avoid and for which they can seldom offer a satisfactory solution, and second, that the ~~falling~~ production of that degree of populousness in the world, which is most to be desired, is not to be expected from the working of natural order, ~~and~~ that the natural degree of populousness is likely to exceed the ideal, and that the question of population is the first and perhaps the most urgent and important of the problems facing those who seek to improve the material condition of mankind. All these conclusions were true in Malthus's time and are true now. It is not in accordance with Malthus's position to suppose that a day will actually arrive either in the near future or at any time when population will have become so dense that all the inhabitants of the world will live on the margin of starvation. Before that happens, some check is likely or certain to intervene. But such an admission does not affect

[Fo. 21.3]

two judgements of pessimism,—that, even as it is, the maintenance of a proper equilibrium generally involves misery; and that in most places the material condition of mankind is inferior to what it might be if their populousness were to be diminished.

I shall maintain then, having reached at last what was, when I sat down to write, to have been the central topic of my paper that in many, if not in most, parts of the world there actually exists at the present time a denser population than is compatible with a high level of economic wellbeing. I regard the tendency of the birthrate to decline in countries inhabited by the races of Western Europe as one of the most hopeful signs of the times,—as presaging a possible escape in the future from the toils of Malthusian pessimism. In thinking in this way I am in agreement with an older tradition. But at present I probably stand in a small minority. What is the explanation of this astonishing reversal of opinion? and can it be justified?

[Fo. 22]

~~What is the explanation of this astonishing reversal of opinion? and can it be justified? Here at last I have reached what was, when I sat down to write, to have been the central topic of my paper. As it is, I must deal with it with the utmost brevity.~~

The causes of this change of opinion are, I think, mainly four:—

(1) the opening up of food supplies from parts of the world hitherto uncultivated
(2) allied to this, the dependence of countries not on their own food supply but on the world's food supply
(3) the actual decline of the birthrate in European countries mainly due to economic causes and to the widespread use of artificial methods for the prevention of conception
(4) the opportunity, given by the first three causes, for the forces of superstition in regard to these matters to reassert themselves.

[Fo. 23]

Let me take these in order and consider how far they justify the change of opinion.

First, the opening up of new sources of food supply.

It must be plain to the meanest intelligence that this factor is temporary. The opening up of the world did, so far as the nations of Europe were concerned, to some extent postpone the problem. Improvements in the science of agriculture and in methods of transport may postpone its full urgency a few years more. But they can only postpone it. We have been living for the last fifty years in a period of economic transition, probably unexampled in the history of the world; and there is hardly a single feature of our economic life the long continuance of which we are justified in anticipating.

Moreover, ~~in my own opinion,~~ as I have already said, although we are still some

[Fo. 24]

way off the time when the average individual amongst the more prosperous nations of the west will be on the margin of subsistence, we are already ~~about to be~~ faced by the problem in the sense that there would be more happiness in the world if the population of it were to be diminished. The world can be overpopulated, in the sense that every addition to this population is so much to the bad, long before the starvation point is reached. Up to about the year 1900 the law of diminishing return was to this extent suspended that every year a given quantity of manufactured product tended to be exchanged for a *larger* quantity of agricultural product. Since 1900 there has been a tendency for this to be reversed; and a given quantity of manufactured product tends to be exchanged for a smaller and smaller quantity of agricultural product.

[Fo. 25]

Besides this, there are other indications which ought not to be overlooked. From 1850 to 1900 the rate of real wages was rising in the principal western nations at a peak rate. Since 1900 there has been an unprecedented addition to the wealth of the wealthy largely due to the exploitation of the unearned increment of new countries; but real wages have been stationary or have risen but slowly.

Moreover the United States have now reached the point of consuming all the food they produce. They no longer export it.

It is very doubtful, therefore, even in the case of the West, much further postponement will be possible. If we turn to the East, I ~~am inclined to think~~ believe that the Malthusian doctrine has never ceased to be applicable there to its fullest extent. It seems to me to be certain that

[Fo. 26]

India, Egypt and China are gravely overpopulated. In the two former, I believe that the advantages of settled, humane and intelligent government have been very nearly counterbalanced by the tendency of population to increase. It would not be true to say that the material condition of the ryot and the fellah has not been somewhat improved by the British occupation of their countries; but this improvement has not been very great and certainly not so great as it would have been if the population had not so much increased. Since 1881 the population of India has increased by more than 60 million persons or about 25%. ~~The density of population in Egypt (nearly 1000 to the square mile) is about two and a half times as great as in the United Kingdom. The (administration) governments of these countries deliberately ignore, so~~

[Fo. 26.1]

The moral is pointed more precisely by reference to conditions in the Punjab. This is the one province of India in which in quite recent years the rise of real wages and of the standard of living is marked and certain. The change is not due to a single cause,—the British Government's irrigation works must have played a part. But I believe that the chief part of this explanation is to be found in the vital statistics of the Punjab. In this province the population actually fell between 1901 and 1911 and stood in the latter year about where it had been twenty years earlier. The reason for this decline is certain. Within the decade in question 10 per cent of the population was swept away by plague. Without the assistance of this beneficent visitation, twenty years of humane and settled government, the building of railways, and an expenditure of £12,000,000 in irrigation in that province alone would have availed, as we can judge from experience elsewhere, very little. Mr Haffkine's prophylactic against plague ~~will~~ may be expected to destroy in ~~another~~ the next decade the benefits of a generation of engineers and administrators.

[Fo. 27]

The density of population in Egypt, excluding the desert (nearly 1000 to the square mile) is about two and a half times as great as in the

64

United Kingdom. The governments of these countries, India and Egypt, deliberately ignore, so far as I have observed, all Malthusian considerations. It is a point of honour with the Government of India to keep skeletons just alive. When I was in Egypt ~~this~~ last year, I found Lord Kitchener engaged in a great scheme for the drainage of parts of lower Egypt and in a new Midwives bill for the diminution of infantile mortality.[14] The two measures will about cancel one another, and leave the material prosperity of the individual where it is.

The present huge population of China is not, as is commonly believed, a matter of immemorial antiquity, but is of quite modern growth. Great density of population is as recent a thing in China as it is in England. Statistics are naturally untrustworthy; but it is probably true that, whereas before the year 1700 the population of China proper did not exceed 100,000,000, it has been for the last century, and is now, somewhere

[Fo. 28]

between 300,000,000 and 400,000,000. I believe that the decay of civilisation in China is to be attributed more to this enormous growth of population than to any other single cause. The Golden Age of China, the age of her philosophers and poets and of discoveries in the arts of government and of life, was not an age of teeming and overcrowded population. It is difficult to believe that this Age can be recovered so long as those to enjoy it are so many. In Asia, at any rate, civilisation has always tended to throttle itself in a surfeit of population,—to be overlain by its own babies. It has been revived from time to time only by the various agencies of sudden death.

So much for the first influence. Three quarters of the world have never ceased to live under Malthusian conditions. And the period of postponement for the rest may possibly be coming to an end.

[Fo. 29]

The second influence is the dependence of western countries not on their own food supply but on the world's. This has ~~to a large extent~~ vastly changed the nature of the problem by internationalising ~~the problem~~ it. Formerly each country could settle the question for itself. So long as a country lived on the produce of its own soil, the real cost of food chiefly depended on the relation of a country's own population to its methods and opportunities of production. Now the real cost of food to the Englishman depends on the growth of population, not of England, but of all those countries which buy food in the same market in which she buys it. A country hardly bears a greater part of the burden of its own growth of population than it bears of the burden of the growth of population elsewhere. Thus for England to reduce her birthrate is of little use to herself; while in the race struggle as to what type shall chiefly populate the world it may possibly weaken her. The advantage of a fall in the birthrate in any country is shared

[FO. 30]

by the whole world, while there may be a racial ~~and~~ or military disadvantage to the country where it occurs. Racial and military feeling now runs high, and every patriot urges his country forward on a course of action in the widest sense anti-social. And the patriot has something on his side. What is the use of weakening internationally the stock which we think is the best, by a course of action which, if it is isolated action, will have but a negligible effect on the material prosperity of the world. It would have no more sense in it than for everyone, who has the intelligence and the imagination to appreciate the terrors of Malthusianism, to remain a bachelor. Kant's criterion of moral action does not break down least in a case like this.

The problem, therefore, is made much worse and far harder of solution by having become, since Malthus's time, cosmopolitan. It is no longer possible to have a *national* policy for the population question.

[FO. 31]

The third influence I mentioned is the actual decline of the birthrate in European countries.

In the first place the extent of this decline must not be exaggerated. From the Norman Conquest until the time of the Stuarts the population of England varied from about 2 to 4 m. When Malthus wrote it was about 9 m. It has now increased, fourfold in four generations, to 36 m. In the same period the increase in USA has been from 5 m to 92 m.; it has doubled, that is to say, in almost exact accordance with Malthus's anticipation, every generation.

If the population of the world were to increase ~~so fast as~~ no faster than that of Europe during the last 25 years, we should at the end of 1000 years be standing shoulder to shoulder over the whole habitable globe. And if we were to take the American rate . . . Even to-day, Saturday May 2, nearly twice as many people have been born as have died in such countries as Germany and England.

[Fo. 32]

The decline in the rates of increase is nevertheless very significant. The birthrate has *not* consistently advanced; as according to Malthus it should, when economic pressure is removed. On the whole it has *declined*; and a fall in the death rate, a fact which cannot possibly continue much further, has had, lately, a good deal to do with the increase of population. Also the more we see of human beings in the mass in conditions somewhat removed from those of extreme economic pressure, the more doubtful does Malthus's psychological assumption seem as to the unlimited propensity of the human race to ~~propagate~~ procreate.

I do not think there is much evidence to show that increased material prosperity brings with it a great diminution in the physical capacity to bear children, though many of the circumstances of modern life no doubt make childbirth more dangerous. I should attribute the decline mainly to three causes.

The first affects the *desire* to produce offspring. The economic disadvantageousness of children is very much greater in industrial than in primitive or agricultural communities. In Egypt I should judge that a child begins to earn something substantial towards its keep at about the age of four. The transition comes when, by the change from agriculture to industry, a large family instead of being an advantage, begins to occasion great expense.

The raising of the

school leaving age and strict regulation against the industrial employment of children may thus exercise a profound influence over the birth rate.

The second cause, which affects the *opportunity* to produce offspring, is much less important because it concerns only the upper and middle classes. It is the tendency towards the postponement of the date of marriage. This is to be explained partly by the advanced age at which a man in these classes now reaches his maximum earning power, partly by the increasing expense of social requirements, partly by the altered position of women and the greater demands which the educated classes now make of marriage, so that a~man~ men and women desirous of marriage may spend many years before an opportunity, which they are willing to take, occurs to them.

The third cause, which affects *the ability to avoid* offspring, namely the use of artificial checks, is of enormous importance. This solution, while plainly repudiated by Malthus himself, was not absent from the minds of all of his followers. Artificial checks had a place, I believe, in the ideal commonwealth of Condorcet. Owen's attitude towards them was ambiguous. James Mill, ~covertly supported them~ whose life was embittered by the financial burden of 9 children, covertly supported them. The precocious John Stuart Mill got into trouble with the police, at the age of 17, for distributing street-pamphlets which explained the nature of their use. In the countries of Europe their use and sale is open, and a considerable literature has grown up to discuss their social consequences.

In England, after characteristic fashion, the whole problem has been driven underground. The present position appears to be that a practice actually followed by enormous numbers of the most respectable persons is publicly branded as the height of immorality, and that a question of immense social significance is barely regarded as a proper subject for candid discussion. The law itself interferes half heartedly. But attempts might be made at any moment to strengthen it. These might even be successful;—for public spirit with the courage to ignore quite footling prejudices within the sphere of morals is in this country extraordinarily rare,—especially among members of Parliament. ~~One hesitates whether to wonder at the folly or at the hypocrisy of our legislators.~~ I do not know enough about this subject, it is difficult for any Englishman to know enough, to discuss it adequately. This much, however, is certain, that to put difficulties in the way of the use of checks increases the proportion of the population born from those who from drunkenness or ignorance or extreme lack of prudence, are, not only incapable of virtue, but incapable also of that degree of prudence which is involved in the use of checks.

[Fo. 35]

~~My~~ The last ~~cause~~ influence for discussion is the strength of superstition in these matters. ~~Probably~~ For thousands of generations survival has been the fortune not only of the fittest but also of the most prolific; and those races have tended to persist whose superstitions have favoured a very numerous offspring. But under modern conditions, these superstitions, while they still aid the persistence of a race, powerfully diminish its happiness. I do not see what hope there is of much improvement, moral or material, for the races of India and China, so long as the popular religions of these countries attach so great an importance to early marriage and numerous offspring. Christian doctrine on this matter is less extreme, and, partly because religion is not ~~taken so strongly~~ so influential in western countries, has not had consequences so evidently disadvantageous. ~~Indeed I agree that a greater decline in the birthrate of one Western country than in that of others is probably contrary to its interests. But the present doctrine on these matters is not permanently compatible with 19th century humanitarianism; it is also more and more out of touch with the current practice of decent people. I believe that the matter deserves fuller and more open debate, free from prejudice and distasteful abuse, than it has yet received in England. The *great* argument against checks is, of course, that they may easily go too far and involve race suicide. There are many more matters I intended to discuss, but I must now sum up. There are dilemmas in every direction. One hopeful line of possible progress can be detected—at any rate for the UK. If custom and practice develop along their present lines, it is just possible that~~

69

~~western nations may reach of their own accord a position more or less of equilibrium. They may protect themselves from the fecundity of the East by very rigorous immigration laws and other restrictive measures. And eventually they may be in a position to mould law and custom deliberately to bring about that density of population which there ought to be.~~

[Fo. 36]

Nevertheless progress must greatly depend in modern conditions on freeing the settlement of this question ~~being freed~~ from superstitious influences. Present orthodox doctrine on these matters affords no permanent or consistent line of policy. It is certainly incompatible with 19th century humanitarianism. It is also more and more out of touch with the current practice of decent people. The Church may declare that it deliberately prefers overcrowding, ignorance, poverty and disease to the employment of artificial preventives of conception; and it may bring to an end its nineteenth century flirtation with ideas of progress. Some such choice ~~in my opinion~~ is being presented to us. Anyhow let it be agreed that the matter deserves fuller and more open debate, free from prejudice and distasteful abuse, than it has yet received in England.

[Fo. 37]

I have left myself no time in which to sum up. I do not think we ought to be frightened by the fear of what is called race-suicide. I have seen no evidence of its probability. The love of children is powerful, and most normal persons will continue to desire to have children, so long as they can afford to support them. The view, that the birth of children is mainly due at present to the inadvertent consequences of sensuality, is, for England at any rate, quite unfounded.

Further we ought not to be unduly influenced by so-called patriotic or militarist arguments. While large parts of the world fit for a white population were waiting to be filled up by European emigration racial arguments rightly carried considerable weight. This temporary state of affairs is rapidly coming to an end. In the future we can act with our attention chiefly directed towards the economic wellbeing of the population of our own country, with but secondary regard to the numerical position of our race in the world as a whole. National and military advantages are at least as likely to be diminished as increased by the evils of over-population. On the other hand cosmopolitan humanitarianism

[Fo. 38]

must be indulged in but very moderately if evil consequences are to be avoided. Almost any measures seem to me to be justified in order to protect our standard of life from injury at the hands of more prolific races. Some definite parcelling out of the world may well become necessary; and I suppose that this may not improbably provoke racial wars. At any rate such wars will be about a substantial issue. Countries in the position of British Columbia are entirely justified in protecting themselves from the fecundity of the East by very rigorous immigration laws and other restrictive measures. I can imagine a time when it may be the right policy even to regulate the international trade in food supplies, though there are economic reasons, which I cannot go into now, for thinking this improbable.

[Fo. 39]

~~There are~~ Though awkward dilemmas confront in every direction those who would influence action, for progress in the West ~~it is possible to~~ one can feel some hope. If custom and practice are encouraged to develop along their present lines, it is just possible that western nations may reach of their own accord a ~~position~~ state more or less of equilibrium. Eventually they may be in a position to mould law and custom deliberately to bring about that density of population which is the best.

[notes and name list on back of manuscript]

Withers—I am not pessimistic provided checks etc. not discouraged. Quite prepared to admit that new food supplies may keep us from getting worse off

But can we get better off

additional fecundity of lower classes due to expense of checks

Ind. G of. stats. Landowners

I begged the question that if the economic well-being of the British lower classes would be improved if their numbers were reduced it would be a good thing.

1900 turning point

Is birth rate falling too far

> quantity v quality not commensurate
>
> But economic v moral considerations
>
> If any moral consideration absolute
> it must be the greater good

J. A. Hobson
Henley Withers
Gilbert Murray
Graham Wallas
W. H. Beveridge
Bishop of Bedford
W. T. Layton
J. A. Smith
Hastings Rashdall
Cadbury
A. J. Carlisle
Barker

NOTES

1. Gilbert Wakefield (1756–1801), after a brilliant undergraduate career, became in 1776 a Fellow of Jesus College, Cambridge. He resigned from his Fellowship and from the Church of England in 1779. He became a leading and controversial figure in the Unitarian movement. In 1782, Robert Malthus was sent by his father to the Dissenting Academy in Warrington, where he lived and was taught by Wakefield. He made a new translation of the New Testament, and published an edition of Lucretius' *De Rerum Natura*, which is now regarded as his finest work. After publishing a pacifist pamphlet in 1798, he served two years in prison for seditious libel.

2. Henry Gunning (1768–1854) was a contemporary of Malthus, and

a Fellow of Christ's College, Cambridge. In his old age, he wrote *Reminiscences of the University, Town, and County of Cambridge from the Year 1780*, which was published in 1854.

3. The 'Lake School' is a dubious category, a label applied by others to the poets concerned, simply because Wordsworth, Coleridge, and Southey all lived in the Lake District of Britain. Southey shared Coleridge's antipathy to Malthus's views on population (Winch, 1987: 52).

4. In the 1933 version of his essay on Malthus, Keynes added the following note: 'Before which I read, on 2 April 1924, an earlier version of this essay under the question, "What sort of man was the Reverend Robert Malthus" '. The London Political Economy Club is not to be confused with the Political Economy Club that Keynes himself founded in October 1909 for Cambridge economics undergraduates. Harrod gives a colourful account of Keynes reading the 1922 version of his Malthus paper to the Cambridge Political Economy Club, illustrating how sensitive the topic of birth control was then (Harrod, 1972/1951: 174, 385–7).

5. David Ricardo (1772–1823), banker, economist, and Member of Parliament. This is the sole reference in the text of 'Population' to Malthus's friendship with David Ricardo and the prolonged correspondence between the two men about the right way to analyse economic production and distribution. This is probably because in 1913–14, most of Malthus's side of the correspondence still remained to be rediscovered. The final version of Keynes's essay on Malthus has much more to say about the Malthus of *The Principles of Political Economy* (1820), and it says less about Malthus the population theorist than does 'Population'. The Malthus–Ricardo correspondence is to be found in Ricardo (*Works*: vols. vi–ix). For further discussion, see Ch. 5.

6. Jean-Jacques Rousseau (1712–78), the Geneva-born social and political philosopher, is best known for his *Le Contrat social* (1762). Earlier, in 1757–60, he had written *Émile*, which is aptly described by the words that Rousseau put in the mouth of a potential critic, namely 'not so much a treatise on education as the visions of a dreamer with regard to education'. In it, he advanced a radical view of child-centred development in harmony with nature, completely at odds with established systems of formal instruction. He never prescribed a single educational method or programme to be followed at all times and places.

7. William Otter (1768–1840), a leading Evangelical divine, Bishop of Chichester, and Malthus's biographer.

8. The Directory was the name of the five-man oligarchy that ruled France briefly (from 1795 to 1799).

9. William Pitt the Younger (1759–1806), the prime minister of the day.

10. William Paley (1743–1805), author of *Principles of Moral and Political Philosophy* (1785) and other works.

11. Edward Daniel Clarke (1769–1822), who became a Fellow of Jesus College, Cambridge in 1795, was a close friend of Malthus, and a personality that dominated College life in the first two decades of the 19th century. On his extensive travels, he made collections of minerals, antiquities, paintings, drawings, manuscripts, plants, and seeds (*CW*, x. 79).

12. Edwin Cannan (1861–1935), Professor of Economics at the University of London, whose *History of the Theories of Production and Distribution* went into three editions between 1893 and 1924.

13. My efforts to identify the American economist whose view of Malthus is quoted by Keynes have failed completely.

14. What was the source of Keynes's knowledge of the Midwives Bill? During his brief visit to Egypt in April 1913, he had discussions with both Robin Furness, an official in the Ministry of Finance, and Maurice Amos, a Judge of the Egyptian Court of Appeal. Furness was a old friend from undergraduate days in King's College. Amos appears the likelier source of the two (Harrod, 1972/1951: 66, 192; Skidelsky, 1983: 274).

3

'Population': A Commentary

I. EARLY TWENTIETH-CENTURY
PRO-NATALISTS AS KEYNES'S
RHETORICAL TARGET

The argument of Keynes's lecture on 'Population' was polemical
in intent. Its rhetorical purpose was to persuade his hearers of
the dangers of population growth, and of the practicality of
actively limiting the size of Britain's future population. Keynes's
intended wider audience was thus those pro-natalists who, at
the turn of the twentieth century, were making increasingly
energetic and strident efforts to turn public opinion in their
direction, and who were having a growing success in the political arena. In 'Population', Keynes memorably categorized the
sources of early twentieth-century pro-natalism as **English
bishops, French politicians and German economists** (Fo. 21). In
order to have an understanding of some of the ideas and
political pressures that Keynes was concerned to weaken through
his critical assault, this commentary begins by examining each of
these three categories.

In England, the decade before 1914 had witnessed a series
of pronouncements by members of the Anglican episcopate
directed against marriages that avoided parenthood. Many of
these statements expressed anxieties about the future of the
British empire, which were formulated in the language of race.
For example, in 1904, William Boyd Carpenter, Bishop of Ripon,
warned that 'it is left to the tramp, to the hooligan, and the
lounger to maintain the population. This is not the way to rear

up a great Imperial race'. In 1905, Arthur Foley Winnington-Ingram, Bishop of London, claimed that artificial prevention of births had 'spread like a blight over the middle-class population of the land'. George F. Browne, Bishop of Bristol, chaired a committee which produced a resolution approved by the 1908 Lambeth Conference calling upon 'all Christian people to discountenance the use of all artificial means of restriction as demoralising to character and hostile of national welfare'. The Lambeth Conference resolution lacked any formal authority, but created considerable public controversy. In 1911, the Bishop of London described family limitation as a 'sin'. Cosmo Gordon Lang, Archbishop of York, and Edgar Gibson, Bishop of Gloucester, defended this pronouncement. The Bishops of London and Ripon circulated in 1913 a memorandum entitled 'The Misuse of Marriage' to the clergy and laity, in which they sought to clarify the practical implications of the 1908 Lambeth Conference resolutions. The Bishop of Southwark dissented from this, because he objected to natural as well as artificial means of family limitation. That most of the leaders of the Church of England opposed birth control need not be doubted (Soloway, 1982: 90–111).

Only W. R. Inge, Dean of St Paul's, spoke out in favour of deliberately chosen small families, in 1912. He did so on negative eugenic grounds, taking a position similar to Keynes's. Keynes later recognized this exception in *An Economist's View of Population* (*CW*, xvii: 442). There he again referred to 'the utterances of English bishops, French politicians, German economists', added 'and Bolshevik Russians', and appended a footnote to 'English bishops' which said 'I except deans (Inge, the gloomy Dean)'.

The pro-natalism of **French politicians** was more fervent than that of the English bishops, and was an accurate reflection of the anxieties of many of their constituents. These arose from powerful fears of the military consequences of the exceptionally rapid decline in fertility in France. After her 1870 defeat in the

Franco–Prussian war, the slow rate of population growth caused widespread concern because of its serious implications for French military strength relative to that of the new German empire. Although this concern extended to the need to reduce infant mortality, its main thrust, symbolized by Zola's novel *Fécondité* (1899), was the need to reverse the decline in fertility (Teitelbaum and Winter, 1985: 18–30). Thus French opposition to neo-Malthusianism was broad-based in the period 1870–1914. It certainly included the Roman Catholic Church, which was as an institution more hostile than the English episcopate, basing its opposition on the moral value of chastity and periodic abstinence within marriage, as Malthus himself did. The French medical profession was also hostile, basing its objections both on the defence of 'family values', and the alleged medical ill consequences of using contraceptive methods. The legal profession aided and abetted the prosecution of writers of contraceptive manuals under the laws against pornography.

The political offensive against neo-Malthusianism in France took two forms. One was active campaigning and the organization of direct action in support of repressive laws against public discussion and sale of contraceptives. Among the leaders of this activity were Senator René Béranger (1830–1915), who founded the Fédération des société's contre la pornographie in 1905, and his successor, Professor Charles Gide. Another was Jacques Bertillon, a statistician who directed the Alliance nationale pour l'accroissement de la population française, and wrote *La Dépopulation de la France* (1911). The membership and Funds of the Alliance nationale grew very rapidly in 1913 and 1914. Other similar leagues sprang up. For example, in 1912 a new league called La Race française was established. Apart from meetings, propaganda, and street demonstrations, the main outcomes were the mounting of prosecutions against individual neo-Malthusians on charges of handling pornography, and the gift of child-care supplies to young unmarried mothers to encourage them to keep their babies (Ronsin, 1980: 121–31).

The second political thrust against French neo-Malthusians was conducted in the legislature. In 1900, the French Senate had voted for an inter-parliamentary Commission on Depopulation, and this was set up by Waldek-Rousseau early in 1902. Work went on very slowly, but eventually a sub-commission on Mortality, which held several sittings between 1908 and early 1911, reported in favour of outlawing the sale and distribution of all abortifacient and contraceptive materials, including manuals and information thereon. This report was then debated in the Senate and Chamber of Deputies, with ministers being accused of excessive toleration of contraception. In 1910, one Professor Lannelongue introduced proposals in the Senate to impose additional military obligations on bachelors and to create incentives for officials to marry. These were laid aside in favour of the bill criminalizing abortion and contraception. The Senate held further hearings on this in January and February 1913, which might have been fresh in Keynes's mind when he wrote 'Population'. The bill was not finally approved until after the Great War, when nationalist and pro-natalist passions reached high tide. Among those who voted in favour of the Loi du 31 juillet 1920 were Aristide Briand, Maurice Barres, Edouard Daladier, Leon Daudet, Paul Reynaud, and Robert Schumann. Those opposed were mainly socialists, led by Vincent Auriol and Léon Blum (Ronsin, 1980: 137–48).

In Germany, after unification in 1870, nationalism also created an unfavourable atmosphere for neo-Malthusianism, which was expressed by **German economists** among others. Friedrich List's best-known work, *The National System of Political Economy*, had already set this trend. List applied his habit of energetic contradiction to his notion of the ideas of Malthus. He argued that it is narrow-minded to worry about the disproportion of population growth to the growth of subsistence 'so long as on the globe a mass of natural forces still lies inert by means of which ten times or perhaps a hundred times more people than are now living can be sustained'. He also castigates Malthus's doctrine as an unnatural one 'which seeks to destroy a desire which nature uses as the most active means for inciting men to exert mind and body, and to awaken and support their nobler feelings' (List, 1977/1885: 127).

Keynes's understanding of the views of German economists on population probably derived from an article in the *Economic Journal* by Gustav Cohn. Soon after Keynes became its editor, the *Economic Journal* carried an article by Professor Cohn of Göttingen University on the increase of population in Germany. Given its anti-neo-Malthusian content and the short gap between its appearance in March 1912 and the start of Keynes's editorship in late December 1911, it was almost certainly accepted for publication by his predecessor, Francis Ysidro Edgeworth. Cohn's name did not appear on the list that Keynes kept of contributors to the March 1912 *Economic Journal* with whom he had corresponded (EJ/1/1/83). However, Keynes did receive a postcard from Cohn in early April 1912 thanking him for improving the English of the article.[1] So we can be sure that Keynes did read it.

Cohn's view of the state of German opinion was that

Thirty to forty years ago some leading German statistical authorities held that a population of between forty and forty-five millions was too large for the country. To-day many critics are of the opinion that sixty-six millions can very well be accommodated. There is even a widespread anxiety, since population no longer increases at quite the same rate, respecting the exploitation of the available resources for increasing the means of subsistence. . . . This anxiety becomes intelligible when we find that it generally coincides with the belief that the neo-Malthusian movement is gaining ground, and that a rapid development that would approximate to the French condition of affairs might ensue . . .

To-day our views on the whole subject of numbers and future development have been transformed . . . Not only have favourable experiences destroyed the bogey of over-population, not only have we been convinced that we can provide the means of subsistence for a much larger population, but we have developed . . . a national ideal of progress both as regards the quantity of life and the quality of its sustenance (Cohn, 1912: 35, 40).

Cohn concludes by pointing to the ill consequences of neo-Malthusianism in France, although admitting that Bertillon's *La Dépopulation de la France* contains some 'bold exaggerations'.

Keynes seems to have taken Cohn's description of German economists' opinions at face value. In fact, not all German writers of the time were in the anti-Malthus camp. At least two German authors who were favourable to neo-Malthusian views had published their work just before 1914 (Petersen, 1964: 53–4). One was Jessie Marburg (1912). The other was Siegfried Budge (1913). In the 1920s, German economists swung more in this direction, possibly influenced by Keynes's own writings (as Petersen suggests), but no doubt also mindful of the post-war economic circumstances of their country.

Clearly, Western Europe in the years before 1914 exhibited a wide and powerful range of opinion, spiritual and temporal, practical and academic, that supported the pro-natalist movement of his day. The contemporary currents of nationalism and imperialism were running strongly in favour of natalism. How could Keynes persuade his hearers of the necessity of neo-Malthusianism in this political and ideological context?

II. POPULATION THINKING BEFORE MALTHUS

'Population' has its own rhetorical strategy. It is to represent the modern pro-natalists as hardly distinguishable from pre-Malthusian thinkers and writers on population. By them, **Malthus was forgotten or disbelieved** (Fo. 21). Pro-natalism was, on this account, a regression to an earlier, pre-scientific age, in that it disregarded truths that were **simple, clear and irrefutable** (Fo. 21.1). This line of argument involved an important assumption. It was that Malthus's views marked a clear break with all the writing on population that had gone before him. If they did not constitute an intellectual leap forward, the charge of scientific regression would lose its persuasive force. Accordingly,

Keynes argues that Malthus's contribution to the population debate was historically decisive.

Keynes drew on two main sources for his information about, and his understanding of, the eighteenth- and early nineteenth-century intellectual background to Malthus's population principle. The first and most important was Edwin Cannan's history of English political economy (1924/1893). The second was James Bonar's book on the life and work of Malthus (1966/1885). Edwin **Cannan** (1861–1935), Professor of Political Economy at the London School of Economics, is probably most noted now as an editor of the works of Adam Smith. But he also wrote *A History of the Theories of Production and Distribution in English Political Economy from 1776 to 1848*, which was first published in 1893.[2] Cannan's *Theories* was the basic source from which Keynes took his account of eighteenth-century views on population before Malthus. The most obvious evidence of this is the fact that the same quotations from *The Vicar of Wakefield*, Adam Smith, Pitt, and Paley which Keynes uses in 'Population' (Fos. 18–19) all appeared first in Cannan's book (1924/1893: 124–5). Moreover, they appear there in the same order as in 'Population', with only Cannan's quotation from Hume being passed over.

These four quotations are used by Keynes as evidence of erroneous thinking on population which Malthus overturned, but which the pro-natalists had revived in his own time. Keynes implies that his (and Cannan's) exemplars are typical of eighteenth-century pro-natalists who, ignorant of what Malthus would prove, favoured population expansion without regard for the availability of the means of subsistence. In order to bolster this implied suggestion, for nowhere is it stated in so many words, Keynes ignores the template provided by Cannan's text. He does not go on to discuss the work of individual pre-Malthusian writers who did, in many important ways, anticipate Malthus's principle of population. The effect of this is to reverse the priorities of Cannan, who devoted more space to them than to those he found to be in pre-Malthusian error. Keynes's selective use

of Cannan over-emphasizes the originality of Malthus in pro-
pounding the basic principle of population, and at the same time
misses his truly original contributions.

It is highly unlikely that Keynes took the trouble to check the
contexts from which Cannan took his allegedly pro-natalist
quotations. The quotation from **The Vicar of Wakefield** is the
opening line of Oliver Goldsmith's only novel, *The Vicar of Wakefield* (1766). Dr Primrose does indeed exhort the bachelors of his
parish to matrimony. However, the criticism of the good pastor
is much weakened when Keynes himself grants later in the text
that it makes no sense 'for everyone, who has the intelligence and
the imagination to appreciate the terrors of Malthusianism, to
remain a bachelor' (Fo. 30).

The source of the quotation from **Adam Smith** is chapter VIII
('Of the Wages of Labour') in *The Wealth of Nations* (Smith,
1976/1776: 87–8). The context is Smith's argument that 'it is not
the actual greatness of national wealth, but its continual increase,
which occasions a rise in the wages of labour'. Smith contrasts
the rapid economic growth of (poorer) North America with the
slower growth of (richer) England. His statement that 'the most
decisive mark of the prosperity of any country is the increase of
the number of its inhabitants' thus has to be read in a dynamic
sense. The rate of population growth is an indicator of a
country's 'thriving', the rapidity with which it is advancing to the
further acquisition of riches. Moreover, it is such an indicator
because 'the produce of the soil maintains at all times nearly that
number of inhabitants that it is capable of maintaining', as Smith
had said in his *Theory of Moral Sentiments* (Smith, 1976/1759: 184).
This was a widely held view in the eighteenth century, shared by
Smith and Malthus, not to mention Godwin. That Smith quali-
fies the congruence of population and subsistence by the word
'nearly' shows that he did not deny that population could sometimes run a little ahead of subsistence, giving rise to the 'oscillations' that Malthus later elaborated, or could sometimes run a

little behind, as both he and Malthus believed was the case in North America.

Smith's further point was that labour in North America is 'so well rewarded that a numerous family of children, instead of being a burthen, is a source of opulence and prosperity to the parents [since] the labour of each child, before it can leave their house, is computed to be worth a hundred pounds clear gain to them'. It is exactly the same point about the impact of the economic value of children on fertility that Keynes himself makes later in 'Population' (Fos. 32–3). As with the Vicar of Wakefield, he had more in common with Smith than he realized.

The strong contrast that Keynes, following Cannan, draws between the positions of Smith and Malthus on population size as an indicator of prosperity is exaggerated. Malthus, in the appendix to the 1806 edition of the *Essay on the Principle of Population*, says:

It is an utter misconception of my argument to infer that I am an enemy to population. I am only an enemy to vice and misery, and consequently to that unfavourable proportion between population and food which produces these evils. But this unfavourable proportion has no necessary connection with the quantity of absolute population which a country may contain. On the contrary, it is more frequently found in countries which are very thinly peopled than in those which are populous. (Malthus, 1989/1803: ii. 205).

The more densely a country is populated, the *less* likely it is to suffer a Malthusian subsistence crisis. In support of this view, the first *Essay* itself says that 'there is not a truer criterion of the happiness and innocence of a people, than the rapidity of their increase' (Von Tunzelmann, 1986: 90–1).

Undoubtedly, Malthus shared Smith's position that at all times the produce of the soil maintains *nearly* that number of inhabitants it is capable of maintaining. What concerned Malthus especially, however, was the process of population growth somewhat overshooting subsistence, and that overshoot then having to be corrected. Malthus saw that, even when population growth is accompanied by wages that are rising in nominal terms, it is possible that the nominal price of provisions could rise faster, depressing the real wage rate, and thus checking population growth. He did not dissent from Smith's analysis of the labour market in North America, but thought this outcome was a result of the fact that there 'the means of subsistence have been more ample' (Malthus, 1989/1803: i. 11, 22).

Paley is taken by Keynes, as by Cannan, as another pronatalist. According to Keynes (Fo. 16), Malthus was **proudest himself of having converted Pitt and Paley.** William Paley was a 'fellow and tutor of Christ's, . . . Archdeacon of Carlisle, author of the *Principles of Moral and Political Philosophy*, which anticipated Bentham, and of what is generally known as "Paley's Evidences" *(Natural Theology, or Evidence of the Existence and Attributes of the Deity collected from the Appearances of Nature)'* (*CW*, x. 232). Malthus's disagreement with Paley originated in the former's first unpublished essay of 1796, 'The Crisis, a View of the Recent Interesting State of Great Britain by a Friend of the Constitution'. Paley's statement, quoted on Fos. 18–19, that 'the decay of population is the greatest evil that the state can suffer' is part of his discussion of the aims of rational politics. He maintains that the maximization of happiness within a territory is done more effectively by increasing the number of inhabitants with a healthy subsistence than by increasing the level of opulence of a given number of inhabitants (Paley, 1799: 347). This evidently is not the same as saying that population should be encouraged to grow without any regard for the availability of the means of subsistence. It is simply that Paley has a different trade-off between increased numbers and increased living standards than Keynes who, as we have seen, 'inclined, with some compromise, to prefer a high level to numbers' (UA/6/9/25).

Paley's account of population is, as Waterman (1996) claims, very similar to that of Malthus. Paley had already stated that 'nature has provided for an indefinite multiplication', so that the key question must be 'what are the causes which confine or check the natural progress of this multiplication?', and that the answer must be that 'the population of a country must stop when the country can maintain no more, that is, when the inhabitants are already so numerous as to exhaust all the provision which the soil can be made to produce' (Paley, 1799: 348–9). Paley did not think that the population of England had yet reached the maximum ultimately possible, because there was considerable scope, in his view, for raising both the extent of cultivation and the level of agricultural productivity. To say this is not to say that he believed that this population growth would be limited only in the future. He stated quite clearly that 'the rapidity, as well as the extent of the increase' in population 'will be proportioned to the degree in which these causes exist', namely, the confinement of sexual intercourse within marriage and the ease and certainty experienced by each class of people in procuring its conventional standard of subsistence (ibid. 350–1).

Given this degree of anticipation of Malthus's doctrines by Paley, what was left for Malthus to convert Paley to? Paley held a particular belief about the danger of the diffusion of luxury consumption. On the one hand, as has been pointed out, he did not think that it added much at the margin to the sum of happiness. On the other hand, he thought that it would raise the cost of conventional subsistence, and by so doing deter marriage and thus deter population increase—which he did rate highly for its incremental contribution to the sum of happiness in a country.

It was this view that Malthus claimed to have persuaded Paley to abandon, by arguing as follows:

If, indeed, it be allowed that in every society not in the state of a new colony some powerful check to population must prevail; and if it be observed that a taste for the comforts and conveniences of life will prevent people from marrying under the certainty of being deprived of these advantages; it must be allowed that we can hardly expect to find any check to marriage so little prejudicial to the happiness and virtue of society as the general prevalence of such a taste; and consequently that the spread of luxury in this sense of the term is particularly desirable; and one of the best means of raising the standard of wretchedness . . . (Malthus, 1989/1803: ii. 193–4)

Paley was converted by the above argument to abandon his opposition to the diffusion of luxury throughout the population, not to abandon some primitive pro-natalist creed, as implied by Cannan and Keynes.

That Malthus's population doctrine was **largely anticipated in a clumsier way** by earlier writers was indeed acknowledged by Keynes, although he departed from Cannan by not mentioning any of these anticipations. Apart from Paley, we may note two other clear anticipations of Malthus's principle. Robert Wallace, a Scottish clergyman and amateur economist, argued in his *Various Prospects of Mankind, Nature and Providence* that 'under a perfect government, the inconveniences of having a family would be so entirely removed . . . that . . . mankind would encrease so prodigiously, that the earth would at last be overstocked, and become unable to support its numerous inhabitants' unless 'some wise adept in the occult sciences, should invent a method of supporting mankind quite different from anything known at present', and even then 'there would not be sufficient room for containing their bodies upon the surface of the earth' (Wallace, 1969/1761: 114–16). In the preface to the 1803 edition of his *Essay*, Malthus acknowledged the influence on it of Wallace, as well as of Hume, Smith, and Price. These were objections to the communism of property that **William Godwin** had already addressed in his *Political Justice* (Marshall, 1984: 112).

Joseph Townsend, in his *A Dissertation on the Poor Laws* (1786), argued against instituting the communism of goods while leaving everyone free to marry, on the ground that 'they would first increase their numbers, but not the sum total of their happiness, till by degrees, all being equally reduced to want and misery, the weakly would be the first to perish'. This argument implies a maximum level of food production (Halevy, 1960/1928: 228–30). The Marquis de **Condorcet** (Fo. 33), in his *Sketch for an Historical Picture of the Progress of the Human Mind* (1955/1795: 189), conceded that 'it is possible . . . that there should be a limit to the amount of food that can be produced and, consequently, to the size of the population of the world'. However, he thought that the progress of reason would ensure that 'men will know that, if they have a duty towards those who are not yet born, that duty is not to give them existence but to give them happiness', a clear enough hint that birth control should be used to adjust births to the maximum sustainable population. Condorcet was not so much advocating an **ideal commonwealth,** as suggested by Keynes, as making a forecast of the forms that future human progress would take.

These anticipations carry significant implications for Keynes's view of Malthus. In the first place they weaken the force of the contrast he presents elsewhere in the text between pre-Malthusian and post-Malthusian thinking on population, as in **Then came Malthus** (Fo. 19). Second, they show that Malthus was entering into a well-established eighteenth-century debate, and that his chosen opponents—Godwin and Condorcet—had already considered, and on various grounds rejected, his principle of population (Winch, 1987: 16, 26–7). Third, the question arises of the sense in which Malthus's formulation of the principle was less clumsy than that of Wallace and Townsend. Since Keynes explicitly rejects the **analogy of the geometrical and arithmetical ratio to describe the rates of growth of population and subsistence** (Fo. 21.1), what is the nature of Malthus's superiority? Keynes makes it appear as if it was largely a matter of presentation, Malthus's smashing emphasis on a simple generalization. It seems more correct to argue, following Winch, that Malthus's special contribution was to elaborate 'the precise ways in which population growth *had in fact been limited* by the operation of a series of checks which entailed vice and misery in one form or another' (ibid. 19; emphasis added). For Malthus, the limits to population growth were not something that would happen in the future: they were already in operation.

III. KEYNES ON MALTHUS

To contrast Malthus with the supposed naïve pro-natalism of his predecessors, he himself is raised to great heights. Just how high is a matter of a little equivocation. On the one hand he was the author of **a very great book** (Fo. 13). On the other hand, although he has a place in the English scientific pantheon, he is **not quite in the first rank of it** (Fo. 16). However, his is **no case of a man of second-rate powers** (Fo. 13). One senses the examiner at work, slightly unsure of the exact mark to be awarded. Malthus is evidently to be placed somewhere near the top of the list.

When one reads the justification for this placing, it seems unconvincing. Although one does not disagree much with the mark, the reasons given for it prove to be inadequate and unpersuasive. Keynes favoured the youthful inspiration of the original 1798 edition, explaining this judgement later by claiming that the importance of the *Essay* 'consisted not in the novelty of its facts but in the smashing emphasis [Malthus] placed on a simple generalisation arising out of them' (*CW*, x. 86). The second (1803) edition added very substantially to its empirical content, including country and area studies of an astonishing range—the South Seas, Africa, Siberia, Turkey, Persia, 'Indostan', Tibet, China, and Japan—to mention only those in book I. This greatly expanded empirical material is rich in historical scholarship and sociological and anthropological insights. Nevertheless, the qualification and attenuation of the force of the original principle which the case-studies required did not appeal to Keynes. He thought, mistakenly as it has turned out, that posterity would join him in the view that the 1798 edition was 'a superior book'.

Within the framework of that fundamental and unchanging

judgement, the 1913–14 manuscript on 'Population' provides a distinctly more nuanced appreciation of Malthus's work on population than does the 1933 biographical essay. The latter praises Malthus's simple generalization, but it does not specify precisely what he understood that generalization to be. 'Population' had in fact already provided what the essay omitted. First of all, it rejects two of Malthus's well-known propositions, saying that **subsequent writers have rightly discarded** them (Fo. 21.1). It declares that there is no just foundation for the attribution of geometrical growth to population and arithmetical growth to the means of subsistence.[3] Second, on the basis of British experience in the second half of the nineteenth century, it rejects the proposition that *any* increase in economic well-being tends to increase the rate of population growth, thus following his line of argument in the first half of his 1912 lectures.

Keynes then again followed Cannan by criticizing Malthus for not seeing how his principle of population depended on the existence of **diminishing returns in agriculture.** Keynes endorsed the view, already long established by 1914, that Malthus erred in relying on his arithmetical ratio of the growth of the means of subsistence, but that his population principle could be salvaged by substituting for it 'the tendency to diminishing returns in agriculture'. This doctrine is attributable to John Stuart Mill's *Principles of Political Economy* (Mill, 1904/1848). As a criticism of Malthus it is misguided, in the sense that the two notions are not substitutes but complements, and Malthus himself, as already discussed in Chapter 1, had in fact arrived at the principle of diminishing returns in agriculture in the 1798 edition of his *Essay.*

Mill believed in an optimum level of population, which, if surpassed, reduces average welfare:

After a degree of density has been attained sufficient to allow the principal benefits of a combination of labour, all further increase tends in itself to mischief so far as regards the average condition of the people. (ibid. 118)

Mill allows that the progress of improvement may validate an actual population increase beyond the optimum, in the sense that it may prevent actual agricultural costs from rising, or it may temporarily reduce them. However, once the optimum has been passed in this way, reducing the population until the optimum level is regained can increase average welfare. Mill puts this proposition, with some obscurity, as follows:

But though improvement may, during a certain space of time, keep up with or even surpass the actual increase in population, it assuredly never comes up to the rate of increase of which population is capable; and nothing could have prevented a general deterioration in the condition of the human race, were it not that population has in fact been restrained. Had it been restrained still more, and the same improvements taken place, there would have been a larger dividend than there now is for the nation or the species at large. (ibid. 119)

Cannan points out tartly that Mill regarded the population density of 1848 as optimal, and that, if population had in fact been restrained to that level, the improvements that had occurred since then would have been perfectly inconceivable (1924/1893: 181–2). Hollander's conclusion is that 'Mill was on occasion carried away by his concern with population growth and stated his case more strongly than either the historical cost data or the analytical model and its methodological status or his own appreciation of the contemporary impact of new technology merited' (1985: i. 237).

Mill further defined the optimum size of population as a population density 'sufficient to allow the principal benefits of combination of labour' and 'necessary to enable mankind to obtain, in the greatest degree, all the advantages both of co-operation and of social intercourse' (Mill, 1904/1848: 118, 454). This in turn provided a definition of overpopulation, namely population density in excess of the optimum. In all this we can see a clear departure from Malthus, for whom the existence of overpopulation was an impossibility, except in the very short run. His model of dynamic 'oscillations' presented a regulatory mechanism that prevented the growth of population beyond the available means of subsistence, while acknowledging that the amount of vice and misery (and, post-1803, prudential restraint) necessary to achieve this adjustment would vary across space and time, according to the general state of development of the economy and society.

Keynes in 'Population' takes up Mill's idea of an **ideal** level of population (Fo. 21.2) and says that *in most places* the material condition of mankind is inferior to what it might be if their populousness were to be diminished (Fo. 21.3; emphasis added). To make the distinction between this generalized or endemic overpopulation and the condition of India, Egypt, and China, he describes the latter three countries as being *gravely* overpopulated (Fo. 26; emphasis added). Keynes took up the occasional population concerns of Mill, based on the tendency to diminishing returns in agriculture, and drew from them some very strong conclusions.[4] Once this had been done and an imperative to reduce existing populations had been set up, it was only one more step to welcoming the positive checks to population, and the misery they bring, as **beneficent visitations** (Fo. 26.1).

Keynes's second major criticism of Malthus's population principle was its **failure to anticipate** (Fo. 21.1) the size of future increases in food supplies. Although this failure of anticipation was seen as a flaw in the doctrine, Keynes (like Marshall before him) did not think that it was a culpable one, presumably because he judged the foresight required to avoid it as extraordinary. However, to say that Malthus should not be blamed for failing to anticipate the subsequent great increase in food supplies betrays a misunderstanding of Malthus's principle of population. It is exoneration for not taking account of something that he believed to be utterly irrelevant to the soundness of his principle. He believed that, however rapidly the supply of food increased, population would soon inevitably increase even more rapidly. He says this quite explicitly:

The allowing of the produce of the earth to be absolutely unlimited, scarcely removes the weight of a hair from the argument, which depends entirely upon the differently increasing ratios of population and food: and all that the most enlightened governments, and the most persevering and best guided efforts of industry can do, is to make the necessary checks to population operate more equably, and in a direction to produce the least evil; but to remove them, is a task absolutely hopeless. (Malthus, 1989/1803: i. 445)

What Malthus failed to anticipate, then, was not that the food supply could greatly increase, but that the power of population could be checked before it fully adjusted to the available food supply, thereby allowing the average standard of living to rise.

Furthermore, as has already been pointed out in Chapter 1, it is not even true that Malthus wholly failed to anticipate the great increase in the sources of food supply that occurred in the nineteenth century. He did address this possibility, in the form of a thought experiment based on the assumption that North America could still be expected to produce food in excess of the immediate needs of its population, and that this surplus could be exchanged for European manufactures. Admittedly, he regarded this as an 'extravagant supposition'. In strictest logic, it was more than this. It was a direct contradiction of his own principle that population will *always* catch up with the available means of subsistence. Nevertheless, he did make it.

What is remarkable about this argument is that it is almost identical with the one that Keynes himself goes on to sketch at Fos. 23–5. Yet it is nowhere referred to in 'Population', although it could have been used to give credit to Malthus for farsightedness. The passage was, however, later quoted in this sense by Wright (1923: 170–1), who was writing under Keynes's editorial supervision. Did Wright know his Malthus better than Keynes? Did Keynes stumble on it later? Or had he already absorbed it, and made it his own?

Having acknowledged these supposed errors of Malthus,

'Population' proceeds to embrace the three elements of Malthus's thesis that Keynes found simple, clear, and irrefutable. Leaving aside the mathematical formulation, it remained true that the limits on the growth of supplies for subsistence were of quite a different kind from—thereby implying that they were much more stringent than—the limits on human propagation. Thus, societies face a central problem which creators of utopias do not squarely address. Moreover, the equilibrium between demand for and supply of subsistence has been achieved only by the operation of various unpleasant checks on population growth, so that an optimum population level cannot be expected to occur from the working of the natural order. Therefore, all those who want to improve the material conditions of mankind should treat the reduction of the growth of population as their most urgent and important problem, in 1914 just as in Malthus's day.

Here we have a clearer and more comprehensive statement than anywhere in his published writings of what Keynes believed to be the enduring contribution of Malthus to population studies. In his later writings on population, Keynes used a shorthand phrase to represent this set of ideas. This phrase is 'the Malthusian devil'. 'Population', though innocent of the words, provides the content of that phrase: a persistent propensity for population growth to exceed that of the means of subsistence, leading to positive checks that add to human misery and that indicate the desirability of interventions aimed at protecting the economic standard of living.

Keynes's judgement of the superiority of the first, polemical edition over the second gives the clue to his preferred interpretation of Malthus on population:

The polemical first edition . . . became thereafter synonymous with 'Malthusianism' . . . The reality of Malthus's model is not only more optimistic but far richer in its historical and predictive content. For this reason we should clearly distinguish Malthus's model from 'Malthusian' models. (von Tunzelmann, 1991: 274)

Keynes's definition of the enduring truths of Malthus in 'Population' shows him to have been, in von Tunzelmann's sense, a Malthusian, rather than a connoisseur of Malthus's population model. In 'Population', that model of 'oscillations'—the dynamic sequence of population spurt, falling real standard of living, population stagnation, increased demand for labour, and recovery of living standards—is alluded to only once, and then brushed aside (Fo. 32). Yet that is the basis of his reputation at the end of the twentieth century (see for example Hollingsworth, 1973: p. xxv; Winch, 1987: 95; Wrigley, 1988: 38).

IV. NEO-MALTHUSIANS AND ARTIFICIAL CHECKS

The designation 'Malthusian' was in widespread use in Keynes's time to describe the sort of views that he espoused in 'Population'. It is therefore a perfectly correct usage from an historical point of view. Nevertheless, it has the potential to mislead. It implies a closer identity between the views of Malthus and the views of turn-of-the-century 'Malthusians' than actually existed. Their views diverged from Malthus in two very important respects. One of these concerns opposition to or acceptance of birth control by artificial means. The other concerns attitudes to the role of divine providence in human affairs. These two subjects are closely interlinked in both Malthus's and Keynes's discussions of population.

There is no doubt that Malthus was opposed to all forms of deliberate birth control, other than that of postponing the age of marriage and abstaining from sexual intercourse outside marriage. In a supplement to the original appendix of 1806, he stated that 'if it were possible for each married couple to limit by a wish the number of their children, there is certainly reason to fear that the indolence of the human race would be very greatly increased; and that neither the population of individual countries, nor of the whole earth, would ever reach its natural and proper extent' (Malthus, 1989/1803: p. xiii). His opposition to birth control was grounded on a combination of economic arguments about its potential to increase the incentive to choose leisure rather than work and natural law arguments about the proper use of the environment.[5]

Even during his own lifetime, however, Malthus's population principle was taken up by the Philosophic Radicals and deliberately given a completely opposite intellectual and practical twist. This manoeuvre was later described by John Stuart Mill in a famous passage in his *Autobiography*. Describing the influences acting on the young Philosophic Radicals in the early 1820s, he wrote that

Malthus's population principle was quite as much a banner, and point of union among us, as any opinion specially belonging to Bentham. This great doctrine, originally brought forward as an argument against the indefinite improvability of human affairs, we took up with ardent zeal in the contrary sense, as indicating the sole means of realising that improvability by securing full employment at high wages to the whole labouring population through a voluntary restriction of the increase in their numbers. (Mill, 1924/1873: 88–9)

In 'Population', Keynes briefly reviews some of the early advocates of birth control, particularly among the classical political economists. He is interested here specifically in their advocacy of artificial checks, and not merely of forms of sexual behaviour that are inimical to conception, although the latter were by far the most important means by which sexually active couples at that time attempted to control their fertility.

Keynes does not explain why he thought that Robert **Owen's attitude** towards the use of artificial checks to conception **was ambiguous**. If he were relying on Bonar's work, he would have read that 'it is beyond all doubt that the Neo-Malthusians are the children, not of Robert Malthus, but of Robert Owen' (1996/1885: 14). Admittedly, this statement was softened somewhat in the second edition to say 'it is probable that . . .' But Bonar's view of Owen on this point remained basically unchanged: that Owen was an advocate of artificial checks. An article by James A. Field (1911) advanced the same view in a much more guarded and circumspect way. The prevailing view, at the time Keynes wrote, was, in the words of Cohn (1912: 36), that 'Robert Owen heard how small was the number of children in French as compared with English families. He visited France, and ceased to be afraid of too rapid an increase of the people in his communities'. This may be reticent, but there is no real ambiguity of meaning here.

Thanks to the careful research of Himes (1928: 627–40), it is now clear that the anecdote of Owen worrying about population growth, going to France, and returning with specimens of the contraceptive contrivance in use there was an invention of Francis Place, as part of his neo-Malthusian propaganda campaign of 1823–6. Owen originally failed to notice the appearance of the anecdote in various radical publications. When it was drawn to his attention, he wrote a comprehensive letter of denial, published in the *Morning Chronicle* of 8 October 1827. There is no reason not to accept this denial at face value. Keynes may have thought otherwise, and thus arrived at the supposed 'ambiguity' of Owen's attitude.[6]

James Mill's covert support for birth control, as Keynes put it, can be deduced from the article 'Colony', which he published in the supplement to the *Encyclopaedia Britannica* in 1818. His *Elements of Political Economy* (1821) also hinted in the same direction. His son, **the precocious John Stuart Mill,** was, unlike Robert Owen, involved in Francis Place's neo-Malthusian propaganda campaign. His involvement has proved not to be mythical. It became public knowledge after Mill's death, when Abraham Hayward QC circulated a paper claiming that the young Mill had come to the notice of the police for distributing handbills, Place's so-called Diabolical Hand Bills, that gave actual contraceptive information. Hayward also claimed that Mill's neo-Malthusian opinions persisted throughout his mature life. Circumstantial evidence suggests that Hayward's first charge was correct, the only doubt being whether Mill was personally distributing the handbills, or merely accompanying others who were doing so. It seems that young Mill and the others were brought before a magistrate, but that the charges were dismissed or the indictment dropped. The most likely date of the incident was 1823, when, as Keynes states, J. S. Mill was only seventeen (Himes, 1928: 629–32). His precocity extended to authoring three of the articles in *Black Dwarf* in 1823 and 1824 that advocated the use of artificial checks.

Hayward's other claim, that Mill maintained his early approval of artificial contraception, does not admit of such a clear answer. His publications are ambiguous on how a voluntary restriction of numbers is to be achieved, whether by moral restraint or by artificial methods. Possibly the ambiguity was deliberate. It has been suggested that he might have withheld his true opinion, because any advocacy of birth control by him might have influenced public perceptions of his long friendship with Harriet Taylor prior to their marriage in 1851 (Hollander, 1985: 970).

Keynes's purpose for citing these advocates of artificial methods of contraception was to establish that there were respectable predecessors in the line of English economists who had departed from Malthus on this issue, and had pioneered a position that was his own.

A second departure from Malthus was on the question of divine providence. Thanks to the work of Donald Winch and others, the characterization of Malthus as a Christian moral theorist and social scientist is now well established. He was an ordained clergyman whose conceptions of vice and virtue were, for the most part, orthodox in terms of the Anglican Book of Common Prayer. He was trained in the Cambridge of Paley to reconcile the findings of science with the doctrines of theology. Having demonstrated that the existence of the positive checks to population growth wrought human misery, he believed that he was required to justify the ways of God to man. He did so by

arguing that evil exists in the world not to create despair and passivity, but to stimulate human efforts to avoid the evil (Winch,
1987: 34–5).

Keynes, like the Philosophic Radicals, operated by contrast in
an explicitly secular framework of thought. He was well aware
that Malthus intended a 'justification of the methods of the
Creator, in spite of appearance to the contrary' (CW, x. 84). He
never saw that as part of his own agenda. For him there was no
divine providence. It has been suggested that he was a believer
in natural law, albeit some ill-defined secular version of it
(Fitzgibbons, 1988: 69–72). That goes beyond what is warranted
by his assertions that **that degree of populousness in the world,
which is most to be desired, is not to be expected from the
working of the natural order** and that **the natural degree of
populousness is likely to exceed the ideal** (Fo. 21.2).

When he referred in 'Population' to the Punjab plague as a
benevolent visitation, he meant this in a social-scientific sense,
not a providential one. When he criticized attempts at medical
intervention, he did so because he thought they were unreasonable, not because he thought them impious. After the First World
War, however, there is a change in his tone and language. The
term 'devil', as a shorthand for Malthus's positive checks, makes
its first appearance in his population writings, and then recurs
(see Chapter 5). This suggests that after 1914 he ceased to believe
that positive checks were benevolent and should be accepted passively.[7] Rather, active intervention was required. This latter was,
ironically, what Malthus believed for religious reasons, although
he could hardly have agreed with Keynes's terminology of the
'Malthusian devil' to describe the positive checks. Nor would
Malthus have agreed in the least with Keynes that the appropriate form of countervailing human action was the widespread
adoption of birth control, rather than the cultivation of prudential restraint on reproductive fertility.

Because of these two major differences between Malthus and
Keynes on population, I have tried to adhere to the convention

of referring to the latter's views on population as 'neo-Malthusian', despite the fact that the term 'Malthusian' was the contemporary designation. The aim of this convention is nothing more than to avoid confusion. Keynes himself was insufficiently explicit about his divergence from Malthus on these two issues, both in 'Population' and in the 1933 version of the essay on Malthus.

V. THE MALTHUSIAN THREE-QUARTERS OF THE WORLD

What then does 'Population' have to say about the larger picture within which neo-Malthusian ideas, European food security, and contraception have to be set? Keynes argues that **three quarters of the world have never ceased to live under Malthusian conditions** (Fo. 28). He takes as paradigmatic of that three-quarters of the world the countries of India, Egypt, and China. He does not allude at all to any of the then thinly populated poor countries of Africa and Latin America. Not only are the paradigm countries overpopulated, he argues, but the efforts of colonial governments (in the cases of India and Egypt) to raise the standard of living are regularly negated by population increase.

The example of rising real wages in the Punjab is cited as the exception that proves this rule. Keynes claimed (although without any attempt at proof) that the colonial government's investment in canal irrigation in Punjab would have had hardly any effect on real wages if the population had not been decimated by plague between 1901 and 1911. The plague, according to him, raised living standards. In these circumstances, he claims, specific medical interventions to reduce the mortality rate from epidemic diseases are misguided, since all that they do is weaken the positive checks and thereby prevent any rise in living standards. Here then the neo-Malthusian view of misery (famine, disease, and war) as a welcome safety valve for overpopulated societies is advanced by Keynes in its simplest and starkest form.

Keynes's knowledge of **conditions in the Punjab** derived from his employment, between October 1906 and July 1908, as a clerk in the India Office. In January 1908, he began the task of editing the Office's *Annual Statement Exhibiting the Moral and Material Progress and Conditions of India* for the year 1906–7. Two pages of Keynes's draft that dealt with the plague epidemic in India (pp. 4–5) were criticized by his superior, Sir Thomas Holderness, not for factual inaccuracy, but for giving the impression 'that the country has been terribly ravaged by plague, and that the government has done nothing beyond issuing a circular and carrying on a coldblooded scientific inquiry'. To avoid giving comfort to 'persons who want to find fault with the Government', Holderness suggested that 'some economy in statement is reasonable on our part' (*CW*, xv. 11). That little lesson in the official urge to be economical with the truth evidently made an impression on Keynes.

After he had resigned from the Office, he wrote a review of the following year's *Annual Statement* for 1907–8. The review appeared in the 3 July 1909 issue of *The Economist*. It began by suggesting that 'a too rigid economy of statement' on controversial subjects could be counter-productive, by failing to generate an informed public understanding of the government's problems and difficulties. It instanced the treatment of plague: 'the account of plague dwells on the remedial measures of Government, and does not emphasise the extraordinary mortality in certain districts'.

Despite noting the unreliability of Indian statistics of crop production, wages, and prices, Keynes continued by giving this account of real wages in some Punjab districts:

Where . . . the ravages of plague have been worst, wages have risen even more than prices. It is not fully realised in this country how devastating plague has been in particular localities, especially in the Punjab.

The population of large tracts of land has been more than decimated, and in a few places nearly half the population have perished since the first outbreak of the disease. Under such conditions there have been districts in which the crops were left standing on the ground for lack of labourers to harvest them, and the favourable harvests of this year have naturally caused a demand for labour which exceeds the supply . . . (*CW*, xv. 36–7)

Keynes then conjectured that the permanent effect of such conditions might be profound, like those of the Black Death in fourteenth-century England, making the labourer the master of his economic situation.

In describing plague in the Punjab as **this beneficent visitation** (Fo. 26.1), Keynes very definitely parts company again with Malthus. In his appendix to the 1817 edition of the *Essay*, Malthus explicitly rejects the attribution to him by James Grahame's *An Inquiry into the Principle of Population* of the view of 'the vices and follies of human nature, and their various products, famine, disease and war, as *benevolent remedies* by which nature has enabled human beings to correct the disorders that would arise from that redundance of population which the unrestrained operation of her laws would create' (Malthus, 1989/1803: ii. 233). Malthus replied:

These are the opinions imputed to me and the philosophers with whom I am associated. If the imputation were just, we have certainly on many accounts great reason to be ashamed of ourselves . . . It would not be easy to compress in so small a compass a greater quantity of absurdity, inconsistency, and unfounded assertion. (ibid. ii. 233–4)

Malthus would therefore also have taken the opposite view to Keynes in the matter of **Mr Haffkine's prophylactic against plague.** Waldemar Mordecai Wolff Haffkine (1860–1930), a bacteriologist, made important scientific contributions to public health in British India in the 1890s. Born in Odessa as Vladimir Aronovitch Chavkin, in 1888 he left Russia for Geneva and then Paris, where he was an assistant librarian at the Pasteur Institute.

In 1892, he developed an anti-cholera inoculation that he was permitted to test in northern India between 1893 and 1895, allegedly with some success, primarily in reducing the incidence of mortality from cholera rather than preventing its spread. However, the Indian authorities were concerned that Haffkine's experiments could antagonize the inmates of the prisons where the tests were conducted, and his Russian origins put him under some political suspicion. Nevertheless, when plague broke out in Bombay in 1896, Haffkine was invited to return to India by the government and was sent to Bombay as a member of the newly formed Plague Research Committee, with special responsibility for investigating the transmission of plague and preventive inoculation. In December 1896, Haffkine announced that he had devised a suitable vaccine and by May 1897, some 7874 volunteers in Bombay and 4352 elsewhere had been inoculated, although no follow-up was done to check results. However, a smaller experiment at Byculla jail, Bombay did reduce both the incidence of plague and mortality among its victims. Programmes of anti-plague inoculation were carried out later in Mysore, Bangalore, and Punjab.

The Indian Plague Commission was created in 1898 to inquire into 'the effects of the preventive inoculation of M. Haffkine'. It reported in 1900 that Haffkine's inoculation 'can and does exercise some immune effect' and that no serious ill effects had been produced so far (see Harrison, 1994). From 1901–02, the rural districts of Punjab began to suffer severely from plague. Sir Charles Rivaz, Lieutenant-Governor of the Punjab, asked Haffkine to embark on a programme of mass inoculation. Half a million Punjab villagers were inoculated in 1902–03. Then, in October 1902, nineteen villagers in the Punjab village of Malkowal died of tetanus as a result of inoculation with contaminated serum. This incident cast a shadow over inoculation for some years. The Indian government was quick to pin the blame on Haffkine and procedures taken at his laboratory in Bombay, although in reality the source of the contamination was far from certain. An unpopular outsider, and a convenient scapegoat, Haffkine was suspended from duty for three years. Following an active campaign on his behalf in the British press, he was re-employed by the Bombay government, though not in his old position (Waksman, 1964). Haffkine 'spent most of his remaining time in India, before his retirement in 1915, brooding in a small laboratory in Calcutta . . . He made little further contribution to the struggle against plague'. He also remained opposed to the rat-flea theory of the transmission of plague (Catanach, 1988 and Waksman, 1964).

Keynes's prediction that Haffkine's prophylactic against plague would destroy in the next decade the benefits of a generation of engineers and administrators was to be proved wrong. Even after the rat-flea theory of plague transmission had been vindicated experimentally by Glen Liston and others, plague in India did not diminish rapidly. It began to decline in the 1920s and 1930s as rats became more immune to the plague bacillus. It was not until the 1940s and 1950s that the big decline came, with the use of DDT on the rats and streptomycin on the human victims of the disease.

For Keynes's rhetorical purpose, Haffkine is presented as if his medical skills were capable of abolishing visitations of nature. This was far from the reality. In fact, plague had been unknown in India for two centuries before 1896 and neither British doctors nor Haffkine himself knew at that time how it spread. As Chandavarkar has said:

Probably never before or since has such an imposing array of epidemiological talent assembled in one place for research on a specific disease. Their findings were to throw as much darkness as light on the subject while thousands continued to die. At times, their investigations proceeded along lines determined less by scientific evidence than by social assumptions. (1992: 215)

Although Haffkine made a start on preventive measures, his progress was cut short by official victimization. Of this circumstance Keynes himself was perfectly well aware. Keynes knew of

Haffkine's victimization through his employment in the India Office, and referred to it in a letter to Lytton Strachey of 13 September 1907. The context of this letter is Keynes's youthful frustration with the ways of bureaucracy. He complains to Lytton that

This theory that if even a tolerable face can be put on the matter Government never withdraws anything—even in matters of justice—seems to me quite wrong and very dangerous. It was the same in the Haffkine affair . . . Haffkine is apparently censured for negligence in his laboratory. Of this he is demonstrably innocent. But Government maintain their position because an entirely different reason renders it undesirable to employ him again in his old position. It is quite clear to me that, whatever they do subsequently, censure for the thing of which he is innocent should be freely withdrawn first. (Don't mention this in public, please.)

The version of this letter in Harrod's biography omits both mentions of Haffkine's name (1973/1951: 144). His biographer Waksman, on the other hand, seems to have guessed that the reference was to Haffkine, but he failed to check the original letter, because he inserted the word 'Malkowal' incorrectly in place of the first mention of Haffkine (Waksman 1964: 60).

In this incident, an enduring aspect of Keynes's personality is evident. He was well capable of liberal indignation on behalf of a particular individual who had suffered injustice. However, in his mind such principled indignation about injuries to individuals was entirely dissociated from the prejudices which he held about the characteristics of groups, what would today be called collective stereotypes. For the purposes of depicting Indians as feckless, reckless breeders, Mr Haffkine's vaccine is portrayed as an immensely powerful prophylactic. As a matter of fact, Keynes knew all along the true story of this brilliant but tragic man.

The collective stereotype of Indians that Keynes espoused had its origins within the Indian civil service of the last quarter of the nineteenth century. The recurrence of famines in the 1860s had provoked the official perception that India was overpopulated, but thereafter official opinion diverged:

Some thought that the population problem in India was not insurmountable, and with proper measures such as emigration it could be contained for a long time to come. On the other hand, there was an equally strong body of officials who were sure that India had already reached the Malthusian limit, and no government measures could alter the fact. These differing views in turn exercised tremendous influence, not only on the suggested policies, but also on the measures taken to alleviate distress during the famines. (Ambirajan, 1976: 6)

One policy approach was that generous relief provided right at the start of a famine would succeed in minimizing excess mortality, while the other was that minimal relief would be most favourable to agricultural recovery.

Scorning the humanitarian measures taken by the imperial government of India, Keynes said that **It is a point of honour with the Government of India to keep skeletons just alive** (Fo. 27). This is his way of disparaging the Famine Codes, adopted by the government of India after 1883, that gave provincial administrations detailed instructions about monitoring the onset of scarcity and famine, the type of relief works to be constructed, categorizing relief labour and the wage scale, the organization of gratuitous relief (doles and free kitchens), the remission of land revenue, the granting of loans, the relaxation of forest laws, and the protection of cattle (Bhatia, 1991/1963: 184–5). Keynes clearly regarded these Codes as evidence of excessive zeal for saving native lives on the part of the government of India. He sided with those Indian officials who believed that the population had reached an upper bound set by the possibility of producing subsistence goods, and that government famine relief was self-defeating.

There were a number of different strands of thinking behind this belief. A prominent one was the anxiety that British rule had disturbed a 'natural' equilibrium of population and resources which had existed in pre-British India. As Sir Evelyn Baring put it in 1888, 'the natural checks on the population which existed in the old Mahomedan days are taken off . . . the survival of the fittest argument does not hold good in India any longer'.[8] Or, as Sir George Couper had advised the Viceroy, in 1881:

If we are to secure that a class of men—so low in intellect, morality, and possessions, the retention of which makes life valuable, as to be absolutely independent of natural population checks—shall be protected from every cause, such as famine or sickness, which tends to restrain their numbers by an abnormal mortality, they must end up by eating every other class in the community. (Ambirajan, 1976: 7–9)

The Indian Famine Codes, as they were administered in practice, were far from an ideal system of famine relief. Contrary to the more generous approach that had been used in the 1870s, the Codes were implemented in a way that minimized government expenditure, based on the argument of the need to avoid market disruption and dependency or pauperization. The fear of encouraging dependency stemmed 'more from moral or racial interpretations of people's character than from real economic analysis' (Hall-Matthews, 1998: 107). This fear undermined the previous practice of giving 'early and generous relief [that] can serve precisely to enable people to protect their long-term entitlements and therefore incline them to maintain their livelihoods with as little help as possible' (ibid.). The Codes provided minimalist relief, to which people resorted only after they had exhausted all other entitlements. Such people were dependent on others well before they availed themselves of government relief. The government's only choice then was between helping them to survive and letting them die (ibid. 108, 117–21). So Keynes was right that what the government was actually doing was 'keeping skeletons just alive'. There was not a great deal of honour in this parsimonious and misguided approach to famine relief. No doubt there was more honour in it than in the alternative course, which Keynes would have preferred, of letting the skeletons die.

That preference was based on the assumption that a significant portion of the total population is economically redundant or surplus, and its loss through sudden death will not diminish (or, strictly, will not diminish *pro rata*) total production. Passivity in the face of positive checks thus becomes a short-cut to an increase in living standards for those who survive. This is a far cry from Malthus's own treatment of the checks to population in India (Indostan). Malthus is clearly sympathetic to the suffering inflicted by recurring famines, particularly noticing their especially severe impact on the labouring castes and those outside the caste system. He also described some of the preventive checks adopted in India, and approved of attempts by the East India Company to reduce those he regarded as cruel and inhuman, like female infanticide (Malthus, 1989/1803: i. 113–20). He saw the misery of positive checks in a moral and social frame, and not in terms of a purely economic calculus. But he had economic reasons, too, believing that any temporary rise in the standard of living would induce an offsetting increase in population growth, unless religious and cultural patterns were to change in a way that supported reproductive prudence.

Keynes by contrast seems to assume that a rise in the standard of living occurring through some positive check to population would be a once-for-all gain, and that repeated checks would ratchet up income per head, at least to the point where all of the surplus population had been eliminated. He also fails to consider any interactions between mortality and fertility, and particularly the possibility that medical interventions that succeeded in reducing mortality might thereby induce lower fertility. The option of losing surplus population by encouraging international migration is not mentioned, presumably because, as we shall see, Keynes was frankly hostile to it, at least if it was directed to Europe or other 'white lands' such as Australia. Here is another difference from Malthus, who was willing to countenance international migration, at least as a short-run expedient, while pointing out that it could not abate the overpopulation of the whole of the Earth. Finally, although unlike Malthus, Keynes favoured the spread of birth control, he does not allude to it as a remedy for overpopulation in India, Egypt, and China.

The one ray of hope with which Keynes lightened this arche-typal neo-Malthusian scenario was the prospect of a reversal of inter-generational income flows. He believed that **the transition comes when, by the change from agriculture to industry, a large family instead of being an advantage, begins to occasion great expense** (Fo. 32). In contrast to his objection to intervention in health matters, he argued that, when this transition begins, certain types of public policy could indeed assist it: **The raising of the school leaving age and strict regulations against the industrial employment of children may thus exercise a profound influence on the birth rate** (Fos. 32–3).[9] The mechanism by which couples respond to incentives created by public policy (whether by changing age of marriage, or increased abstinence, or some other means) is not discussed. The possibility of extending the use of birth control in the paradigm countries is not considered. This invites the speculation that Keynes did not believe that his ray of hope would be shining on the paradigm countries for many years to come. He had certainly stated that the future development of India was to be sought in the improvement of agriculture, rather than of industry (*CW*, xi: 27–8).[10]

VI. THE 1900 TURNING POINT

For the remaining quarter of the world—Europe and North America—the previous fifty years had already been a period of reprieve from Malthusian pressures. This was because new sources of food supply had opened up from parts of the world hitherto uncultivated, and an international market in foodstuffs had developed. Unlike Marshall and other economists cited in Chapter 1, Keynes thought that **it must be plain to the meanest** intelligence that this factor is temporary (Fo. 23). Keynes cited one economic indicator as his evidence of a 1900 **turning point**:

Up to about the year 1900 the law of diminishing returns was to this extent suspended that every year a given quantity of manufactured products tended to be exchanged for a *larger* quantity of agricultural product. Since 1900 there has been a tendency for this to be reversed; and a given quantity of manufactured goods tends to be exchanged for a smaller and smaller quantity of agricultural product. (Fo. 24)

No numbers are cited in 'Population'. He was presumably relying on those in the *Economic Journal* note of 1912. From this alleged reversal in Europe's commodity terms of trade, he concluded that food security is likely to diminish just at the moment when **in the principal states of Europe an enormous literature is growing up . . . to call on all patriotic citizens to propagate** (Fo. 21). To Keynes's mind this was folly, which would undermine the European standard of living.

But at the same time, and contrary to Malthus's oscillation model, the rate of population growth had responded by declining, rather than rising. This was primarily because the birth rate had declined. Keynes correctly diagnosed that the ability to avoid offspring, namely the use of artificial checks, is of enormous importance in explaining the continuous fall in the birth rate. Having understood the effectiveness of artificial checks for adjusting voluntarily the rate of population increase to economic circumstances, he nevertheless still foresaw imminent danger to the standard of living because of the ending of abundant food supplies from North America and Australia.

What was to be done? How could he show the patriotic pronatalists that they were wrong? This was more difficult than it at first seemed. The difficulty he saw was that policies which encouraged the English rate of population growth to decline further would have only a very slight impact on the protection of the English standard of living. The significance of the development of an international market in foodstuffs, on which

England had become dependent, was that food prices were set in a global market, in which England's demand was but only one element of total demand. If world food supplies had reached a plateau, while world demand was expanding because the over-populated countries were failing to restrict their population growth, a moderation of English demand would hardly arrest the rise in food prices, and the consequent loss of welfare. As Keynes put it, **the advantage of a fall in the birth rate in any country is shared by the whole world** (Fos. 29–30). By the same token, a rise in the birth rate in any country will, *ceteris paribus*, cause a welfare loss to the whole world. This loss cannot be offset by small countries that do attempt to restrain their own population growth.

From an analytical viewpoint, this sketch of a model of the welfare implications of differential population growth in what today would be known as the North and the South is the most interesting thing to be found in 'Population'. It is not fully worked out. It assumes that the extra food demand of the South's additional population, as well as the North's, will all be met from the international market. It ignores the fact that the strength of the South's additional food demand will be mediated by income, of which by definition the South has less per head. There is no attempt to try to calculate empirically the welfare effects of plausible differentials in the rate of population growth. In empirical terms, Keynes underplayed England's dominance in the world food market: at that time, England was much the largest food importer in the world.

What Keynes presents is an early example of an 'isolation paradox', a paradox of population growth that prefigures his later famous paradox of thrift in *The General Theory*. As he puts it, **every patriot urges his country forward on a course of action [that is] in the widest sense anti-social** (Fo. 30), just as he was to argue much later that the more virtuous people are in exercising thrift, the further the national income will have to fall. Such paradoxes, based on the insight that the structure of individual incentives is inconsistent with the achievement of the social good, have characterized political economy and economics from at least the time of Mandeville to the modern environmentalists' concern for the 'tragedy of the commons'. They provide one link between the intellectual approaches of Keynes and Malthus.[11]

In his final summary of the argument in 'Population', Keynes concludes against the patriotic pro-natalist case, but with some heavy reservations. Notwithstanding his population paradox, he suggests that 'In the future we can act with our attention chiefly directed towards the economic wellbeing of the population of our own country, with but secondary regard to the numerical position of our race in the world as a whole [because] [n]ational and military advantages are at least as likely to be diminished as increased by the evils of over-population' (Fo. 37).

The effect of the population paradox is felt in the immediate qualification of this conclusion by what Skidelsky calls 'a typical Edwardian Yellow Peril coda' (1992: 430). Keynes warns that **cosmopolitan humanitarianism must be indulged in but very moderately if evil consequences are to be avoided** for the English standard of life (Fos. 37–38). Appropriate protective measures against economic injury at the hands of more prolific races are specified as **some definite parcelling out of the world** by means of rigorous immigration laws, or even regulation of the international trade in food supplies. The former, however, would not in all logic mitigate the welfare loss to the North postulated by the population paradox, while the latter, as Keynes himself conceded, might well be economically infeasible (Fo. 38). The conclusion was hasty and highly ambivalent, many interesting dilemmas having been stated and then left unresolved (Fo. 39). Perhaps the most intriguing dilemma on the moral plane is how Keynes arrived at the judgement that cosmopolitan humanitarianism is a form of self-indulgence.

NOTES

1. Cohn sent Keynes a postcard from Göttingen dated 1 Apr. 1912 (EJ/1/191).
2. Two further editions appeared in 1903 and 1917, with reprints of the third edition in 1920, 1922, and 1924. The new editions varied in only a few minor ways from the original text. Thus nothing turns on which of the first two editions Keynes used.
3. This is a strong statement, particularly its first part. Malthus did take some trouble to try to establish a realistic figure for the rate of population increase in a country where the means of subsistence were relatively abundant, the manners of the people relatively pure, and the checks to early marriage fewer compared with Europe. He found that in North America, population was doubling every 25 years. He then argued that, *taking one generation as a unit of time*, population growth had the 'power' or 'tendency' to produce a series of population totals which advanced in geometric progression *from generation to generation* (Malthus, 1989/1803: i. 11–15). His understanding of the North American experience was accurate, and the inference that he drew from it was formally correct.
4. The Mill doctrine, as adapted by Keynes, is restated by Wright (1923: 30–40). This includes a side-swipe at Cannan, who had criticized Mill's version in 1893, but in a 1916 book review endorsed neo-Malthusianism to the extent of echoing Keynes's hostility to pro-natalist English bishops.
5. Nevertheless, 'Malthusian' had become a synonym for 'contraceptive' by the 1920s. This usage is recorded in Naomi Mitchison's memoir (1979: 34): 'Before my marriage my mother had spoken vaguely of "Malthusian capsules" which perhaps she had used herself'.
6. A recent, more general discussion of the relation between Owenism and the population question is to be found in Dean (1995: 579–97), who agrees that Himes discredited the case for Owen being a pioneering advocate of contraception in England, despite its reappearance in Claeys (1987: 41).
7. The adoption of this somewhat Manichaean description of positive checks might be connected with Keynes's post-war shift of focus on population questions away from the East, and towards Europe.

8. Another exponent of this view of population growth in India was Sir Robert Giffen, the statistician who identified the concept of the Giffen good, or inferior good, for which demand increases as its price rises. Staple foods in times of famine are the usual examples.

9. Unlike Adam Smith, Malthus, and John Stuart Mill, Keynes found an additional justification for state education in its effect in reducing the birth rate; see Weiner (1991: 121–6).

10. This statement, in a 1911 review for the *Economic Journal* of Sir Theodore Morison's *The Economic Transition in India*, included a sentence that anticipated the idea of the 1900 turning point in the terms of trade of industrial and agricultural goods. Keynes wrote: 'Nor is it unlikely that manufacturing nations have now reached the highest point of their *relative* advantage, and the balance of exchange will move in future in favour of those countries whose advantage lies in the fertility and the extent of their soil' (*CW*, xi: 28, emphasis in original).

11. Malthus had turned public opinion against the 'Speenhamland system', the pre-1834 English Poor Law which allowed poor relief to be given in proportion to the number of children in each poor family. He argued that the virtue of charity to the poor could become a source of misery. This kind of paradox was attractive to Keynes, who later traced it back to Mandeville (1970/1714). Strictly speaking, Mandeville claimed that private vices created public benefits, where Malthus and Keynes both claimed that private virtues could create public disbenefits.

4

The Rapid Multiplication of the Unfit

I. THE LANGUAGE OF SOCIAL DARWINISM AND EUGENICS

How is the young Keynes's writing on population to be located within the field of neo-Darwinian and eugenic thinking of his own day? To what extent does he merely articulate an existing contemporary consensus? To what extent did he achieve his own individual synthesis? If there was, somewhere in the early twentieth-century aether, an ideology that brought together population growth, the fear of the 'rapid multiplication of the unfit', and a belief in the inevitability of race conflict, how did Keynes's distillation from the aether resemble or differ from those of other intellectuals? To see Keynes's contribution on these issues in isolation is to risk judging it only by the liberal standards that hold general sway at the end of the twentieth century. It is impossible for us to suspend or set aside our knowledge of what these standards are. However, a more comprehensive and satisfactory evaluation requires them to be balanced by the additional knowledge of the standards of judgement that prevailed on these matters in the late Victorian and Edwardian eras. Otherwise, our evaluation runs the risk of anachronism.

How then do Keynes's remarks on population growth and race conflict compare with what others were saying around about the same time? Limitations of space prevent anything but a highly selective approach to historical comparison. Moreover, that selection itself allows some scope for the introduction of subjectivity. Who are the appropriate objects of comparison? I have chosen to rely on two major intellectual leaders of Keynes's youth. One is Alfred Marshall, then England's leading economist and Keynes's intellectual mentor. The other is H. G. Wells, journalist, writer of what would now be called science fiction, and social prophet. Between them, these two give some contemporary perspective on the young Keynes's position.

The better to understand the thought of the late Victorian and Edwardian period, the discussion is conducted with the aid of the terminology that was in use at the time. The term 'racism' is deliberately omitted, for example, since its current sense was unknown before the 1930s and reflected the emergence of ideas and behaviour that were absent in the earlier period (Williams, 1976). The other side of the coin is that much of the language of Social Darwinism and eugenics has fallen out of use in the last fifty years and it demands some effort to revive it. It should help the clarity of what follows to begin by defining some essential terms from these old discourses. In the eugenics area, Field (1911) has been chosen as the main guide. He was a supporter of eugenics, but at the same time sufficiently sober and scholarly to view the topic with considerable detachment.

Although the extent of the shock that the theory of evolution gave to the Victorian mind has no doubt been exaggerated and mythologized, for some it was real enough. Darwin himself found it very difficult to acknowledge publicly the implications that he drew from his own discoveries. When the discoveries themselves had been published, their implications for religious beliefs and human values more generally may not have touched many outside the intelligentsia, but they did provoke spiritual crises in some of the best and most sensitive minds of the age. In these circumstances, it is not surprising that the route of Alfred Wallace and to some extent Darwin himself, of representing evolution as a process of human developmental advance, became fashionable. This strategy tried to establish evolution as the mechanism for driving forward the Enlightenment idea of progress.

What then was Social Darwinism? It was an expression of anxiety about the weakening of the process of natural selection in humans. If evolution and only evolution were progressive, any inhibition of natural selection would limit human progress. And there lay the first difficulty. Nobody could be sure *how* natural selection worked in humans. The Social Darwinists saw it as working, as in other animals, by the winnowing out of weak individuals who were badly adapted to survival in their changing environment. Social Darwinists could emphasize the importance of policies of *laissez-faire*, allowing competition between individuals to do its winnowing work unimpeded. They could also advocate intervention and government action to remove existing social and institutional obstacles to effective winnowing, or they could even recommend that the government lend evolution a helping hand, for example by organizing to prevent the procreation of the feeble-minded. Whether preferring *laissez-faire* or intervention, Social Darwinists valued the fierceness of the struggle for survival among individuals. At the turn of the century, this attitude was gaining ground from the older tradition, which thought that evolution drove forward human progress by favouring the growth of social sympathy and the emergence of a sense of collective responsibility.

In the field of eugenics, the first and most fundamental distinction that needs to be made is between positive and negative eugenics. Positive eugenics involves increasing the fertility of the 'best' types of human stock. The first modern exponent of positive eugenics was Charles Darwin's cousin, the young Francis Galton, who published his *Hereditary Genius* in 1869. This argued for the hereditary nature of genius and talent, sounding a note of alarm about the erosion of aristocratic privilege. It suggested that selective marriages among the talented would be a possible route to future human improvement, and pointed the way to 'eugenics' and the voluntary development of a caste of the naturally gifted, among whom intermarriage would be socially encouraged, and exogamy socially discouraged. Positive eugenics soon fell into the doldrums, however. It was not that inter-marriage among the gifted was unpopular. On the contrary, it was a flourishing practice, not least among the great literary and scientific families of the last half of the nineteenth century, including the Darwins and the Keyneses. Rather, one problem was that these marriages had continuously falling fertility rates; and the other problem was that there was nothing much which could be done to increase intermarriage among the gifted or to raise the fertility of such unions.

The revival of interest in eugenics after 1900 therefore centred more on negative eugenics. Negative eugenics involves decreasing the fertility of the 'worst' types of human stock. It is worth noting that both eugenic approaches assume that the grading of human stocks along a single continuum from 'best' to 'worst' is not problematic. Few people at the time seemed to question this assumption. One exception was the young Gwen Darwin, the daughter of Sir George Darwin, who challenged the views of her uncle, Leonard Darwin (another of the five sons of the great Charles), on this question:

Uncle Lenny used to shock me when, in talking about Eugenics, he maintained that a money standard was the *only possible* criterion in deciding which human stocks should be encouraged to breed . . . I said that money had little importance for such people as artists, philosophers, inventors, gypsies. It would be an irreparable loss to the human race if those valuable strains were bred out altogether . . . But Uncle Lenny could not see this at all. He had very little use for artists; and gypsies were generally dirty and dishonest. [Aunt Mildred] was driven into the definite statement, that a man who successfully held a small job in a post office was worth more than the greatest artist in the world! And Uncle Lenny sat there, listening and amused; but in substantial agreement with her. (Raverat, 1952: 199–200; emphasis in original)

The absence of a practical criterion of 'fitness' did not dampen the enthusiasm for negative eugenics in the first decade of the twentieth century. The failure of the 'best' to propagate sufficiently was still bemoaned, but now more usually as a preliminary to discussing what to do about the excessively rapid multiplication of the unfit. The poor specimens that were rejected in such quantities in the recruiting booths for the South African war became worrying evidence for the reality of this phenomenon. Here, at least, something could be *done*! The increased use of contraception among the poor would be helpful. However, many in the upper ranks of British society were resistant to legalizing the sale of artificial devices for this purpose, and many more doubted whether the poor would or could use them, even if they were made readily available. Where these doubts were the strongest, for example in the case of the feeble-minded, the enthusiasts for negative eugenics advocated sterilization, either without the consent of the individual or with 'consent' being regarded as acceptable even when obtained under duress.

In principle, both positive and negative eugenics could be advanced by both non-coercive and coercive measures. For positive eugenics, it is hard, as already suggested, to envisage coercive measures. Perhaps the closest one can get to this is the organized marriage festivals of the Guardians in Plato's *Republic*. In practice, it is very hard to coerce the 'best' stock of society on any issue, but particularly in the matter of reproduction. However, for the purposes of negative eugenics, choosing a coercive approach is more feasible. The 'worst' stock is more open to some coercion, and the object with them is to prevent reproduction, not make it happen. In principle, coercion can be applied whatever the method of negative eugenics. People can be coerced into the use of contraception. By the same token, sterilization can be genuinely voluntary, and need not be coercive. However, since in Edwardian Britain the distribution of birth control devices was illegal, state coercion in support of their use was out of the question. Thus, compulsory sterilization, and even (as some of the medical lunatic fringe of the day recommended) involuntary euthanasia, were the coercive measures of last resort that some negative eugenicists advocated.

Leaving positive eugenics out of consideration at this point, negative eugenics could be pursued by the adoption of different strategies of action at home and abroad. The option of application abroad was relevant for countries that had responsibilities for overseas territories. This option was relevant for Edwardian Britain, which still had extensive imperial and colonial jurisdictions. Thus, there was nothing to prevent Britain and other colonizing countries choosing to apply different negative eugenic regimes to domestic and foreign populations.

Finally, negative eugenic regimes can be operated on non-racial criteria, or they can be based on distinctions of race, as in Leonard Darwin's view of gypsies. Just as negative eugenics is not inherently coercive, so it is not inherently discriminatory by race. From the modern liberal point of view, the more coercive the measures become, and the more differentiated by race the measures become, the more objectionable they are. In the 1930s there were those in England who remained enthusiasts of negative eugenics, while condemning the application of eugenics on a racial basis in Germany.

This alerts us to the fact that eugenics as such was not the sole preserve of Social Darwinists, but attracted support from some socialists and liberals as well (Freeden, 1979). Since the political implications of an enthusiasm for eugenics are not straightforward, it is important to avoid prior assumptions. Keynes's association with the eugenics movement does not *ipso facto* ensure that he was a Social Darwinist. By the same token, it does not *ipso facto* prove that the eugenics movement attracted liberals, given that our question precisely is how liberal Keynes was at different times.

II. KEYNES'S VIEW OF THE INFLUENCE OF MALTHUS ON DARWIN

Keynes gave Charles Darwin a pivotal position in his account of the changing analyses of population. Darwin appears in the 1912 lecture notes in two roles. The first role is as a great thinker inspired by Malthus. The second is as the source of a new, post-Malthus dilemma of population. In 'Population', too, his significance is acknowledged, but it is done more broadly. Darwin is included in Keynes's great 'tradition of Scotch and English thought' on Fo. 15. Malthus's role in Darwin's mental development is discussed on Fo. 17. On the other hand, Darwin as the source of early twentieth-century dilemmas of population slips out of focus. Keynes's thematic statement of 1912 that Malthusian ideas stimulated Darwinian ideas, and the latter now lead us to modify the former (UA/6/9/22) is not explicitly repeated in 'Population', although it remains the key to understanding some of the main arguments of the lecture.

Keynes's claim that Darwin was a thinker inspired by Malthus was a common Edwardian view, one that was shared, for example, by H. G. Wells. Darwin himself had said as much in his *Autobiography*. The relevant paragraph, which Keynes first quotes partially and then deletes from his text, runs in full as follows:

In October 1838, that is, fifteen months after I had begun my systematic enquiry, I happened to read for amusement Malthus on *Population*, and being well prepared to appreciate the struggle for existence which everywhere goes on from long-continued observation of the habits of animals and plants, it at once struck me that under these circumstances favourable variations would tend to be preserved, and unfavourable ones to be destroyed. The result of this would be the formation of new species. Here, then, I had at last got a theory by which to work; but I was so anxious to avoid prejudice, that I determined not for some time to write even the briefest sketch of it. In June 1842 I first allowed myself the satisfaction of writing a very brief abstract of my theory in pencil in 35 pages; and this was enlarged during the summer of 1844 into one of 230 pages, which I had fairly copied out and still possess. (Darwin, 1995/1892: 40)

Keynes had derived great pleasure from reading Darwin's *Autobiography* in 1908. He thought it was 'superb' (Harrod, 1972/1951:

24). However, he did not realize that it is not wholly reliable. In fact, Darwin read Malthus's *Essay* at that time not for amusement, but as part of a programme of reading on vital statistics and fertility behaviour (Browne, 1995: 384–90).

The 'theory by which to work' was not the idea of evolution itself. What Darwin took from Malthus was the idea of the struggle for existence as the mechanism of natural selection. In the struggle for existence, variations that favour survival would be preserved and handed on to the next generation, while unfavourable variations would die out. (Even this idea was not wholly new, because a version of it in which *unfit* species *fail* to survive is to be found in book V of *De Rerum Natura* by the Roman author Lucretius.) However, Darwin went further and drew the conclusion that gradually a given species could change, and ultimately a new species could be created. Naturalists had previously considered that struggles for existence occurred only *between* species, a perception consistent with the idea of the fixity of species. Predation by a different species was thought to reinforce the original character of the species preyed upon, by eliminating weak or deviant specimens (Kingsland, 1989: 169–71). This was Malthus's view, in line with the natural theology of his own time. Of plants and animals, he said the following:

In plants and animals the view of the subject is simple. They are all impelled by a powerful instinct to the increase of their species; and this instinct is interrupted by no reasoning or doubts about providing for their offspring. Wherever, therefore, there is liberty, the power of increase is exerted; and the superabundant effects are repressed afterwards by want of room and nourishment, which is common to plants and animals; and among animals, by their becoming the prey of each other. (Malthus, 1989/1803: i. 10)

Darwin saw that the process of repression might occur through differential mortality within a species, according as types (or sub-species) possessed characteristics that improved or worsened their survival chances. This process of natural selection could act, in the same way as the artificial selection of animal breeders, to change the character of a species and, ultimately, to create new ones. Therefore, Darwin actually stood Malthus's account of plants and animals on its head, a point that Keynes did not emphasize. Indeed, Darwin did not emphasize it either, but rather stressed, in chapter 3 of *The Origin of Species*, that his own account of the struggle for existence was 'the doctrine of Malthus applied with manifold force to the whole animal and vegetable kingdoms; for in this case there can be no artificial increase of food, and no prudential restraint from marriage' (quoted in Bowler, 1980: 116–17). However, the struggle for existence *within* species was taken by Darwin to be much fiercer than that *between* species, because it was a competition between near equals for the same resources. That was why the fixity of species became the evolution of species.

In this, Darwin may have been influenced, less by what Malthus actually said, than by the 'Malthusian' *Zeitgeist* which flourished in England when Darwin returned from the long voyage of the *Beagle* in 1837:

Darwin's biological initiative matched advanced Whig social thinking. This is what made it compelling. At last, he had a mechanism that was compatible with the competitive, free-trading ideals of the ultra-Whigs. The transmutation at the base of his theory would still be loathed by many. But the Malthusian superstructure struck an emotionally satisfying chord; an open struggle with no hand-outs to the losers was the Whig way, and no poor-law commissioner could have bettered Darwin's view. He had broken with the radical hooligans who loathed Malthus. Like the Whig grandees—safe, immune, their own world characterised by *noblesse oblige*—Darwin was living on a family fortune, and thrusting a bitter competition on a starving world for its own good. From now on he could appeal to a better class of audience—to the rising industrialists, free-traders, and Dissenting professionals. (Desmond and Moore, 1991: 267)

Unlike Malthus himself, this Malthusian *Zeitgeist* interpreted the struggle for existence as a struggle between individuals. Malthus never did use the phrase 'struggle for existence' in this sense. When considering human society, he spoke of 'this perpetual struggle for room and food' only in relation to conflicts between primitive tribes (Malthus, 1989/1803: i. 62). Darwin was probably more influenced by current general ideas about the benefits of economic competition than by Malthus's precise views on human populations. Since Malthus himself distinguished carefully between the law of population in plants and animals, and in human society, it was probably Malthus's phrase 'repression afterwards' that was his greatest personal contribution to the idea of natural selection.

Malthus's influence on Darwin did not extend to religious and moral questions. On the contrary, Darwin took a huge step away from the morality of Malthus's Anglicanism. Under the influence of Harriet Martineau and others, he secretly shifted to a moral relativism that denied any divinely implanted, universal moral sense. All cultures, moralities, and religions (including Christianity) were interpreted as the product of the evolution of useful social instincts (Browne, 1995: 398–9; Desmond and Moore, 1991: 268–9). He was unable to confide this great change of view to his orthodox Anglican wife, Emma.

As long as the belief persisted that cultures, moralities, and religions embodied *useful* social instincts, and were among the products of evolution, the socially corrosive power of the idea of moral relativism was neutralized. What would happen, however, when this belief was questioned, and when moralities and their manifestations came to be regarded as impediments to the vast meta-historical forces that have made, and will make, the universe what it is? That doubt, which had already formed in Darwin's own lifetime, was the seed from which 'Social Darwinist' views would grow, to attract the young Keynes and many others of his generation.

III. THE 'FAILURE OF NATURAL SELECTION' IN CIVILIZED NATIONS

We may now assess Darwin in the second role that Keynes assigned to him, as the source of a new post-Malthus dilemma of population. As we shall see, Darwin was not so much the source of this dilemma as a commentator on it. Darwin's theory of evolution in plants and animals sparked off a great debate about the relevance of the process of natural selection to mankind, well in advance of the publication of his own conclusions on this topic in 1871. The re-importation of the idea of natural selection into social thinking was occurring in earnest in the 1860s. A new social anxiety entered the arena of public debate; or possibly, it was an old anxiety re-expressed in what were generally taken to be Darwinian ideas. This was the problem posed by William Rathbone Greg in *Fraser's Magazine* for September 1868. Greg was a writer who has been called 'a sort of all-purpose pundit on everything' (Hoppen, 1998: 323). His punditry in this instance came in an article called 'On the Failure of "Natural Selection" in the Case of Man'.

His choice of title was a misleading one, because in fact Greg's argument was that the operation of natural selection in man was a failure only in part. According to him, natural selection *did* operate in man with respect to the survival of 'races and nations'. However, it did not operate on the different types of men within *civilized* 'races and nations'. Particular institutions of civilized nations blunted the force of the mechanisms of natural selection. These were systems of support for the weak and defective and property rights that allowed great wealth to be inherited by the incompetent among the aristocracy. Thus the members of the middle class, those 'most qualified to continue the race, are precisely those who do so in the scantiest measure' (quoted by Field, 1911: 8). In these ways, civilized nations put themselves at a disadvantage in the fierce struggle for survival with other, uncivilized 'races and nations'. That, in short, was the Greg Problem. However, for reasons already mentioned, he regarded the solution of imposing positive eugenic reproduction as impractical.

Darwin himself had avoided all discussion of man and human society in *The Origin of Species* (1859). All he would say there was that his findings could be expected to have some implications for man and his history. In *The Descent of Man* (1871), he finally broke his silence to argue that man had indeed evolved from the lower primates. In the course of so doing, he turned aside briefly from this main theme to consider the role of natural selection both within civilized nations, and between civilized and barbarous races. In this digression into amateur sociology, Darwin simply took over Greg's basic distinction between civilized nations, on the one hand, and barbarous races or savages on the other. It was a distinction that he never properly defined, but used unthinkingly to denote 'higher' and 'lower' stages of evolution. In other ways, too, Darwin's discussion in chapter 5 of *The Descent of Man* of the effect of natural selection on 'civilized' nations is highly derivative from the ideas of Galton, Greg, and Wallace. He restates the Greg Problem that the civilized condition interferes with natural selection in various ways: for example, 'we institute poor-laws; and our medical men exert their utmost skill to save the life of everyone up to the last moment . . . vaccination has saved thousands, who . . . would formerly have succumbed' (Darwin, 1981/1871: 168). Among other interferences with the operation of natural selection in the civilized condition were the inheritance of property and the law of primogeniture. Thus, the morally inadequate would prevail over the morally excellent in the civilized society, because the former marry earlier and are more fertile than the latter.

Darwin quoted Greg directly, including without any hint of embarrassment Greg's use of racial stereotypes:

The careless, squalid, unaspiring Irishman multiplies like rabbits: the frugal, foreseeing, self-respecting, ambitious Scot, stern in his morality, spiritual in his faith, sagacious and disciplined in his intelligence, passes his best years in struggle and in celibacy, marries late and leaves few behind him. . . . In the eternal 'struggle for existence', it would be the inferior and *less* favoured race that had prevailed—and prevailed not because of its good qualities but its faults. (Darwin, 1981/1871: 174; emphasis in original)

Darwin did, at the same time, advance some contrary arguments that he thought would tend to mitigate the quantitative effect of the Greg Problem. He thought that higher mortality among the morally inferior was a countervailing tendency. However, there was no guarantee that this tendency would be sufficiently powerful. If not, 'the nation will retrograde . . . We must remember that progress is no invariable rule' (ibid. 177). He added that the strengthening of the social instinct of sympathy was a positive good, so that 'we must bear without complaining the undoubtedly bad effects of the weak surviving and propagating their kind' (ibid. 169). The socially and medically assisted survival of the unfit was thus something required by an evolved instinct of social sympathy. On the other hand, Darwin seemed to concede that social sympathy was less than wholly useful in promoting progress. Hence his attempts to draw the sting of the Greg Problem were intellectually indecisive and ambivalent. It survived and grew to become the key problematic of social Darwinism in the generation after his death.

From the modern perspective, Darwin was right to separate his biological theory from a moral evaluation of its consequences, by insisting that 'progress is no invariable rule'. Natural selection itself—never mind interference with natural selection—is quite consistent with 'the weak surviving and propagating their kind'. There are certain diseases, for example, that stimulate an abnormal level of sexual activity at an early age, but then cripple their victims in middle life. It is unlikely that the genes of these sufferers would ever be eliminated by a process of natural selection. There is thus no special fitness about the characteristics of the types that survive, over and above the fact that they do survive. Spencer's phrase 'the survival of the fittest' is nothing but a tautology. The fittest to survive, survive. They may survive by evolving from free-living beings into parasites that are no longer capable of independent existence. They may survive by adapting to their environment so closely that once that environment alters even slightly, they will become extinct.

Notwithstanding all these implications drawn by later generations from the theory of natural selection in plants and animals, the 'problem' of the rapid multiplication of 'unfit' human beings continued to grip the imagination of Victorian and Edwardian social thinkers who thought of themselves as followers of Darwin.

Greg himself referred quite casually to 'races and nations'. What was Darwin's own view of the 'races of man'? He argued that each of the races of man (or, sometimes, 'so-called races of man') is not a distinct species, but a sub-species of a distinct human species. He thought that, when any of these races became extinct, it was not because of harsh environments but because of the consequences of competition and conflict with other races, contact with Europeans being particularly destructive. Likewise, the formation of races with different physical characteristics is not a direct result of different environmental influences, but of prolonged cross-breeding between existing races, and the effects of sexual selection. The significance of this account of 'race' was double-edged. On the one hand, it retreated from earlier accounts of races as distinct species, defined by specific physical characteristics. On the other, it made 'race' the site of community altruism, and posited competition between 'races' as a mechanism of natural selection. Most important of all, Darwin took over from Greg a moral hierarchy of 'civilized nations' and 'lower races', based on a simple stereotyping. In this way, conflicts between races *were* after all legitimized in terms of morality, progress, and the spread of civilization (ibid. 166).

Darwin assigned countries like India, which today are thought of as 'older civilizations', to his category of barbarous races. He agreed with Malthus 'that the reproductive power is actually less in barbarous than in civilised races' (ibid. 132). This he attributed to longer lactation periods, less nutritious food, and cultural practices of prudential restraint. He also believed that less fertile savages could experience sudden bursts of rapid population growth in particular conditions. In support of this belief, he cited an anecdote from W. W. Hunter's *The Annals of Rural Bengal* (1868):

Notwithstanding that savages appear to be less prolific than civilised people, they would no doubt rapidly increase if their numbers were not by some means rigidly kept down. The Santali, or hill-tribes of India, have recently afforded a good illustration of this fact; for they have increased, as shewn by Mr Hunter, at an extraordinary rate since vaccination has been introduced, other pestilences mitigated, and war sternly repressed. (ibid. 133)

This example goes against the idea that conflict and competition with Europeans is particularly destructive for the savage races, at least in the medium term. Hunter's anecdote suggests the reverse, that improved public health and public order measures had promoted population growth. But could the situation last? Was it sustainable? Would not the Indian population become adapted to its new environment so closely that the smallest change would repress its growth severely? Darwin thought so. Subsequent famines in India lent some credence to this view. The problem for British officialdom was then what to do, whether to intervene further with famine alleviation measures, or to stand back and let Nature take its course. Even after the first course of action had been adopted in one form or another, its wisdom continued to be questioned, not least by the young Keynes.

IV. ALFRED MARSHALL AND THE GREG PROBLEM

There is no direct evidence that Keynes read the original Greg article, or even the 'transmission' of it in a qualified form by Darwin in *The Descent of Man*. Yet, the Greg Problem is stated quite clearly in both the 1912 lecture notes and in 'Population'. How did Keynes acquire the idea? One possibility worth examining is that it was something that he imbibed from his mentor in economics, Alfred Marshall. When Keynes began to study economics with Marshall, the latter was already in his sixties, having started his own study of political economy in 1867. He made important contributions to economic theory as a young man, but did not publish them until after Jevons had published his own researches on the same topic. The publication of Marshall's *Principles of Economics* in 1890, which was originally intended as the first of a two-volume work, established him as the dominant force in British economics from then until the First World War. In 1906, Keynes described Marshall, in an arresting contrast, as 'a very great man, but I suppose rather a silly one in his private character' (Harrod, 1972/1951: 136).

That Herbert Spencer, together with Darwin, exercised a profound influence on Marshall's mind can hardly be doubted. The 1860s, the period of his intellectual formation, was a period of great intellectual ferment in which many lost their Christian belief. Keynes himself later identified both Spencer and Darwin as important influences on the thought of the young Marshall (Pigou, 1925: 9).[1] However, it was Spencer, and not Darwin, who was given pride of place by Marshall himself. In this eulogy of Spencer published in 1904, Marshall wrote that

There is probably no one who gave as strong a stimulus to the thoughts of the younger Cambridge graduates thirty or forty years ago as he. He opened out a new world of promise; he set men on high enterprise in many diverse directions; and though he may have regulated English intellectual work less than Mill did, I believe he did much more to increasing its utility. (ibid. 507)

In the 1870s, Marshall had lectured on moral and political philosophy, including among the works he discussed Spencer's *Social Statics* and *First Principles* (Marshall, 1975/1867–90: i. 11). At this time, he was interested in the extent to which ethical life was determined by economic conditions, in particular by the different forms of industrial organization. He thought that the speculations on this theme would be 'of fundamental importance and vital concern to those who are working their way, as I am, towards that ethical creed which is according to the Doctrine of Evolution' (ibid. ii. 377). The idea of evolutionary ethics had several distinguished exponents in Cambridge and elsewhere in the 1870s (Chadwick, 1990/1975: 231). The content of that ethical creed was never fully stated by Marshall. It would almost certainly have differed little in substance from the ethics embedded in Christianity, although it would have been expressed in terms of the central ideas of Herbert Spencer.

Spencer held on to an essentially pre-Darwinian conception of the struggle for existence.[2] Following Lamarck, he believed that acquired characteristics could be inherited, and that faculties that were not used were not inherited. This belief supported his contention that evolution, both physical and social, was 'progressive', moving away from simple homogeneity and towards a combination of greater differentiation of parts and a greater integration of those more differentiated parts, or a mixture of increased complexity and increased co-ordination. Spencer strongly supported *laissez-faire*, but he opposed militarism and colonialism. He embodied evolutionary thinking as it was before Darwinian arguments came to be deployed as a justification for imperialism, war, and race conflict.

It was from Spencer that Marshall drew his ideas of the organic nature of economic life (Hodgson, 1993: 408). Despite his repeated protestations that the biological analogy was more useful than the mechanical analogy, especially for the more difficult problems of economics, the inadequacy of Spencer's philosophy relegated Marshall's idea of economics-as-biology to the status of an impracticable research programme. Marshall sometimes warned against imposing a progressive interpretation on the struggle for survival. However, he then proceeded to soften this hard truth by telling his readers that altruism within one's race improves that race's chances of survival:

Thus the struggle for existence causes in the long run those races of men to survive in which the individual is most willing to sacrifice himself for the benefit of those around him; and which are consequently the best adapted collectively to make use of their environment. (Marshall, 1920/1890: 243)

This passage, which shows the clear imprint of Spencer, is in effect a direct denial of the existence of the Greg Problem. It asserts that a more highly developed altruism, far from being a handicap in race conflicts, on the contrary makes a race stronger than others in war, and in contests with famine and disease.

It was probably from correspondence and discussions with William Bateson that Marshall came in the 1890s to abandon the Lamarckian doctrine of the inheritance of acquired characteristics. However, that change of scientific view did not inhibit Marshall from trying to salvage his understanding of evolution as potentially progressive. Now he appealed to the influence of environmental conditions, especially in the early years of life, as a force making for improvement in human beings. He argued the point with the Social Darwinist Benjamin Kidd in 1894:

As things are, I am inclined to think that the race which has prospered under the influence of natural selection through struggle, in spite of bad provisions for the health of mind and body of young and old, might *conceivably* continue to progress under the influence of better physical and moral conditions of life, and in spite of the cessation of the struggle for survival. (Groenewegen, 1995: 484; Prendergast, 1998: 96–7; emphasis in original)

Given this background of belief, it is no surprise that when in 1910 Karl Pearson and Ethel Elderton, the leading lights of the biometric school of eugenics, wholly denied *any* environmental effect of parents' alcoholism on the welfare of their children, Marshall entered into public debate on the opposite side. His basic principles of economic and social progress were under attack. It was not just an issue of the validity of environmental-ism in general. The significance of parental responsibility and early nurturing and child care, on which he had written so much over his career, was being brushed unceremoniously aside. Keynes's role in this public debate, which was mentioned in Chapter 1, was strictly as an auxiliary. As he told Lytton Strachey on the morning after Marshall's opening salvo was published in *The Times*, 'I didn't put Marshall up to his letter' (PP/45/316/4/166). It was Marshall's own choice. The quarrel soon became personal as well as public. As Keynes reported a month later to his father, 'K. P.'s insolence has at last roused the old Prof.'s blood' (PP/45/168/7/69). His citadel had come under a powerful attack by a very confident enemy, and he responded with less than total academic scruple.

We could end the matter here, and classify Marshall as a 'Social Lamarckian' who migrated to environmentalism, if he had not introduced one significant qualification to his argument. Marshall applied the biological distinction between free-living organisms and parasites to the 'races' of mankind:

though biology and social science alike show that parasites sometimes benefit in unexpected ways the race on which they thrive; yet in many cases they turn the peculiarities of that race to good account for their own purposes without giving any good return. The fact that there is an economic demand for the services of Jewish and Armenian money-dealers in Eastern Europe and Asia, or for Chinese labour in California, is not by itself a proof, nor even a very strong ground for believing, that such arrangements tend to raise the quality of human life as a whole. For while a race entirely dependent on its own resources can scarcely prosper unless it is fairly endowed with the most important social virtues; yet a race, which has not these virtues and which is not capable of independent greatness, may be able to thrive on its relations with another race. (Marshall, 1920/1890: 244)

Marshall's belief in the vigour of the English and the 'spiritless-ness' of the Chinese has already been mentioned *en passant* in Chapter 1. These further comments on the Jews and the Armenians suggest that Marshall's vision of evolution as at least potentially progressive was confined to the 'independent' races, within which an ethical creed of altruism could evolve; in the others (the 'spiritless' and the 'parasitic' races) it could not.

Despite dismissing the Greg Problem at the level of race conflict, Marshall did acquiesce in part of Greg's diagnosis at the level of the quality of national population. He argued that the pressures of competition and struggle have abated (which, presumably, they must have done, if altruism has increased) and that the strongest and most vigorous no longer leave the largest number of progeny behind them. This brought him to the positive eugenic remedy. He thought that the principles of eugenics could be applied to ensure that the race was replenished from its higher rather than its lower strains, but that the improvements from any intervention of this kind would necessarily be gradual and slow (ibid. 207).

As Freeden (1979) has successfully argued, eugenics was never a unified doctrine, and individuals' enthusiasm for eugenics could survive strong disagreements about the respective roles of environment and heredity in contributing to the superior quality of the future population. Despite the length and animus of the controversy with Pearson on exactly that point, Marshall maintained his personal enthusiasm for the eugenic movement. This is demonstrated by a letter which he wrote to Keynes from his holiday retreat in Devon in May 1911:

As you may have heard we have decided to study the evolution of Spring in Devonshire this year; . . . So I shall not be able to attend the meeting of the C.U. Eugenics Society on Monday.[3] But I am hugely delighted that it has been formed & inclose a life composition fee. (Marshall, *Corr.*: iii. 284)

All things considered it is most unlikely that Keynes acquired from Marshall his understanding of, and attitudes towards, the Greg Problem. Marshall's formative influence was Herbert Spencer, who had fallen out of favour by the start of the twentieth century. Social Lamarckianism, maintaining as it did the doctrine of inheritance of acquired characteristics, saw evolution as progressive for humanity as well as for the animal kingdom, since co-operative behaviour of the type that would now be called generalized reciprocity was seen as an evolutionary advantage, not as an evolutionary handicap. Civilized nations, in their relations with others, could therefore well afford, from the viewpoint of the survival of the fittest, to rely on policies of social co-operation at home and free trade abroad, while avoiding policies of militarism and imperialism. These mid-Victorian values were the foundations on which Marshall built his intellectual house. After reading the new edition of Marshall's letters, a reviewer rightly commented that 'there is really nothing in the papers to compare, on the scale of Political Incorrectness, with the recent sensational release from the Keynes Papers', i.e. the manuscript of 'Population' (O'Brien, 1997: 1865).

As was shown in Chapter 1, Marshall did believe that in terms of race, British was best, and he rejoiced in the emigration of British stock to occupy new territory. This stopped him from worrying about overpopulation in Britain, except to the extent that it led to overcrowding and poor living conditions, especially for young children. He found his belief in the formative influence of the environment quite compatible with enthusiasm for eugenics. Unlike Keynes, after 1870 or so he was no neo-Malthusian. While he acknowledged the existence of what he called 'the residuum of population', he was not a strong advocate of negative eugenics. Indeed, it seems likely that he disapproved of birth control on moral grounds (Groenewegen, 1995: 260–1). All of this put him at some considerable distance from the positions that Keynes was to adopt on population issues. At the same time, Marshall's remarks in the *Principles* about parasitic races, applied to the Jews and others, did give a foretaste of the darker mood that was to prevail in the first half of the twentieth century.

V. KEYNES AND THE GREG PROBLEM

(a) *Keynes's Faith and Morals: 'Egoism' (1906)*

Owen Chadwick noted, with brilliant insight, that 'in the 1880s [there] passed over Western Europe one of those movements of mind that history perceives but cannot easily analyse or define':

> More a breath of spirit than a reasoning of intellect, you find it in the new movements of English and Scottish philosophy as they turned away from Herbert Spencer and John Stuart Mill . . . The extremist who was typical of no-one and yet (because an extremist) symbolized the entire mood, was Nietzsche . . . The noises were confused; a Babel of voices, moral and religious and philosophical, but amidst the din one thing was clear; the generation put aside the serene hopes and optimisms of the mid-Victorians. (Chadwick, 1990 / 1975: 239–40)

This was the spiritual mood of the young Keynes and his generation.

In the philosophical Babel of the *fin de siècle*, a very radical question had been raised about the morality that this generation had inherited from Christianity and from the (partly opposed) tradition of Western liberal thinking. It was Nietzsche's question from the preface to his *On the Genealogy of Morality*:

> up till now, nobody has had the remotest doubt or hesitation in placing higher value on the 'good man' than 'the evil', higher value in the sense of advancement, benefit and prosperity for man in general (and this

includes man's future). What if the opposite were true? What if a regressive trait lurked in 'the good man', likewise a danger, an enticement, a poison, a narcotic, so that the present *lived at the expense of the future?* . . . So that morality itself were to blame if man, as a species, never reached his *highest potential power and splendour?* So that morality itself was the danger of dangers? (1994/1887: 8; emphasis in original)

This doubt, that the old and familiar morality, the conventional Christian morality, was not only a form of self-indulgence, but was positively harmful to the future prospects of mankind, is, when couched in the Darwinian accents of 'traits' and 'species', the very essence of Social Darwinism. With the provocations of Nietzsche, the Greg Problem entered moral philosophy, and sparked a critique of religion as profound as any that had been thrown up during the Enlightenment.

Like Nietzsche, the young Keynes was both very aware of religion, and hostile to it. Formally speaking, in religion he was an aggressive agnostic. As described by his younger brother Geoffrey, 'he always felt an intellectual interest in religion, but at the age of seventeen or eighteen passed painlessly, as did my sister and I, into a natural state of agnosticism' (Keynes, 1981: 20). Painlessly perhaps, but not passively. Already at Eton, 'the serious-minded Christians soon grasped that his free-thinking went deeper', and that religion was a more dangerous ground for discussion with him than politics. As an undergraduate at King's, he led a successful campaign to secularize the College's social mission. He was heartily contemptuous of Henry Sidgwick; because the latter could not reconcile himself to the logic of his own arguments against Christianity (Harrod, 1972/1951: 39, 109, 135). He attacked the churches, and the conventional morality that they propagated.

As we have already seen, Keynes told his undergraduate audience of 1912 that his own sympathies were with the cosmopolitans. Sympathetic he may have been, but he rightly did not say that he himself was a cosmopolitan or Kantian in his ethics. That would have been untrue. He and his close friends were keen, albeit rather unorthodox, disciples of G. E. Moore, whose *Principia Ethica* appeared in 1903. Moore there argued that the notion of 'good' was indefinable in terms of any other idea or combination of ideas, but that it could be applied to describe different states of mind which people experience. Looking back from the vantage point of 1938, Keynes recognized that he and his friends had been mainly occupied with trying to apply Moore's ideas to their personal experiences of love, beauty, and truth (*CW*, x. 436). However, Moore, though venerated as the spiritual centre of their small world, had a curiously mixed effect on their understandings. His belief in the goodness of conventional morality was the part of his philosophy that they simply rejected. Thus their philosophical beliefs led them to an introverted and egotistical sensibility that, for most practical purposes, restricted concern for others within the limits of their own small élite group. Among the members of the group, there was, as Harrod put it, 'in fact a good deal of disdain for' the majority of mankind (1972/1951: 94 n. 25). They practised an aristocratic aestheticism much more consonant with the thrust of Nietzsche's philosophy.

Keynes may have retrospectively exaggerated the degree of amorality in his and his group's early beliefs. Nevertheless, they were consciously engaged in a revolt against the conventional ethics of Christianity. Keynes remembered that 'we used to regard the Christians as the enemy'. In developing their anti-Christian critique, they became inward looking, élitist, and self-obsessed. As he later recalled, 'the divine resided in a closed circle' (*CW*, x. 445–6, 437). Keynes and his friends believed that Darwin had destroyed both Christian and liberal ethics, and that they were engaged in some immensely exciting and far-reaching philosophical and moral reconstruction.

It is within this context that Keynes's declaration of sympathy with cosmopolitanism must be viewed. His sympathy was quite different from a personal commitment to the active furtherance of a definite principle of justice on a universal scale. This was because Keynes never succeeded in resolving the philosophical problem of our duty to others, as he believed it to arise from Moore's theory of goodness. This is clear from the paper that Keynes read in 1906 to the Cambridge Apostles on 'Egoism'. In this, he discussed the conflicting moral claims of 'my goodness' and 'the goodness of the Universe' in the light of Moore's *Principia Ethica*. The implication of Moore is taken to be that it is necessary to make a clean sweep of all previous principles of justice, all formulations of laws of morality. Therefore,

goodness no longer consists in the formation of character, or in obedience to the laws of God or the so-called Laws of Nature or in Categorical Imperatives or Laws of any kind. It is to be found only in certain specific states of consciousness, any one of these states being logically independent of any other . . . My goodness and your goodness no longer consist in obedience to a Common Law . . . (UA/26/8–9)

The next step was to realize that, if this were so, then deciding between the competing claims of self and others becomes quite problematic, given our inability to inspect other people's states of mind. In Keynes's words:

my goodness and the goodness of the Universe both seem to have claims upon me which I cannot easily reduce to common terms and weigh against one another upon a common balance. I am a good friend of the Universe and I will do my best for it: but am I willing to go to the devil for it? (UA/26/11)

In the 'Egoism' paper, Keynes gave an example of going to the devil for the sake of the universe, which illustrates the anti-Christian context in which he thought about this problem:

I wonder if in our heart of hearts we would blame a man who chose the most splendid flights of passionate and mutual affection or who elected to sup with Plato and Shakespeare in Paradise, *rather* than linger through eternity in a state of sordid and disgusting pain combined with the lowest and most degraded feelings and with the foulest and most malignant desires . . . although the sacrifice were to lead to the enlightenment of two negroid negroes from Central Africa and to their participation in the paradisaic supper party. (UA/26/5; emphasis in original)

Having posed the question of moral obligation in this extreme form, Keynes digressed to blame 'the dreadful Stoics' and 'their semitic founder' because 'they introduced the negroid negro question into morality' (UA/26/6). Skidelsky calls this remark 'an unconscious echo of Nietzsche' (1983: 151). However, it is not clear that the echo is unconscious, rather than conscious. The parallelism of ideas is so close that it is hard to believe that Keynes was not deliberately alluding to the relevant section of Niet-zsche's *The Will to Power*. Both passages make the same argu-ments about the dual nature of Stoicism as a religion and a philosophy, and about the historical significance that should be accorded to the alleged Semitic origins of the founder of Stoicism, Zeno of Citium.[4] Keynes seems here to be quite con-sciously affirming the Nietzschean argument that Christianity is a morality based on resentment, a morality of slaves. By contrast, the master morality spontaneously defines its own activities as good, then labels what it sees as inferior to itself as bad.[5] Niet-zsche on religion provided the link between Moorean philoso-phy, in its reduced form, and Social Darwinism. The 'masters' are the fit who will survive the process of natural selection. They have the right to impose their criteria of civilization and judge all others by themselves. Keynes, though he was clear about what he had rejected—the conventional morals of Christianity—was less definite about what he was embracing. Even at the end of his discussion in 'Egoism', Keynes remained in a bind about sac-rificing one's own goodness: 'we ought, but we can't. Rationally we ought, psychologically we can't' (UA/26/12).

As late as 1938, Keynes said that he intended to remain an immoralist, rejecting the universal ethics of Kant, as well as Christianity. Although for him, unlike the others of his set, 'the outside world was not forgotten or forsworn', he never solved the intellectual problem of how to balance doing good against his ideal of being good, that is, embodying in oneself what Nietzsche would have called 'culture', and Keynes called 'civilization'. In another part of *My Early Beliefs* (1938), Keynes described in retrospect how, having rejected the goodness of conventional morality, he departed still further from the views of Moore. He says that he became aware that the view of human nature underlying Moore's moral idealism was 'disastrously mistaken', specifically in believing that human nature is wholly reasonable. He tells how he came to see, in the years just before the manuscript of 'Population' was written, that, on the contrary, there were insane and irrational springs of wickedness in most men. If that was the case, he concluded that civilization was a precarious crust erected by the personality and will of a very few:

as the years wore on towards 1914, the thinness and superficiality, as well as the falsity, of our view of man's heart, became, as it now seems to me, more obvious . . . (*CW*, x. 449)

The civilization of the few, who included Keynes and his Bloomsbury group, was thus perceived by them to be more vulnerable to external threat than they had previously imagined. One of the key presuppositions of Harvey Road gradually seemed doubtful. Thus, sympathy for a universal ethic like cosmopolitanism had to be increasingly balanced by the need to defend their civilization against the eruption of irrational forces within the majority. Yet, they knew of no interpersonal standard by which this might be done. From the immoralist standpoint, if civilization were to be threatened by population growth and the consequent intensified competition with 'uncivilized' countries for food and living space, there need be no moral compunction about the means used to defeat the threat. Keynes makes this very clear in 'Population' when he says that it may be necessary to parcel out the world, despite the probability of provoking racial wars, but that 'such wars will be about a substantial issue' (Fo. 38). The substantial issue for him was the safeguarding of civilization, as he and his friends had defined it for themselves. His fear, on the other hand, was that Britain's political leaders did not see the forthcoming battle for civilization as clearly as he did himself, lacking as they were in a sufficient conviction of Britain's racial superiority.

(b) *Keynes and Public Policy: Coercive Negative Eugenics*

Marshall sent his life subscription to the Cambridge University Eugenics Society to Keynes, for the unsurprising reason that Keynes was its treasurer (Freeden, 1979: 671). He therefore would have attended the Society's inaugural meeting in 1911, and heard W. R. Inge's exposition of the Greg Problem. However, that would certainly not have been his first introduction to it.

As a book collector, he made his first subject collection in 1906, 'when he assembled a long series of works on probability for the writing of his Fellowship dissertation, mainly modern works' (Munby, 1975: 291). He then acquired a copy of Sir Francis Galton's Herbert Spencer Lecture for 1907, which was entitled *Probability: The Foundation of Eugenics.* Most of this lecture consisted of a brief sketch of a course curriculum on the statistics of variation and correlation. However, in laying out the motivation for developing such a course, Galton restated the Greg Problem, along with the eugenicists' solution. He did so by quoting from a lecture that Karl Pearson had given in 1903. The quotation from Pearson was:

We are ceasing as a nation to breed intelligence as we did fifty years ago. The mentally better stock in the nation is not reproducing itself at the same rate as it did of old; the less able and the less energetic are more fertile than the better stocks. No scheme of wider or more thorough education will bring up, in the scale of intelligence, hereditary weakness to the level of hereditary strength. The only remedy, if one be possible at all, is to alter the relative fertility of the good and the bad stocks in the community. (in Galton, 1907: 10–11)

Here then is one early source of Keynes's understanding of the Greg Problem, if we need to tie it down to a particular document that he owned and read. Another early source was his mother. The problem of the rapid multiplication of the unfit was one of the many concerns of the redoubtable Florence Ada Keynes, the dedicatee of Harrod's biography. She had been a pillar of Emmanuel Church, Cambridge, but fell away from her Congregationalist faith once her children had become agnostic (Keynes, 1981: 20). She became increasingly active in the local community, in the Charity Organisation Society and the local Board of Guardians, earning a reputation for being 'the busiest woman in Cambridge'.

From time to time in her letters to 'Dear John',[6] she inserted a paragraph about eugenics research along with enquiries about his health, news about relatives and friends, and descriptions of parental holidays and holiday plans. In January 1908, she wrote to seek his help in preparing a book, having been 'commissioned' to do so by 'the principals on this project' who, she wrote, were the Horace Darwins and the Whethams. (It would be odd if the Horace Darwins had been involved in a project like this. Horace Darwin had served as the Mayor of Cambridge, but it was his brother, Leonard Darwin, who had the keen interest in eugenics, and became President of the Eugenics Society (Raverat, 1952: 195–208). Did Florence simply confuse the two first names?) William Cecil Dampier Whetham was a physicist and an agronomist who was a Fellow of Trinity College, Cambridge. He and his wife Catherine were early stalwarts of the Eugenics Education Society, which had been founded in 1907. They were also engaged in preparing a book entitled *Family and Nation* that was published in 1909 and became a well-known exposition of negative eugenic views. The Whethams and Leonard Darwin (if it was indeed Leonard who was involved) were well-known conservative and Social Darwinist exponents of eugenics (Freeden, 1979: 652, 656).

The topic of the new Darwin–Whetham book project was 'the Feeble-minded' and the core of it was to be an abstract of a 'recent report' on the subject. An article from the biological point of view was to be solicited from Galton, and one from the economic viewpoint was also wanted, Marshall having been asked to do it and having declined. Keynes was asked to approach Pigou. Florence then indicated the sort of article that she wanted:

we want to impress upon the public that there *is* an economic question involved in our treatment of the feeble-minded. We should like something said about the effect on wages of a large amount of very low grade and unimprovable labour—and the cost to the community occasioned by the unemployables at present at large—or supported in Workhouses and Prisons. Also about the probable ultimate reduction in this cost, although a large outlay might be required at first to establish institutions and colonies. (PP/45/168/13/3; emphasis in original)

The report of the Royal Commission on the Care and Control of the Feeble-minded in 1908 'had backed eugenic fears that their fertility was way above average', and recommended segregation to control them (Weeks, 1981: 136). A campaign led by the Webbs and other Fabians advocated both the 'endowment of motherhood' and, later, the permanent legal segregation of the feeble-minded in order to prevent their reproduction (Himmelfarb, 1991: 368–9). Certainly, the Whethams in *Family and Nation* advocated the 'extinction of the tribe' of the feeble-minded and the incurably vicious, arguing that: 'By legislative reform, we may segregate the worst types of the feeble-minded, the habitual criminal, and the hopeless pauper, and thus weed out of our race the contaminating strains of worthless blood' (quoted in Kevles, 1995: 93). Florence Keynes's mention of the establishment of new institutions and colonies, to be followed by a reduction in the cost of the treatment of the feeble-minded, makes it sufficiently clear that she, like the Whethams and the Webbs, was a supporter of eugenic policies like the sterilization of the feeble-minded, criminals, and paupers.

What Keynes thought or did about his mother's request is unclear to me, not having succeeded in finding his reply. My guess is that he did nothing more than pass on the request, as he had been asked to do. Pigou was sympathetic to the sterilization approach, as we know from his discussion of the issue in chapter 10 of *The Economics of Welfare*, in which he refers to the Whethams' *Family and Nation*. Pigou may not, however, have accepted the invitation to contribute to the Darwin–Whetham project that Florence was trying to launch. Keynes seems to have kept his mother's interest in eugenics and sterilization of the feeble-minded at arm's length. It was his father, Neville, who was the essential parental influence on him at this time (Skidelsky, 1983: 66). He never seriously engaged with Florence's belief in coercive negative eugenics as a method of social reform. There is no evidence that he thought it was a sensible way of doing good, even if he had been sure how much good he ought to do. His only written comment to his mother on the issue was obliquely dismissive. From his holiday address, he wrote to her in August 1910:

Of the seven guests who I have asked to stay with me here, no less than six have a near relative mad or feeble-minded—in three cases a brother. I seem to have a liking for the not quite dotty. (PP/45/168/7/64)

The comment is obviously light in tone. Its implication is clear enough, that the consequences of adopting coercive eugenic policies might not leave the middle classes entirely unscathed.

(c) *Public Policy: Remedying the Greg Problem at Home and Abroad*

The Greg dilemma is stated with admirable clarity and succinctness in Keynes's 1912 lecture notes:

There is a marked process of selection at work in favour of the elements which we regard as least good. In a given country it is the poorest and least intelligent part of the population which reproduces itself most rapidly; and it is in the most civilized countries that the birth rate is falling off fastest . . . We are faced by a dilemma.

The Malthusian Law of Population, when it is in operation, maintains the lower classes of the population in a condition of perpetual misery. But it is an engine of evolutionary progress, and those classes of society, or portions of the world, for which its operation is suspended are liable to be overwhelmed by the rest. (UA/6/9/23)

So much for the problem; what about the remedy? Having split the problem into two parts, the internal problem of the higher fertility of the poor and unintelligent and the external problem of the higher fertility of 'uncivilized' countries, Keynes then makes two totally different policy responses to the two parts of the same basic problem. The 1912 notes have only one sentence about solving the internal problem: 'The problem within a civilized country may possibly be solved in time by the growth of prosperity and education' (ibid.). In 'Population', Keynes looks to a combination of economic pressure, education, and a change in public attitudes to contraception as the appropriate policy answer.

This is a markedly more liberal approach than some of his contemporaries were taking. For one thing, it indicates his confidence in the educability of the poor. This was something that writers like George Gissing and Wyndham Lewis certainly lacked. Florence Keynes herself, given her belief in 'a very large amount of unimprovable labour', also seems to have been doubtful about what education could do for the labour force. For another thing, Keynes succeeds in avoiding the coercive element characteristic of the interventionist negative eugenics of the Webbs. He advocates as the solution to the Greg Problem neither the state segregation of the feeble-minded and other 'undesirables', nor the withdrawal of state social and medical assistance from those in the lower strata of the population. Keynes's more liberal position was underpinned by the belief that the lower strata could be relied on to adopt contraceptive methods, if they are given access to them. He thus favoured negative eugenics over the positive eugenics of Galton, but negative eugenics without the coercion that so many, including his own mother, approved.

However, in all this, recall that Keynes is prescribing a liberal remedy only for the populations of 'civilized nations'. He devoted much more of his discussion to the external dimension of the Greg Problem. This was the aspect that really challenged him. It is obvious that he felt wholly uncomfortable with the idea of applying the same liberal approach that he favoured for the internal problem of adverse selection to 'barbarous races', such as those of India. In 'Population', he highlights the ways in which the imperial state promotes the survival of the unfit. He instances both the Indian Famine Codes and the recent introduction of the practice of inoculation against plague in India. But far from bearing these things without complaining of their bad effects on the fitness of the population (as Darwin proposed), or seeing them as the evidence of an evolving noble instinct of social sympathy (as Spencer and Marshall proposed), they are made the target of his scorn (Fo. 26.1 and Fo. 27). His scorn is directed not at these practices *per se*, but to their use in India and other densely populated countries. It is hard to believe that he would be equally scornful if he were speaking of similar measures designed to protect European populations from the effects of famine and plague. A relative liberal at home, Keynes was clearly a Social Darwinist abroad.

If one were to seek an explanation for this differential ruthlessness, it would be reasonable to refer to what Keynes called 'the race struggle as to what type shall chiefly populate the world' (Fo. 29). He was acutely aware of this struggle in evaluating the population problem. He thought that only so much of the world's available land was suitable for European settlement, and that it was imperative that white settlement should be completed without surrendering any of this ground to people of other races. Only when this process had been completed could the competition between races be downgraded to a secondary consideration in the making of English population policy. That had not yet happened, and the fall of the European birth rate was slowing down the rate of settlement of the available land by European emigrants. Meanwhile, he believed that 'almost any measures' were justified to protect the European standard of living 'from injury at the hands of more prolific races' (Fo. 38). In this way, Darwin's understanding, shared with Malthus, that barbarous races are less fertile than 'civilized' races is reversed by Keynes, who maintains a belief that they are more prolific. Further, Darwin's idea of the competition between races selecting for those with the widest sympathies and noblest instincts is transmuted by Keynes into the idea that almost any measure can be justified if it is needed to safeguard European domination of those parts of the world where Europeans could live.

Once Darwin's ideas have been distorted in these ways, it is understandable that Keynes should feel it necessary to express doubts about Kant's criterion of moral action. Kant formulated his categorical imperative variously. Perhaps the simplest and most familiar of these is: 'Act only according to that maxim by which you can at the same time will that it should become a universal law', i.e. it is only morally permissible to perform an act if the principle by which one would be acting could be adopted by every rational being. Kant's morality is universalist, or (as Keynes calls it) cosmopolitan. For a Kantian, moral obligations to others do not vary depending on whether the others in the case are judged by oneself to belong to a civilized or a barbarous nation. On the contrary, they are derived from a rationality that is assumed to be shared by all human beings. One could go further to suggest that cosmopolitan humanitarianism is the foundation on which any claim to be a civilized nation has to be built. Civilized behaviour in the international arena precisely involves acting within mutually agreed law-like codes of reciprocal rights and duties.

So in what sense can Keynes mean that cosmopolitan human-itarianism will have such evil consequences that it should be indulged in but very moderately? The evil that he foresees is the relative decline of 'the stock which we think is best'. It is hard to interpret these words other than as a euphemism for white people from Europe, North America, and Australia. Once he accepts the validity of the idea that there are superior and infe-rior racial stocks, Keynes and those who think like him *ipso facto* deny that a shared common humanity exists, upon which a uni-versal morality could be based. This is especially so if the desig-nation of racial superiority or inferiority remains the prerogative of different groups (or the leaders of different groups) who con-stitute the undefined 'we' in the phrase 'the stock which *we* think best'.

It would be wrong to suggest that Keynes was using the terms 'race' and 'stock' in a strictly genetic or biological sense. These terms were at that time often, but not invariably, used very vaguely. The sharp dichotomy between biology and culture, for example, was almost certainly not part of his mental furniture, although the distinction is there for all to see in Wells's *Modern Utopia*. For Keynes, a race in the biological sense had its own stereotypical culture, which helped or hindered its survival in the struggle between races. This view is manifest in his declaration (Fo. 35) that those races have tended to persist whose supersti-tions have favoured a very numerous offspring. It was the popular religions of the East which, by encouraging early marriage and large families, frustrated the emergence of civilization: 'In Asia, at any rate, civilisation has always tended to throttle itself in a surfeit of population,—to be overlain by its own babies' (Fo. 28). Therefore, his idea of 'the prolific races' was a compound of bio-logical and cultural stereotypes, one of those crude classifications and false generalizations that were the object of much criticism from H. G. Wells.

VI. WITH PREJUDICE TOWARDS SOME: KEYNES'S ANTI-SEMITISM

As an adolescent, Maynard had introduced his younger brother, Geoffrey, to the science fiction of H. G. Wells.[7] Later, Geoffrey also read some of Wells's social and political works. Maynard himself read *A Modern Utopia* as soon as it was published in 1905. In July 1905, he wrote to Lytton Strachey: 'I have finished Wells's *Utopia*, which rather peters out' (Harrod, 1972/1951: 124). Unfortunately, he did not say anything to indicate how or why he thought that the book petered out. When later, in January 1909, Keynes related to Duncan Grant how J. T. Sheppard had criticized Rupert Brooke 'for admiring Mr Wells', he again was not explicit about his own opinion in the controversy (ibid. 171). This is a pity, because Keynes followed many paths parallel to those found in Wells's social thought, although in one crucial particular, that of race stereotypes, he did not do so.

Wells's early non-fiction work represents a dramatic shift in mood and temper, as well as in content, away from Marshall's ideas on population and eugenics. In many ways Wells is the more relevant object of comparison, whose work allows us to define more precisely Keynes's distinctiveness within his own peer group. Many similarities between Wells's *Anticipations of the Reaction of Mechanical and Scientific Progress upon Human Life and Thought* (1902) and Keynes's outlook on the population question are evident. For both, Malthus was an epoch-making figure of great intellectual originality. For both, too, Malthus's inspiration of Darwin to produce the theory of natural selection had a transforming impact on the moral world. Another similarity between Keynes and Wells was in their attitudes to the birth-control controversy. This showed particularly in their agreement on the need to combat those polite social conventions that stifled public discussion of the issue, and the need to expose the sexual morality of the Church as a contributory factor to the larger social immorality of massive child poverty and misery. Both also agreed that public policy should aim to reduce the opportunity for parents to profit from the earnings of their children.

In relation to the growth of overseas populations, the Wells of *Anticipations* agreed with the Keynes of 1914 in emphasizing the threat that arose from their fecundity, and that it was right to pursue hard-hearted and unpitying policies towards the mass of black, brown, and yellow people who could not assimilate themselves to the efficiency standards of Anglo-Saxon 'civilization'. However, the Wells of *A Modern Utopia* was a reformed character, denouncing this type of imperialism as early as 1905 (ibid. 330–5). It is important to note that in both moods, imperialist and anti-imperialist, Wells took pains to adopt a non-racial stance and to avoid stereotypes (or what he called 'crude classifications and false generalisations'), a course that Keynes did not follow. Thus, although there are broad and important similarities, Keynes differed from Wells on this critical issue. Whether Keynes's enigmatic comment to Strachey about 'petering out' refers to this difference remains obscure.

A Modern Utopia also retreats from the harshness of *Anticipations* with regard to the future prospects of so-called 'inferior races'. Wells still believes that truly inferior races are bound to die out, because they progressively lose the will and means to reproduce themselves. However, he now denies that there are any actual 'inferior races' in that sense. In every race, he now declares, there will be individuals who will succeed in meeting the test of efficiency that the future will pose, even from the rapidly shrinking population of Australian aboriginals (ibid. 323–6). He reaches this conclusion by means of an analysis of 'race' with which any liberal at the end of the twentieth century would feel wholly comfortable. This passage clearly refutes any who might be inclined to claim that all the intellectuals of Keynes's time shared a common race prejudice. For it comprehensively denounces the idea of race purity, distinguishes between differences of race and differences of culture, and insists on the uniqueness and individuality of all people regardless of place and circumstances of birth. It also provides his own cogent explanation of the 'race mania' of the day:

The great intellectual developments that centre upon the work of Darwin have exacerbated the realisation that life is a conflict between superior and inferior types, it has underlined the idea that specific survival rates are of primary significance in the world's development, and a swarm of inferior intelligences has applied to human problems elaborated and exaggerated versions of these generalisations. These social and political followers of Darwin have fallen into an obvious confusion between race and nationality, and into the natural trap of patriotic conceit. (ibid. 314–15)

In addition to the rise of this 'bastard science', Wells notes the effect of 'the dissent of the Indian and Colonial governing class to the first crude applications of liberal propositions in India' in spreading 'the delirium about race and the racial struggle' (ibid.). It seems to me that Keynes's 'Population' is not entirely exempt from the force of this criticism.

That Keynes, like Marshall, subscribed to race prejudice in the sense of the stereotyping of large groups of people can hardly be denied. The stereotypes were usually, but not invariably, negative. The English, not surprisingly, were given a positive stereotype by both, and Marshall did the same for the Japanese. Negative images of the Indians, the Chinese, and the Jews emanated from the pens of both men. Black Africans were automatically 'savages' to Keynes, who thought that it was foolish of governments to guarantee investment loans to countries where they live (*CW*, xix. 275–84). This stands in marked contrast to Wells, even the early Wells of *Anticipations*. He goes to some length to acquit himself of any charge of race prejudice, especially about the Jews. In what could be read as a direct rebuttal of the argument of Marshall about parasitic races, he writes:

the Jew also [the New Republic] will treat as any other man. It is said that the Jew is incurably a parasite on the apparatus of credit. If there are parasites on the apparatus of credit, that is a reason for the legislative cleaning of the apparatus of credit, but it is no reason for the special treatment of the Jew. If the Jew has a certain incurable tendency towards social parasitism, and we make social parasitism impossible, we shall abolish the Jew, and if he has not, there is no need to abolish the Jew. We are much more likely to find that we have abolished the Caucasian solicitor. I really do not understand the exceptional attitude that people take up against the Jews. (Wells, 1902: 316)

Wells here is doing two very important things. He is challenging the identification of undesirable characteristics with ethnic origins, and thereby objecting to stereotyping in general. He is also challenging a particular stereotype, the identification of social parasitism with Jews, by raising the possibility that a non-Jewish professional group like solicitors may be the more successful rent-seekers. Some recent writers who have tried to revive the charge of anti-Semitism against Wells have overlooked this passage. It is important because it indicates the error of those who say that Keynes and Marshall were no different from all the intellectuals of their day in their resort to race-based stereotypes.[8]

Why did Keynes not maintain a clear distinction between the attrition of those who cannot modernize and the attrition of particular races? Owen Chadwick has argued that the idea of evolution had to be simplified, had to be reduced to stereotypes, even for the cognitive purposes of educated men like Keynes:

What stands out is the necessity for symbols, or as they have been called, *stereotypes*; easily identifiable names or persons or pictures or issues. Most men—most educated men—do not understand *evolution*. The word can only be a symbol, a substitute for understanding, a point of adherence for a faith, which bears small relation to what happened (so far as scientists can discover that). (1990/1975: 44; emphasis in original)

Pace Chadwick, it was not really a matter of an intellectual gap between scientists who understood great complexities and educated people in search of a practical understanding. As we have already seen, the discourse of natural selection as it was applied to human society, *even in Darwin's own hands,* required the construction and use of human stereotypes. In the plant and animal world, it was *types* that either survived or failed to survive, not individuals. However, scientific confusion still reigned about what 'type' really meant in plant and animal biology. In Cambridge, Professor William Bateson was making heroic efforts to recover Mendelian genetics from undeserved obscurity. Nevertheless, the implication of Mendel's theory for human genetics was not widely understood. Keynes evidently had no inkling of it, despite the fact that Bateson had befriended his younger brother Geoffrey (Keynes, 1981: 82–3, 152). So, when economists and other social scientists, including Keynes, applied the idea of evolution to human society, 'type' was interpreted to mean racial character. This was, as Wells complained, a wholly unscientific notion.

Keynes's adoption of this interpretation was indicative, not so much of any active hostility to non-European people, but of a profound lack of interest in them and their fate in the world. He thought it unfortunate that Bernard Swithinbank, his best friend from Eton, 'is determined to go to India and refuses to take the opportunity to stay in England' (PP/45/168/51); Swithinbank had to be warned of 'the horrors of India' (Harrod, 1972/1951: 37). When he visited Egypt in 1913, his letters to his parents and to Lytton Strachey show no interest at all in the country, its people, or its contemporary culture. He did indeed think that it might be 'interesting' to become an adviser to the Chinese government, but he told his father that he could not spare the time (PP/45/168/7/240). For the young Keynes, abroad was, in a psychological sense, a very long way away.

Keynes, moreover, was never careful to avoid the negative stereotyping of Jews. One example of this arose when, after visiting Russia in 1925, he wrote three articles about the Soviet system for the *Nation and Athenaeum*. He offered republication rights to several other journals, including the *New Republic* in

New York. The editor accepted the offer, but added the following polite note:

I have made a slight change in the text of the first article. At the beginning of page 40 of the article in the London *Nation* you said Russian Communism doesn't make Jews less avaricious or Russians less extravagant. There seems to be an implication in this phrase which I am sure that you did not intend—that avariciousness is a necessary characteristic of Jews. There are a great many personal friends [and] supporters of the *New Republic* who are themselves Jews and who are sensitive enough to take an implication of this kind seriously. I have consequently substituted the word misers for the word Jews and the word spendthrift for the word Russians. (L/25)

Keynes did not demur. On the other hand, he failed to carry these amendments through to the version republished in *Essays in Persuasion* (1931), where the original wording still stands.

The *New Republic*'s editor may have been right that Keynes did not view all Jews in the same way at this time. However, Keynes certainly had a very low opinion of many German Jews. This is evident from a short essay on Einstein which he wrote after visiting Berlin in 1926, but which he did not publish. The essential passage runs thus:

[Einstein] was the nicest, and the only talented person I saw in all Berlin, except perhaps old Fuerstenberg . . . and Kurt Singer. And he was a Jew; and so was Fuerstenberg. And my dear Melchior is a Jew too. Yet if I lived there, I felt I might turn anti-Semite. For the poor Prussian is too slow and heavy on his legs for the other kind of Jews, the ones who are not imps but serving devils, with small horns, pitchforks and oily tails. It is not agreeable to see a civilisation so under the ugly thumbs of its impure Jews who have all the money and the power and the brains. (*CW*, x. 383–4)

This reference to the Jew-devil draws on an older, medieval tradition of anti-Semitism, while Marshall's reference to the Jew-parasite is a modern version of the same thing. The medievalism is no less objectionable.[9]

Keynes was obviously willing to recognize those he personally liked and respected as exceptions to his general category of impure Jews. It is not difficult to imagine him quite truthfully replying, if criticized for negative stereotyping, that some of his best friends were Jews. Moreover, it is well known that, as the Nazis began their persecution of Jews, Keynes spent time and money to assist the emigration to England of Jewish economists of promise. When the British government decided in 1940 to intern some of these distinguished German émigrés, Keynes also used his influence with Home Office officials to hasten their release from the internment camps. Within the natural aristocracy of talent and culture, racial and religious divisions counted for nothing, as far as he was concerned.

Yet he maintained what Moggridge has called 'a rather generalised anti-Semitism'. He was sufficiently self-aware to be able to see the contradiction between this and his liberal-minded interventions on behalf of individual Jews or even Jews more generally. He wrote to Lydia in April 1933:

I made my usual conversation about the Jews in the Combination Room last night, and then immediately afterwards signed a petition for a great Mansion House Meeting to be called in their favour! (Moggridge, 1992: 609)

But this self-awareness did not always affect his behaviour. Odd manifestations of prejudice continued to flash out from time to time. Despite having written against the barbarism of the Hitler regime, he wrote a special preface to the German edition of *The General Theory* that recommended his theory of aggregate output on the grounds that 'it is more easily adapted to the conditions of a totalitarian state'. This was a quite extraordinary action to take at any time, but particularly so in late 1936, when the horrific nature of the Nazi regime was already apparent to him. Again, when Keynes was leading the British delegation to talks in Washington in the summer of 1943, his anti-Semitic attitudes were made plain in difficult exchanges with Harry White and

E. M. Bernstein. Accusations of 'Talmudism' were the public expression of Keynes's frustrations with the negotiating documents of the United States delegation (ibid. 610–11, 727–8). These incidents are well known, and need not be laboured here. Their significance is as further evidence of a habit of prejudice that Keynes was never able to break with completely. It was a habit that stretched back over forty years, to a time well before the writing of 'Population'.

VII. CONCLUSION

The problem of egoism, which Keynes never seems to have resolved during his life, does have a solution within a Kantian frame of reference. It is that nothing can be a duty to the universe if it cannot be universally willed as a law both for others and for self. On that criterion, the extraordinary self-sacrifice of Keynes's 'negroid negro' example cannot be a moral duty. Given the present state of human nature, it can only be a work of supererogation. However, by the same token, the Kantian does believe that there are *some* duties owed to the 'negroid negroes from Central Africa', and that such people cannot be excluded from the moral universe once it is granted that extraordinary sacrifices on their behalf are not morally obligatory. In Keynes's version of Moore, such duties never are specified because there is no common measure for making interpersonal comparisons of states of mind.

Despite the unavoidable 'immoralism' of a morality that had no way of prescribing our duty to others, the young Keynes did not allow himself to be drawn into the fashionable crusade leading to the Mental Deficiency Act 1913, which recruited many prominent Cambridge eugenicists, including his own mother. The detention and sterilization of the so-called feeble-minded did not receive his support, although his senior colleague Pigou found the idea perfectly reasonable. More generally, Keynes adopted a notably soft policy line towards the 'unfit' who happened to live in Britain. Like John Stuart Mill, he invested much hope in the power of education, combined with the effect of the spreading of contraceptive practices among the working class.

He recommended a very much harsher regime for the proliferating masses of the unfit in India, China, and Egypt. There, social policies of health services and emergency feeding merely encouraged population growth that was unsustainable, and that threatened to make the softer policies advocated for Britain unsustainable also. Such nonsense should be stopped, and plans made for immigration controls and taking control of world food supplies. The basic justification for this lay in the need to protect the future prospects of 'the stock that we think is best', that of (northern) Europe, and of the countries that northern Europeans had settled.

The idea of an inevitable struggle among nation states for territory pre-dates Darwinism, and can be found in mid-nineteenth-century manuals of international jurisprudence (Chadwick, 1990/1975: 132–4). So does orientalism, the belief in radical differences between the people of Orient and Occident (Said, 1978). What Darwinism did was to feed in an equation of nation states with racial types. This seemed to give the doctrine of *Realpolitik*, always an uncomfortable one, both a scientific content and an extra legitimacy, especially for those nations that were at that time extending their rule over others.

Stereotyping by race was an inevitable consequence of applying biological thinking to human politics: positive stereotypes for the colonizers and those that avoided colonization, and negative stereotypes for the colonized. Negative stereotyping by race is a way of denying full humanity to the members of the group that is stereotyped. They are stripped of their individuality, and reduced to instances of some unpleasant characteristic—

spiritlessness, avariciousness, parasitism, savagery, or whatever. They are comprehensively prejudged. 'Tell me your race,' says the peddler of negative stereotypes, 'and I will tell you what is wrong with you.' However, when a favourable stereotype is used, especially about one's own compatriots, this is also objectionably reductionist, in that it amounts to a refusal to acknowledge anything unflattering about the group to which one belongs, although in reality all groups consist of a mixed pattern of good and bad characteristics. To recognize all this is not to fall in with some modern mode of speech, according to rules that are now referred to, with a sneer, as 'politically correct'. Rather it is to show sensitivity to the consequences of a form of arrogant insult, which has all too long, and all too shameful, a history. Wells certainly realized this, but Keynes manifestly did not.

There is some irony in the fact that those who, like Keynes, saw their own civilization, the civilization that they wanted to protect, as a product of extreme individualism should have so lightly devalued the individuality of others. It is only possible to do this by explicitly or implicitly granting oneself a status of privilege or superiority in the world, which cannot or should not also be granted to the mass of 'others'. This privileging of self is all the easier if one has convinced oneself that there is no way of weighing the moral claims of self against the moral claims of the rest of the universe. One of the dangers in propagating this way of thinking was that it is an intellectual tactic that could be used by each of the European imperialist nations once they began to fall out with each other. Indeed, it subsequently was (Carey, 1992: 198–208). The potential of the ideology of population growth, adverse selection, and imminent race conflict for tragedy was increased by the degree of virulence of racial prejudice. However, as Wells's attitude shows, it was not the case that, in those far-off days, everybody was saying the same kind of thing about 'race'. Some at least very definitely refused to go along with the fashionable 'race' stereotypes of the era.

NOTES

1. Groenewegen argues that Darwin's *The Descent of Man* did have a clear influence on Marshall's views on the sexual division of labour, despite the fact that Darwin admitted that his theories in this regard 'lacked scientific precision'. Further, Groenewegen suggests that Marshall used science selectively 'to confirm preconceptions to which he was deeply attached' (1995: 500–1).

2. The idea of the inheritance of acquired characteristics does make a brief appearance in ch. 1 of *The Origin of Species* but more as a vestige of previous thinking than a dominant theme.

3. If Marshall had been able to attend, he would have heard Professor W. R. Inge present the following familiar elements of the Greg Problem and the eugenic remedy:

> One of the most crying necessities is the segregation of feeble-minded women, whose uncontrolled and abnormal fertility is a source of terrible misery and degradation. Another menace is the tendency to shirk parentage on the part of men and women possessing finely developed physical, mental and moral organisms . . . Since in our humanity we inhibit natural selection, it is essential that rational selection should take its place if we are to stem the growing tide of race degeneracy. (Marshall, *Corr.*: iii. 285)

Although Marshall was not there, it is highly probable that Keynes was.

4. Nietzsche says: 'Attempts by antipaganism to found and make itself possible philosophically: predilection for . . . Stoicism, which is essentially the work of Semites (. . . The Stoic is an Arabian sheik wrapped in Greek togas and concepts)' (1968/1901: 114–15).

   Keynes says: 'despite the circumcision of their founder they taught in Athens and consequently claimed allegiance on egoistic grounds. But only I think because their peculiar tenets enabled them to synthesize the two conflicting claims' (UA/26/6).

5. This, incidentally, is but another version of the parasitism of the Jews, in this case a moral parasitism which has no self-affirmation, but only values determined by what it must negate.

6. This is how she addressed him, although Neville Keynes wrote to him as 'dear Maynard'. He signed his letters to both of them 'JMK'.

7. He gave his younger brother Geoffrey a copy of *The Time Machine* in 1898. Geoffrey 'enjoyed all Wells's novels' and 'even read his socio-logical books' at the instigation of Rupert Brooke (Keynes, 1981: 84).
8. Coren (1993: 211–19) makes the charge of anti-Semitism against Wells. Parrinder (1993: 17–18) effectively rebuts it. As Parrinder states, 'there are no dark secrets hidden in his letters or papers'. There is only an isolated prejudiced remark that occurs in a letter he wrote in 1940 (Korn, 1998: 29).
9. According to Alex Bein, 'in the case of the Jews, a semantically created stereotype is dealt with in accordance with the analogy to which the stereotype is tied. Thus in the mediaeval period the Jew-devil is burnt at the stake, while in the modern situation, where the Jew is described as a parasite, he is gassed' (Carlebach, 1978: 353). With this in mind, it is impossible to agree with the statement that 'Keynes's anti-semitism, if such it was, was little more than a theo-logical fancy' (Skidelsky, 1992: 239).

5

Capitalism and Contraception, 1919–1936

I. THE MALTHUSIAN DEVIL IN ECONOMIC CONSEQUENCES

The five and a half years between the delivery of the Oxford lecture on 'Population' and the publication of *The Economic Consequences of the Peace* (1919) involved Keynes, as it did so many of his generation, in a journey across a vast psychological distance. The Great War was simply the most transforming event of his and their lives. Keynes had to deal with complex problems of war finance from his temporary position inside the Treasury, had to come to terms with his own and his friends' attitudes to military conscription and had to assist in negotiating financial aspects of a peace treaty that he realized could never last. Every day taught him the lesson of the uncertainty of human economic affairs, and finally brought him to the nervous breakdown that ended his official duties at the Paris Peace Conference. He recovered. The therapy was 'violent and ruthless truth telling', in his whirlwind composition of *The Economic Consequences of the Peace*.

We are concerned here only with that part of *Economic Consequences* in which Keynes analysed the pre-1914 economic system, and in particular the role of population growth therein. In chapter 2, he described the working of the Malthusian devil on a geographical canvas, which (though still wide) was much narrower than that of Malthus himself in the 1803 edition of the *Essay*. It was also much narrower than the one he had used in 'Population' for his own first intellectual encounter with Malthus. Keynes focused largely on Europe and its economic relations with North America, with the briefest of side-glances at tropical Africa. He chose the one-quarter of the world where, as he had previously argued, 'the cloud had lifted' and the Malthusian devil had been successfully defied. On this restricted canvas, he sketched out a four-phase history of the relation between population and the resources available for the subsistence of Europe's peoples.

Before 1870, Keynes argued, Europe as a whole was self-reliant in food production and population was at appropriate levels for the available food supply, 'adjusted' to it by the standard Malthusian positive checks of famine and disease. From 1870 to 1900, population increase in Europe and North America was more than validated by growth in the available food supply—'as numbers increased, food was actually easier to secure'. This came about because of increasing returns to scale of production in both agriculture and industries, and increasing specialization and division of labour, facilitated by emigration from Europe to North America and transatlantic trade that increased as communications improved. During this phase, the Malthusian devil was effectively 'chained up'.

Keynes then took up again the theme that he had announced in his 1912 Cambridge lectures on Economic Principles and his 1914 lecture on 'Population'. In 1900, a turning point was reached, he claimed, after which 'a diminishing yield of nature to man's effort was beginning to reassert itself', as evidenced by the rising real cost of North American cereals. This was balanced by an inflow of foodstuffs from tropical Africa. The Malthusian devil remained out of sight, but was beginning to threaten what Keynes nostalgically termed 'this economic Eldorado'. No figures to validate the claim of a rising real cost of North American cereals appear in the published version of chapter II.

However, in the original manuscript draft of the chapter, Keynes did at first include a table which listed the price of North American wheat relative to the price of unspecified 'commodities' (reproduced here as Table 2).

Table 2. US labour figures—wheat in terms of commodities [1895 = 100]

1895	100	1899	98	1904	112
1896	76	1900	99	1905	108
1897	95	1902	116	1906	101
1898	103	1903	105	1907	106

He arrived at this index of price relativities by dividing one time series by another. I have not yet been able to identify the origin of the two series, and so cannot comment on the validity of the apparent upward trend in the price of North American wheat relative to the price of 'commodities'. Keynes himself was evidently not satisfied by his calculation, and wrote the word 'omit' next to it in the manuscript (EC/8/47).

He proceeded with his exposition of the sequence of economic history. The war of 1914–18 had then dislocated the accumulation of capital, both physically and psychologically. This dislocation had three dimensions:

1. The pre-war division of labour within Europe was disrupted by the breakdown in transport and the organizational framework for international commerce.

2. The decline of the exportable surplus of food from North America available to feed the industrial populations of Europe, and Europe's decreased ability to pay, threatened basic living standards.

3. The Victorian social psychology had involved a 'double bluff', whereby workers were persuaded to accept as wages an unfair share of their product and the capitalists were persuaded not to consume, but to accumulate and reinvest the profits of such exploitation of labour. This double bluff had now been exposed.

Keynes's thesis was that late Victorian prosperity, which had chained the Malthusian devil, had come to be taken for granted.

It was wrongly assumed to be normal. But, by 1919, it had been revealed as exceptional, an 'extraordinary episode', a 'happy age' whose growth had been unstable. Treating society as a single person, he wrote this about the Victorian capital accumulation process:

Society was working not for the small pleasures of today but for the future security and improvement of the race—in fact, for 'progress'. If only the cake were not cut, but was allowed to grow in the geometrical proportion predicted by Malthus of population, but not less true of compound interest, perhaps a day might come when there would at last be enough to go around, and when posterity could enter into the enjoyment of *our* labour. In that day, overwork, over-crowding and underfeeding would come to an end . . . One geometrical ratio might cancel another and the nineteenth century was able to forget the fertility of the species in contemplation of the dizzy virtues of compound interest. There were two pitfalls in this prospect: lest, population still outstripping accumulation, our self-denials promote not happiness, but numbers; and lest the cake be after all consumed, prematurely, in war, the consumer of all such hopes. (*CW*, ii. 12–13)

This is a slightly confusing, but central, passage. It is worth making two points by way of clarification. The slight confusion arises from the statement that 'one geometrical ratio might cancel another'. If the rate of capital accumulation precisely cancelled out the rate of population growth, then without some other change, the rise in the standard of living to which the Victorians looked forward would not have taken place. Instead, the result would merely have been one of capital-widening, the provision of a growing population with the same average endowment of capital per head. The ending of overwork, overcrowding and underfeeding could have been achieved only by a rising standard of living. Keynes is not explicit about the mechanism which actually raised living standards in the Victorian era, and which, if continuing to operate, might allow the eventual arrival at the stationary state which all the classical economists contemplated. The second, and related, point is that Keynes makes no mention of technical progress in surveying an era which displayed it at an historically unprecedented rate. It could be argued that it is technical progress which raises output per head, permits the wage rate and wages to rise, and thus leads via substitution of capital for labour to a rising capital–labour ratio. By leaving technical progress out of consideration, Keynes's account of economic progress remained underdetermined, even at the most naïve level.

To return to Keynes's historical periodization, 1870–1914 represents the move towards a stationary state with capital accumulation proceeding faster than the rate of population growth. Keynes does not in fact find an historical phase where the two rates were equal, and only capital-widening took place. 1914–18 represents clearly enough the second of the two pitfalls, the consumption of capital in war greater than the losses of population through war, which Keynes regarded as relatively small. But Keynes also expected that in the aftermath of war, Europe would suffer from the first pitfall, that capital accumulation would not recover to equal the rate of population growth and that therefore, according to him, the average standard of living would fall. The Malthusian devil would again be on the loose.

In 1919, Keynes did not see that these two pitfalls clearly bear a very different economic significance. The second pitfall, wartime capital consumption, is a discrete or one-off phenomenon with welfare implications for the short and medium term. The first pitfall, the reversal of the relationship of capital accumulation to population growth, has welfare implications that will persist over the long run. In 1919, there was no lack of empirical evidence for the distress caused by the second pitfall. He could point to the falling output of coal, declining agricultural productivity, the severe disruption of the railways, and the social consequences of malnutrition and increased morbidity and mortality (*CW*, ii. 143–8; 157–9). Neo-Malthusians and their opponents alike would have acknowledged this evidence. The key issue between them would have been that of the speed of recovery and return to the pre-war economic conditions. Had the war caused only a substantial, but brief, loss of economic welfare, or something much more fundamental, such as the first pitfall?

II. POPULATION ISSUES, 1919–1923

The Economic Consequences of the Peace was the work that made Keynes a world-famous figure. Having captured the world's attention, Keynes did not shy away from the subject of population. At some time during the early 1920s, he sketched out the table of contents for a book of essays, under the title of *Essays on the Economic Future of the World* (O'Donnell, 1992: 779–81, 806). Of the proposed ten essays, the first four could have been developed easily by expansion of themes in 'Population' and the second chapter of *Economic Consequences*. The first four chapter headings in the sketch were:

1. Transitional character of the 19th century
2. Relative prices of agricultural and industrial products
3. Population
4. Climate v. Race Patriotism

The project never went beyond this initial sketch. Why not? O'Donnell considers only two possible reasons. He argues that Keynes abandoned his plans either because he changed his mind about the viewpoints they were intended to express, or because he simply lacked the time to complete them. O'Donnell then rejects the former explanation, and embraces the latter (ibid. 804). In the case of Keynes's writings on population, however, this is not convincing. In the first place, as we shall soon see, he did indeed change his viewpoints on population after 1930. It is, therefore, hard to imagine him returning to write a book to the above plan after that date, however much time he had available.

A second reason for scepticism about O'Donnell's explanation is that there is another common reason why a book-writing plan goes unfulfilled. It is that someone else has done almost exactly the same thing already. This renders a writing plan redundant, even if the author retains the original viewpoints and has sufficient time for writing. In fact, Petersen suggested this explanation for the non-appearance of a book on population by Keynes. The pre-empting author was identified as Harold Wright, whose *Population* was published as one of the Cambridge Economic Handbooks in 1923: 'The text of *Population*, which Wright wrote under the editorial guidance of Keynes, can be taken as the fullest statement of the latter's views on population at this time' (Petersen, 1964: 51). In effect, the suggestion is that Keynes used Wright as a quasi-amanuensis for his own ideas on the subject. If this were so, one scarcely need search further to establish why Keynes never wrote the first four chapters of *Essays on the Economic Future of the World*. It was all in Wright until 1930, and, after 1930, Wright was all wrong.

How could one test this suggestion? One indication that Keynes took a special interest in Wright's *Population* is that he wrote an individual preface to it, whereas all the others in the same series carried Keynes's standard preface (*CW*, xii. 857–9). On the other hand, one should not exaggerate the effort that this cost Keynes. A mere half paragraph was all that he added to a shortened version of *An Economist's View of Population* (see below). Apart from the existence of this special preface, Petersen provides no other evidence of Keynes's involvement in the production of this book. He merely asserts that 'Wright could have filled in Keynes' allusions to population theory even without his teacher's personal guidance, for they were in the Malthusian frame of reference' (Petersen, 1964: 64 n. 41).

The Keynes Papers at King's do not contain anything of note relating to Keynes's editorship of the Cambridge Economic Handbooks before the late 1920s. It is therefore not known what personal guidance, if any, Keynes did provide to Wright. Wright obviously expressed very similar views to those of Keynes on many population issues. The similarity could have several different causes. Was Wright's writing influenced or directed by Keynes in any way, or was he selected as author because his population views were previously known to be broadly similar to Keynes's? We do not know, and because we do not know we have no warrant for assuming that any particular part of Wright's text is expressing any of Keynes's own views at the time.

The main point is the simple one that, for whatever reasons, there is too much similarity between the two men's positions on population for it to have been attractive to Keynes to carry out his own book-writing scheme once Wright's effort had been published. This was particularly so as it became clear that the market for books on this subject was weak. Wright's *Population* was the slowest-selling of all the Cambridge Economic Handbooks of the 1920s (letter from Bertram Christian to Keynes, 15 Jan. 1928). So Keynes confined his population work to both academic and popular articles.

In the latter category, 'An Economist's View of Population' appeared in the sixth of the supplements that he edited for the *Manchester Guardian Commercial* in August 1922. It begins by distinguishing, in a way not fully carried through in *Economic Consequences*, between the effects of the two pitfalls in the post-war world. But instead of making an assertion, Keynes now posed a question:

The most interesting question in the world (of those at least which time will bring us an answer) is whether, after a short interval of recovery (sc. from the effects of the war) material progress will be resumed, or whether, on the other hand, the magnificent episode of the nineteenth century is over. (*CW*, xvii. 442)

His answer was one of modified pessimism. The availability of new natural resources, and of unexploited scale economies in production, were both more limited than they were a hundred years ago, he claimed, despite his statement that 'we may still regard the possibilities of scientific improvements as unlimited'. The growth rate of output would therefore be slower and the right policy was 'to prepare the social structure for a return to conditions of quantitative stability' (ibid. 443). This would be difficult because demographic forces affect economic life only after a twenty-year time lag: the post-war labour market would be affected by births determined by pre-war conditions and expectations. It was not clear that people would save enough to finance the capital-widening necessary to prevent the average standard of living from falling. The picture was a gloomy one unless unforeseen developments (presumably the realization of some of the possibilities of scientific improvement) help to restore the equilibrium of population and resources.

In 'The Underlying Principles', the editorial with which Keynes ended the series of *Manchester Guardian Commercial* supplements in January 1923, he used this gloomy analysis to argue for the increased use of contraception, albeit in coded language. He castigated socialists who spoke as if the problem of poverty were soluble only by redistributing existing resources:

> To treat the question of [meeting basic needs] as primarily one of the redistribution of existing resources, without regard to the long-period effect of the new social order on the proportion between numbers and resources, is a far-reaching error. (ibid. 452)

He declared himself unable to see any way of materially improving the average human lot that did not include a plan for restricting the increase in numbers. This plan would not be Malthus's plan for increased sexual abstinence and moral restraint, but a plan for something which both Malthus and many of Keynes's contemporaries found abhorrent, the more widespread use of artificial methods of birth control (Harrod, 1972/1951: 385–7). Keynes was well aware of where the obstacle lay, but persisted in his advocacy:

> If, in Malthusian language, the checks of poverty, disease and war are to be removed, something must be put in their place. It may prove sufficient to render the restriction of offspring safe and easy, and to change a little (not so very much) custom and conventional morals. Perhaps a

more positive policy may be required. In any case, the question must be faced . . . (*CW*, xvii. 453)

It is difficult not to criticize the close link that Keynes made between his positive analysis of population and resources and his advocacy of contraception. There are after all many reasons why birth control is desirable other than an impending Malthusian crisis. In this connection, it is interesting that Keynes himself never advocated the abandoning of contraception once he became convinced in 1937 that 'we shall be faced in a very short time with a stationary or declining level of population' (*CW*, xiv. 125). Yet in the 1920s, it seems that he felt that the campaign for birth control would be undermined if his positive analysis was disproved, and indeed that those who disagreed with it did so because they were opposed to the spread of contraception. It would have been more realistic to argue, as contemporary demographic analysts did, that the increasing use of birth control had already removed the possibility of a future Malthusian crisis in the industrial countries whose prospects he was analysing. As Moggridge has noted, 'Keynes' worries about the reappearance of the Malthusian devil . . . were certainly misplaced in the light of the events he was discussing' (1993: 57).

This, however, was not widely perceived by economists who were Keynes's contemporaries, particularly those with Cambridge connections. Harrod's account of the meeting of the Political Economy Club in the 1922 Michaelmas term, mentioned earlier, is rather misleading on this point. He writes:

[Keynes] also dwelt on modern conditions; the Malthusian devil was still evidently with us. In the discussion Mr Dennis Robertson produced some recent statistics; he was not sure about the Malthusian devil. Indeed he hinted that the modern danger might be the opposite one, a decline in numbers. Robertson seemed to know what he was talking about, and I had the uncomfortable feeling that it was he, and not my master, who was in the right on this occasion. (Harrod, 1972/1951: 385)

However, whatever he was saying to Keynes in private, Robertson was soon mounting a broad, though not wholly unqualified, public defence of the Cambridge neo-Malthusian position, putting in 'A Word for the Devil' (1923: 203–8). He endorsed the conclusions of Wright's *Population*, which, as I have noted, followed fairly closely the main lines of Keynes's own thinking on population as it has been outlined thus far. Hugh Dalton sounded a more sceptical note in his review of Wright's book (1923: 224–8). *Pace* Harrod, Keynes's neo-Malthusianism seems to have enjoyed at least the public support of most of his Cambridge colleagues at this time.

In the serious weekly journals, Keynes's neo-Malthusianism was also making headway. In April 1923, Keynes became Chairman of the Board of the *Nation*, having bought a share in the publication from the Rowntrees. Under a new editor, Hubert Henderson, the *Nation's* editorial line changed from the anti-birth-control line of his predecessor, H. W. Massingham. Although Harrod claims that Keynes never interfered with editorial policy (1972/1951: 396), it was his brand of neo-Malthusianism that now prevailed in the articles that appeared on population questions (Freeden, 1979: 662–4).

In another interesting development, the Family Endowment Council entered the population debate. Its campaign for the endowment of the family by the state drew on one strand of the pre-war pro-natalist movement, the promotion of motherhood. It gained its progressive thrust by combining the championing of maternity with a strong emphasis on freedom of choice and economic independence for women. Its leaders included Eleanor Rathbone, Eva Hubback, and Mary Stocks. They were in opposition to Keynes and his neo-Malthusianism.

In 1924, Eleanor Rathbone commented on 'the brilliant group of younger Liberals led by Mr Keynes' who warned that the world's population was outrunning its natural resources, and whose publicity organ, 'the *Nation*, is popularly supposed to have for its watchwords, "Capitalism and Contraception"' (1924: 223).

She chided them for their offhand dismissal of her campaign for family allowances:

None of these leaders of opinion have as yet condescended to take the proposal for direct [family] provision very seriously or discuss it thoroughly, but when any of them have cast a careless glance at it, I fancy it has seemed to them just another of the many schemes suggested by well-meaning sentimentalists for encouraging the propagation of the unfit and making it easier for the lazy and inefficient to maintain themselves without much work. (ibid. 233–4)

Her estimate of their opinion was well judged, especially their anxiety about the rapid multiplication of the unfit. Not all the leading liberals remained opposed to the policy of family endowment. William Beveridge, for example, was soon to change his mind, for a variety of complicated reasons. Mr Keynes, however, would take a further fifteen years to change his. The story of how he finally came to adopt Rathbone's scheme of family allowances is told in Chapter 6. Before this came about, much else had still to happen. One significant event was already in train: Keynes's debate with William Beveridge, not about family endowment, but about a superficially improbable combination of subjects, namely, the terms of trade and birth control.

III. THE DEBATE WITH BEVERIDGE, 1923–1924

The neo-Malthusian consensus extended to Beveridge at the LSE, as well as to most of Keynes's Cambridge colleagues. Beveridge did not deny the validity of Malthus's fundamental principle that mankind cannot without disaster 'control death by art and leave birth to Nature'. He also shared Keynes's concern, expounded in the 'North–South model' in 'Population', about 'how far the unequal adoption of birth control by different races will leave one race at the mercy of another's growing numbers, or drive it to armaments and perpetual aggression in self-defence' (Beveridge,

1923: 473–4). Beveridge's biographer has therefore suggested there was something 'rather artificial' about his fiercely contested public debate with Keynes in 1923–4, 'since in the last resort they both accepted the [neo-]Malthusian analysis and both were in favour of "rational" family planning' (Harris, 1977: 342). In fact, there was nothing artificial about the debate at all. As explained in Chapter 1, at least since the time of Malthus, the population question had been closely linked to the question of the changing terms-of-trade between manufactures and primary commodities. The debate was about the intensity of Malthusian pressures in post-war Britain, and the urgency of the adoption of birth control. Both of the disputants accepted that (some measure of) the terms of trade between agricultural and industrial goods was a relevant indicator of population pressure. Keynes was on the side of the urgency of birth control, while Beveridge favoured greater caution, and each looked to terms-of-trade indicators to provide the statistical support for his position.

Beveridge had had few personal contacts with Keynes before the Great War. According to Keynes's scribbled list, Beveridge had been a participant at the May 1914 seminar in Oxford. It seems very probable that a disagreement between the two men over the alleged 1900 turning point in the manufacturing terms of trade had already surfaced at that seminar. During the war, they met again when Keynes was in the Treasury and Beveridge was at the Ministry of Food. This encounter was an uncomfortable one for Beveridge, and it stuck in his mind. Thirty years later, at some time in the two or three years after Keynes's death, he dictated a brief obituary memoir, entitled 'Some Memories of Maynard Keynes', in which he recalled this incident:

The war brought him [Keynes] to the Treasury as advisor on problems of foreign expense, problems that were even more difficult in that war than in its successor. One of my first contacts with him as a man of affairs arose through this. When, with the appointment of Lord Rhondda in the middle of 1917 as second food controller, British food control began to be taken seriously, the Ministry of Food in which I was then working decided that the time had come itself to undertake the importation of essential foods which came largely from America . . . We made an order at the end of August stopping all private importation of bacon, hams and lard, and I went on behalf of the Ministry to the Treasury to arrange for dollars with which to begin buying and importing on our own account. In vain I argued that the cessation of private import financed in the ordinary way must lighten the burden of taking the dollar exchange and so release dollars for the direct exchange. Keynes answered that the monthly account of dollars that the U.S. would lend to Britain was fixed and that it was all wanted for other purchases than bacon. Finally, in the face of my despair, he relented a little and threw me a million dollars . . . I remember being impressed with the power that one man could wield (BEV ix (a), 52).

Beveridge added, 'How fortunate that in this case the man was Maynard Keynes'. One cannot help wondering whether Beveridge felt at the time, on the contrary, that Keynes had become somewhat over-mighty. It would have been a natural reaction.

In the immediate aftermath of the war, the two men collaborated on an historical publishing project financed by the Carnegie Endowment for International Peace. Beveridge chaired the British Editorial Board of the Economic History and Survey of the War Period project, and Keynes was a member of the Board (CE/1). In 'Some Memories of John Maynard Keynes', Beveridge also recalled attending another seminar and a lecture given by Keynes.

Beveridge's general reaction to *The Economic Consequences of the Peace* was favourable. Nevertheless, he objected to Keynes's statements in chapter II on the manufacturing terms of trade and their implication for the future welfare of the population. So in 1923, in his Presidential Address to the British Association (Section F), Beveridge publicly denied the occurrence of any 1900 turning point in the industrial–agricultural terms of trade, and thus the pre-war emergence of the first pitfall. After presenting a mass of detailed statistics, he summed up this part of his Address by saying:

Mr Keynes' fears seem not merely unnecessary but baseless; his specific statements are inconsistent with facts. Europe on the eve of war was not threatened with a falling standard of life because Nature's response to a further increase in population was diminishing. It was not diminishing; it was increasing. Europe on the eve of war was not threatened with hunger by a rising real cost of corn; the real cost of corn was not rising; it was falling. (Beveridge, 1923: 459)

Beveridge conceded that for Britain alone, rather than the whole of Europe, the statistics could permit the interpretation of 'some faltering of progress' between the Victorian and the Edwardian age, but this could have been merely a 'transient phenomenon'.

Because of the absence of a '1900 turning point', Beveridge also disagreed with the unqualified advocacy of birth control. His reservations were linked precisely to the problem that Keynes himself had raised about the differential impact of birth control on the European and non-European nations. Beveridge was also concerned about the effect of widening the use of birth control on the future age structure of the British population and on its quality, if adopters were largely upper and middle class—concerns that Keynes did not share. Hence Beveridge denied that 'the authority of economic science can be invoked for the intensification of these [birth control] practices as a cure for our present troubles—unless and until further enquiries were made into the potential agricultural resources of the world, on the one hand, and into the physical, psychological and social effects of fertility restriction on the other' (ibid. 474–5).

In his reply to Beveridge, Keynes shifted his ground. He cited two different indices for the United Kingdom, rather than Europe as a whole. These were Bowley's and the Board of Trade's indices of the 'volume of manufactured exports given for a uniform quantity of food imports'. These showed, not a decline after 1900, but merely a stabilization after a period of improvement. He admitted that such figures 'can never do more than suggest con-clusions,—they cannot prove them' (*CW*, xix. 134). But he then asserted that his conclusion that *Western* Europe was overpopu-lated did not stand or fall with the 'particular point of detail' which he had chosen to discuss, which was 'only one item in a vast field of evidence and argument' (*CW*, xix. 135). Finally, citing newspaper coverage of Beveridge's speech, which (at least in the examples used by Keynes) construed it as a victory for opponents of birth control, he blamed Beveridge, in effect, for the mislead-ing conclusions that had been drawn by the press. He flatly accused Beveridge of sheltering the 'ignorance and prejudice' of the opponents of birth control (*CW*, xix. 137).

Beveridge demolished this audacious but flawed public defence in a further article (1924: 1–20). He showed that Keynes's UK result followed from his splicing of two indices which were not equivalent, which neglected the change in the composition of manufactured exports, and which covered only between 65 and 50 per cent of all UK manufactured exports. The '1900 turning point' was thus shown up as a statistical artefact. More impor-tantly, Keynes's argument confused the falling purchasing power in terms of food of a manufactured item with the falling pur-chasing power over food of a unit of labour applied to manufac-ture. Beveridge correctly pointed out that a downward drift in the former was compatible with an upward drift in the latter when technical progress was achieving increasing returns to labour in manufacturing (ibid. 14–16). Moggridge agrees that Beveridge was right about this:

Keynes's long-standing worry about the secular tendency for the terms of trade between primary products (especially foodstuffs) and manu-factures to turn automatically against the latter to the detriment of European standards of life was certainly misplaced, as well as theoreti-cally incorrect . . . What should really concern one in such cases are not the gross barter terms of trade considered in *Economic Consequences* and elsewhere but rather the single or double factoral terms of trade which relate to the actual resource costs involved. (1992: 345, 345 n. o)

However, unfortunately, in the course of his 'purely destructive and statistical' article, Beveridge made the tactical error of attributing to Keynes 'the definite and immediate advocacy of "birth control" as a means of limiting population' (1924: 1). In fact, Keynes's professionally published pronouncements on this subject had been somewhat indirect and euphemistic, although unmistakable in meaning. This gave Keynes the opening to make the startling claim that he had 'certainly never presented any arguments whatever in favour of' birth control, a claim which deliberately ignores the remarks that have already been quoted from 'Underlying Principles'. In private correspondence with Beveridge, he claimed that (1) he had published only 'three sentences' on population in his life and that (2) what he had written was absolutely right, or would be seen to be so if taken in the context of the vast amount which he knew about population, but had not yet written down. Beveridge then invited him to develop these arguments further for publication in *Economica*. Keynes declined to take up this invitation (*CW*, xix. 119–42). In effect, he retired from the field.

The sharpness of the intellectual clash did not lead to a personal falling out. As Eleanor Rathbone had observed, in the middle of the exchanges in January 1924, the two men were collaborating to prop up the *Nation* (BEV vii 37 (28) and (29)). In 'Some Memories of Maynard Keynes', Beveridge praised Keynes for his ability to raise fundamental questions, while maintaining his disagreement with Keynes's claim of a turning point. The relevant passage is as follows:

It did not seem to me at the time nor does it seem now that the economic data that led Keynes to suggest that the law of diminishing returns was at last reasserting itself and that the immediate danger before economists and the world was that of population really supported that inference. Some of the data which he took from others were as I think I showed at the time in themselves fallacious but whatever the merits of that particular controversy the immense advantage of having it raised by Keynes is beyond question. (BEV ix (a), 52)

Beveridge reflected further on the debate when he wrote his *Autobiography* in the early 1950s: 'A friend later told me that this was one of the few occasions on which Keynes had been shown to be wrong' (1953: 212).[1]

This was indeed the public perception. When Beveridge was criticized publicly, it was not for the unsoundness of his analysis, but for his lack of enthusiasm for the use of birth control by 'all and sundry'. Marie Stopes deplored this at a time when, she claimed, 'the nation was spending £100,000,000 per year on unemployables, including the maintenance of diseased, enfeebled persons whom the proper use of birth control would have prevented from ever existing' (Harris, 1997: 331). Beveridge, however, was more interested in methods of improving the quality of the child population other than the chimerical project of ensuring that the diseased and feeble-minded never get born. In this connection, he reviewed Eleanor Rathbone's *The Disinherited Family* in 1924, and became an immediate convert to her idea of 'family allowances'. His reasons for this were complicated. Apart from the alleviation of poverty, he wanted to prevent any further decline in the fertility rate, and (unlike Rathbone) thought family allowances would have that effect. He also advocated them on the ground that they would hold down wages, something that did not appeal at all to the Trade Union wing of the Labour movement, as Keynes was to discover later (ibid. 332–5).

Beveridge later tried to explain away Keynes's defeat in debate: 'If he was wrong, this was due to a mistake in one of the authorities on which he had relied' (1953: 212–13). This remark certainly shows magnanimity in victory, but it puts a too generous a gloss on Keynes's conduct. It was galling for Keynes, just when *Economic Consequences* was bringing him the most spectacular success, for one of its *obiter dicta* to be picked on by a weighty senior, examined at length, and found wanting. Beveridge probably had the advantage of knowing that Keynes was chancing his arm with a slender piece of unrevised pre-war research. What is so interesting is Keynes's reaction to criticism by an opponent thus forearmed. He could not accept it, because in his mind the question of the correctness of his analysis was entangled much too closely with the success of his campaigning for birth control. So instead of backing off when his analysis was faced by an over-whelming challenge, he pressed on, which only further exposed the weakness of his position.

Despite his defeat in the debate with Beveridge, Keynes main-tained his neo-Malthusian stance on his visit to Soviet Russia in the autumn of 1925. His views on the question of population in Russia had already been stated in his *Manchester Guardian* sup-plement on that country published in July 1922. His picture was one of fast (1.7 per cent a year) and accelerating population growth between 1890 and 1914, generating a total of 150 million people at the outbreak of the First World War, and an annual increment of 4 million at that date. As a result of the war and the Russian Revolution, the economic structure of the country had collapsed and Malthusian checks were operating—'Nature . . . is restoring by her usual weapons the equilibrium between man and his surroundings' (*CW*, xvii. 434–7). Keynes saw 'the swelling body of ever more numerous workers' as 'the deepest disease of the organism' of Russian society (ibid. 439). In a lecture in Moscow on 15 September 1925 he said:

I believe that the poverty of Russia before the war was due to the great increase in population more than to any other cause. The War and the Revolution reduced the population. But I am told that now again there is a large excess of births over deaths. There is no greater danger than this to the economic future of Russia. There is no more important object of deliberate state policy than to secure a balanced Budget of Population. (RV/1)

In the light of modern historical research on Russian demog-raphy, these judgements have to be somewhat modified. The 1914 population total is now put at 140 rather than 150 million. That total was not reached again until 1925, the year of Keynes's lecture. He was correctly informed that the excess of births over deaths was unusually large in 1925 (44.7 births compared with 23.2 deaths per thousand, representing the largest annual net increment to the population since before 1914). Under this stimulus, population did grow rapidly, reaching his 1914 estimate of 150 million in 1928 (Danilov, 1988: 38–40). It seems that Keynes somewhat exaggerated the scale of Russia's pre-war population, and the influence of pre-war population growth (rather than the ravages of the 1914 war itself) on the outbreak of the Revolution. The Russian visit of 1925 proved to be the public swansong of Keynes's neo-Malthusianism.

IV. MR KEYNES AND DR STOPES

As the debate with Beveridge had revealed, Keynes's neo-Malthusianism was far from being merely the product of an academic interest in population questions. It had an underlying 'missionary' purpose. That purpose took Keynes in the 1920s into public campaigning and raised difficult questions about how best to work with others having a similar purpose, but different attitudes and approaches to it. His natural home in the cluster of campaigning groups was the Malthusian League. His views were most closely identified with those expressed in the publications of the League. They combined an acceptance of Malthus's principle of population with a practical activism in promoting contraception on strictly economic grounds (Weeks, 1989/1981: 130). For example, his critique of 'setters forth of Utopias' is reminiscent of the tactic of using Malthus against Marx, which was the frequent resort of C. V. Drysdale, the individualistic and anti-socialist president of the League.[2]

Keynes was temperamentally and philosophically opposed to the championship of a fecund middle class, believing that family life militated against both intellectual creativity and participation in public affairs (Skidelsky, 1983: 223–6). At the same time, he was concerned about the quality of the population. He had made this clear in 'Population', and this concern continued in the 1920s.

Two of his book outlines dating from 1924 provide evidence of his view that both population control and eugenics were legitimate objects of state policy (O'Donnell, 1992: 784, 807–8). In his 1926 lecture on 'The End of Laissez-Faire', he declared that the community must pay attention to the 'innate quality' of the population as well as 'mere numbers' (*CW*, ix. 292). This indicates his continuing interest in negative eugenics. In this, too, he agreed with C. V. Drysdale (1933: 292).

The groups publicly advocating birth control in the 1920s were also divided among themselves. Until 1921 all that had been achieved since the Bradlaugh–Besant trial in 1876 had been the spread of information. It is estimated that between 1879 and 1921 some three million pamphlets and leaflets urging the principle of family limitation had circulated. However, of these, only one million gave usable detail on contraceptive practice (Weeks, 1981: 47). It was not until 1921 that Marie Stopes opened the first birth control clinic in Britain. Stopes's success in softening opposition to birth control during the 1920s depended on her particular socially conservative style and argument. Her main emphasis was placed on two considerations—physical contraception as an aid to marital fulfilment and stability, and as a means to improve maternal and child health. Her crusade also played on the fashionable eugenic concern for population quality. Like Eleanor Rathbone, she deliberately kept a good distance from the neo-Malthusian position adopted by Keynes, and Keynes returned the compliment.

As Keynes was to discover to his discomfort, the politics of the various birth control organizations in Britain in the first half of the 1920s were fairly complicated.[3] The Malthusian League's position as the leading British birth control organization faced a serious challenge when Marie Stopes and her husband opened the first birth control clinic in Britain in March 1921. This was something that Dr Drysdale had been advocating since 1913, but had not done. To respond to Stopes, the Drysdales opened their own clinic in Walworth. It soon closed, owing to a lack of funds, popular hostility, and internal wrangling. In 1922, the Malthusian League was re-launched, without the Drysdales, as the New Generation League, and among its official patrons was J. M. Keynes (ibid. 196).

In mid-1921, Stopes had founded her own support organization, the Society for Constructive Birth Control and Racial Progress. She too sought the sympathetic talented and famous as official patrons of her CBC, as it came to be called. Keynes agreed to become a vice-president of the CBC. Thus by 1922 he had publicly connected himself with two birth control organizations. But they increasingly saw each other as rivals and acted competitively. For example, in July 1922 the Malthusians successfully mounted an International Neo-Malthusian and Birth Control Conference without the presence of Stopes. This conference featured the American birth control advocate Margaret Sanger, whom Stopes already regarded as a personal rival and had earlier dissuaded from pre-empting the Stopes's clinic. Keynes participated actively as the leader of one of the conference sections (ibid. 225). He retained among his papers *The Lancet*'s report of the private medical session (SS/3).

Throughout the early 1920s, Keynes involved himself in various events organized by the Malthusian League and its successor, the New Generation League. Apart from the 1922 international conference, Keynes campaigned within the Liberal Party for more enlightened birth control policies, along the lines of the New Generation League's thinking. Early in 1923 Keynes had aided the League's defence of the publishers of Margaret Sanger's pamphlet on *Family Limitation* when they faced an obscenity charge. He stood surety for them for the sum of £50 (Soloway, 1982: 230). The case caused Keynes considerable vexation, because of muddles between him, Bertrand and Dora Russell, and others about which lawyers should conduct the defence and how they should be paid for. To compound matters, Stopes not only did not assist, but wrote to the Director of Public Prosecutions to condemn the pamphlet's illustrations as 'both criminal and harmful' (Hall, 1977: 210). The case was lost, although the defendants were not punished except by loss of their stock.

The 1922 conference had also discussed the possibility of using the theatre as a medium for the birth control message (ibid. 221). Keynes commented on Stopes's response to this in a letter to his wife Lydia in 1923. Stopes had once again acted decisively to achieve what the neo-Malthusians were still only discussing. The author of *Married Love* and *Wise Parenthood* was putting her gospel onto the London stage. Keynes remarked that

M Stopes has written a play. I wonder how dramatic critics will demonstrate their opinions. I hear that she is so much intraverted [*sic*] in her subject that even when conversation centres around polo, birth control is applied to it by her. (28 October 1923; in Hill and Keynes, 1989: 117)

The play in question was *Our Ostriches*, which was just about to open at the Royal Court Theatre, and the critics generally dismissed it as undisguised birth control propaganda. Keynes's comment about Stopes's personality was, however, prophetic of the difficult, distant, and intermittent relationship he was to have with her.

Shortly before he wrote to Lydia, Stopes had solicited Keynes's help when *The Times* refused to publish an announcement of a forthcoming CBC meeting. She asked him, along with the other vice-presidents, to write a personal letter of protest and request an explanation, which he duly did. In January 1924, Keynes was again approached in his capacity as a vice-president of the CBC, but this time by a Mr G. H. Wales, who complained that the CBC was publishing misleading warnings against the birth control work of a 'Dr Courtenay Beale'. In his own publicity material, 'Dr Beale' had offered the public confidential birth control advice for a fee. As his handbill indicates, 'Dr Beale' was blatantly trading on Marie Stopes's reputation. She hastened to persuade Keynes that the complaint he had received was unjustified, and that on the contrary she was the injured party. She had in fact attempted to take legal action against 'Dr Beale' in 1921, but she was unable to find him or the booksellers who slipped his handbills into her books (Hall, 1977: 204). Now she proposed that Keynes reply to Mr Wales with a catechism of leading questions designed to unmask those who hid behind the pseudonym of 'Dr Beale'.

Keynes was confused by these proposed tactics and wrote her the following reply:

46, Gordon Square
Bloomsbury
30th January 1924

Dear Dr Stopes,

Thank you for your letter. But I am still in ignorance of what the precise ground of complaint is. I gather from your letter that the suggestion is that there is really no such person as Dr Courtenay Beale. At least this seems to be the point of the questions which you suggest that I should ask.

But if so, it seems to me better that I should be free to state in so many words that this is the complaint rather than to ask rather strange questions. May I reply to the complainants that I find on enquiry that one at least of the grounds of complaint is that the doctor in question is a fictitious person?

Yours truly
[*signed*] J. M. Keynes

Dr Stopes
7, John Street
Adelphi W.C.2

(BM Add. MS 58695, Fo. 39)

We can trace the later phases of the relationship with the help of four further letters from Keynes to Stopes which are not in the *Collected Writings*, but are to be found in the Stopes Collection in the British Museum. After the Courtenay Beale affair, he held Marie Stopes and the CBC at arm's length. In 1927, soon after Vera Brittain wrote an article in the *Nation and Athenaeum* on 'Our Malthusian Middle Classes', advocating 'eugenic' rather than 'dysgenic' birth control (meaning larger planned families for the middle class), Stopes wrote a letter to the editor. It seems that her letter was not published, and I have been unable to establish its precise content. She sent Keynes a copy, perhaps taking the opportunity of promoting the eugenic approach of the CBC as against the neo-Malthusianism of the League. In any case, in his reply, Keynes did not bother to disguise his frustration with attempts to foment divisions within the birth control movement:

King's College
Cambridge
26 May 1927

Dear Dr Stopes

Thank you for sending me a copy of your letter to the Editor of *The Nation*. I confess, however, that I wish the various Birth Control Organizations would not spend so much time scrapping with one another! It tends to sap public confidence in all of them alike.

Yours very truly,
[*signed*] J. M. Keynes

(BM Add. MS 58701, Fo. 97 (hand-written))

Undeterred by this rebuff, Marie Stopes continued to try to use Keynes as an occasional facilitator of her activities. In 1929 she sought his signature on a circular letter and in 1930 she asked for his help in setting up one of her meetings in Cambridge. On both occasions, he politely declined.[4]

By this time, much of the energy and excitement pervading the birth control movement in the early 1920s had evaporated. The defences of Church and state were crumbling and contraception was at last achieving some respectability in the eyes of British public opinion. The Lambeth Conference in August 1930 voted by 193 to 67 to adopt a new resolution on marriage and sex. It permitted 'other methods' of birth control than abstinence, when there were morally sound reasons for using them (Soloway, 1982: 252–3). The end of government resistance came when the Ministry of Health was forced to concede that local authorities already had statutory powers under an Act of 1915 to offer birth control advice to married women on medical grounds. A new National Birth Control Council was formed at this time to co-ordinate the various unofficial birth control organizations. This council took it upon itself to inform all local authorities of what they could and could not do under the law. Keynes joined as one of its patrons. So eventually did Marie Stopes, but within three years she had managed to quarrel with others on the Council and resign (ibid. 311).

By the time that the battle for birth control in Britain was effectively won in 1930, Keynes had already embarked on a new intellectual tack that required him to abandon completely his former neo-Malthusian views. There were a number of reasons for this mercurial change, but there can be little doubt that the approaching political victory for the advocates of birth control was a powerful one.

Marie Stopes did not trouble Keynes again, except to enquire in 1939 whether he wished to continue as a vice-president of the CBC. She received this revealing reply:

46 Gordon Square,
Bloomsbury

Miss Marie C. Stopes,   March 26th 1939
The Mother's Clinic,
106 Whitfield Street,
Tottenham Court, [*sic*] Road,
W1

Dear Miss Stopes,

In reply to your letter of March 24th, I am sorry to say that I was unaware that I was still a Vice-President of your organisation. I had meant some little time ago to withdraw from this, and I would be grateful if you would now agree to my doing so.

Yours truly
[*signed*] J. M. Keynes
(BM Add. MS 58721, Fo. 46)

When he agreed to become a vice-president of the CBC, Keynes had evidently badly underestimated the persistent maverick behaviour of Marie Stopes. Once he found out the truth, which he had by 1923, he engaged in what was essentially a damage limitation exercise. He continued to put his support behind the New Generation League's activities while fending off approaches from Stopes. He found his position of being formally at least in both the CBC and NGL camps an uncomfortable and irritating one, but he did succeed in sustaining it until it ceased to be of any importance to him.

V. KEYNES'S RECANTATION OF NEO-MALTHUSIANISM

Keynes wrote a talk in 1928 that later became 'Economic Possibilities for our Grandchildren' (1930). The opening sentences indicate a spectacular *volte-face*:

We are suffering just now from a bad attack of economic pessimism. It is common to hear people say that the epoch of enormous economic progress which characterised the nineteenth century is over; and that the rapid improvement in the standard of life is now going to slow down . . . I believe that this is a wildly mistaken interpretation of what is happening to us. We are suffering not from the rheumatics of old age, but from the growing pains of over-rapid changes . . . (*CW*, ix. 321)[5]

This passage contains no acknowledgement of his own argument ten years before in *Economic Consequences* that Victorian prosperity was 'an extraordinary episode'. It fails to mention his own warnings on the need 'to prepare the social structure for a return to conditions of quantitative stability'. Keynes did not admit that he was himself one of the people whose views he now regarded as wildly mistaken.

What had been the mistakes? First of all, technical progress over the previous ten years had proceeded 'at a greater rate . . . than ever before in history' (*CW*, ix. 325). In 1923, Keynes had argued against Beveridge that it was not safe to leave the question of numbers unregulated in the mere hope that the neo-Malthusian evil day would be postponed by improvements (like the swifter progress of science) which were 'conceivable, but as yet unrealised' (*CW*, xix. 124). By 1928–30, he was predicting that 'in our own lifetimes . . . we may be able to perform all the operations of agriculture, mining and manufacture with a quarter of the human effort to which we have been accustomed' (*CW*, ix. 325). What had happened to the Malthusian devil? In spite of the enormous growth in the population of the world, and the widening of capital that this had made necessary, technical progress had been so rapid that the average standard of life in Europe and the United States had risen very substantially. This was despite the fact that technical progress had been labour-displacing in its effects, and a new 'disease' of technological unemployment had manifested itself. Furthermore, population growth was actually decelerating: 'from now on we need not expect so great an increase in population' (ibid.).

Keynes's focus on the population question had now narrowed again, from Europe and North America to England and Wales. The bald brief statement that in future those countries need not expect so great a population increase was indeed correct. The broad tendency of their population growth in the second half of the nineteenth century was one of deceleration, as the crude birth rate fell more rapidly than the crude death rate. In 1870 population growth was 1.4 per cent a year. By 1914, it had come down to about 1 per cent. Under the impact of the First World War, which both disrupted normal fertility patterns and temporarily pushed up the crude death rate, the growth rate slumped to 0.4 per cent (1915–19). In the first half of the twenties it returned to its pre-war trend (0.9 per cent). Thereafter the deceleration became somewhat sharper, but even at its lowest point before the mid-1970s, it never pushed the rate of population growth below about 0.2 per cent a year (1935–44) (Woods, 1987: 284). The entire century from 1870–1970 is one of slowly decelerating growth (from 1.5 to just below 0.5 per cent), with two major downward deviations, caused by the two world wars.

By 1930, the post-war demographic rebound from the First World War had taken place, and the forces of deceleration had reasserted themselves on population growth. At the same time, Keynes had rediscovered the immense powers of technical change to raise productivity. This dramatic readjustment of the respective strengths of the growth rates of capital accumulation (embodying technical progress) and population allowed him to resurrect the scenario of the stationary state, which supported (as he had previously argued) the social psychology of Victorian capital accumulation. His conclusion, that the economic problem would not be the permanent problem of the human race but might be solved, or within sight of solution, within a hundred years, echoed very clearly the view which he rejected as outdated in 1919—that 'a day might come when there would at last be enough to go round . . . [and] overwork, overcrowding and under-feeding would come to an end'. Although Keynes distinguished in a modern way between absolute and relative deprivation, or between normal consumption goods and what Hirsch calls 'positional' goods (1977: 25 n. 13), and recognized that the problem of relative deprivation (or the availability of positional goods) was not soluble in principle, he argued that

this is not so true of absolute needs—a point may soon be reached, much sooner perhaps than we all of us are aware of, when these needs are satisfied in the sense that we prefer to devote our further energies to non-economic purposes. (*CW*, ix. 326)

Thus the stationary state was put back at the centre. Keynes was now devoting himself to re-establishing in the public mind the very psychology that ten years before he had held to be so exploded that it could never be re-created. Appreciating, as he did, the importance of expectations and conventional beliefs in a world of pervasive uncertainty, he became in 1930 the somewhat disdainful exponent of the very same 'double bluff' which he had exposed to view a decade before. The broader significance of 'Economic Possibilities' in Keynes's thought goes beyond the way in which the balance between population and resources is handled (see Catephores, 1991: 5–15, 40–5). But on this issue alone, 'Economic Possibilities' marks a complete but unacknowledged recantation of his neo-Malthusian views.

But what of the two pitfalls which he had earlier found on the route to the stationary state? They had not disappeared, but remained in vestigial form as limiting assumptions. The economic problem may be solved 'assuming no important wars and no important increase in population'. In 1923, our deep instincts were a profound threat. At that time the working of one particular fundamental instinct needed to be brought under social control (*CW*, xix. 124). In 1930 it seemed to Keynes that, on the contrary, 'we have been expressly evolved by nature—with all our impulses and deepest instincts—for the purpose of solving the economic problem' (*CW*, ix. 327).

VI. KEYNES, MALTHUS, AND THE LACK OF EFFECTIVE DEMAND

Having rediscovered the lost draft of his essay on Malthus in October 1930, Keynes rewrote it between October 1932 and late January 1933 for inclusion in *Essays in Biography*. He told Lydia on 13 October 1932 that

I have been completely absorbed in re-writing my life of Malthus, and sit by the hour at my desk copying bits out and composing sentences and wanting to do nothing else with stacks of books round me. What a relief not to be writing arguments! What an easy and agreeable life fanciful writers must lead! (quoted in Moggridge, 1993: 563)

One result of this revision was to reduce considerably the discussion of Malthus the population expert. Another was to add a concluding discussion, amounting to one-third of the final text length, of Malthus as 'the first Cambridge economist'. In this section, Keynes uses extracts from the Malthus–Ricardo corre-spondence to attribute to Malthus an understanding that unem-ployment can originate in the lack of effective demand, and that a deficiency of demand can result from 'an attempt to accumu-late very rapidly'. Keynes then laments the fact that Malthus's line of thought was almost totally obliterated in subsequent nineteenth-century economics, and Ricardo's became the parent stem of his and others' misguided education in economics. He credited Malthus with being not only the first Cambridge econo-mist, but also the source of an alternative tradition in economics, whose neglect has permitted a malign Ricardian dominance of the subject. These strong assertions led to a considerable revival of interest in Malthus as an economist, but also to a tendency to exaggerate Malthus's differences with Ricardo, and to promote what Winch has called 'a Keynesianised Malthus' (1996: 26–7).

The timing of the composition of this final addition to the essay on Malthus has been cited as evidence in the attempt to date (at late 1932 or early 1933) the point when Keynes integrated in his own mind the key basic ideas of *The General Theory* (Mog-gridge, 1992: 562–3). It has also prompted an extensive debate among historians of economics about the relation between Malthus's political economy and the economics of *The General Theory*. Was Malthus indeed the true precursor, or the inspira-tion, of Keynes's theory of effective demand?

The question of whether Malthus anticipated Keynes's macro-economics has attracted a great diversity of answers. Malthus has been accused of inconsistency and muddle. Harrod (1972/1951: 543) could not 'believe that Malthus, splendid as he was as a population theorist, contributed much of value to economics, in which he was always muddled'. Subsequently, Corry (1959: 717–24) and Balassa (1959: 272) both argued that Malthus did not break with the classical doctrine of the equality of *ex ante* saving and *ex ante* investment in his analysis of overproduction, and therefore was not in fact an analytic forerunner of Keynes. On the other hand, others have taken a diametrically opposite view.

They have found in Malthus's *Political Economy* a set of analogues of Keynes's ideas on underconsumption, excess saving, and sticky wages. Some have even argued that Malthusian political economy is more Keynesian than Keynes himself ever realized (Black, 1967: 59–60 n. 5). This claim is useful in that it alerts us to the difference between a precursor and an inspirer. It is possible to be a precursor of a later thinker, even when the later thinker does not realize that her work has been anticipated. By contrast, it is impossible for a later thinker to be inspired by an earlier thinker unless she is aware of the source of inspiration.

Taking first the question of Malthus as a precursor of Keynes, the answer depends on what is to be regarded as the central analytical contribution of *The General Theory*. In my opinion, it is the reconciliation of differences between *ex ante* saving and investment by means of an alteration in the level of output and employment, rather than by changes in the interest rate, that is its central analytic innovation. Malthus's discussions in the *Principles of Political Economy* or his letters to Ricardo show clearly enough that he believed that effective demand in an economy can be deficient. So did Keynes, although he made the error of inconsistently assuming Marshallian perfect competition in his analyses of the labour and goods markets (Hahn, 1996). Malthus further believed that such a deficiency of demand could be injurious to an economy, in that 'the value of the produce' would fall lower than it otherwise would. Keynes also argued that deficient demand was injurious, in the specific sense that it led to an equilibrium situation with involuntary unemployment. The problem in going beyond these very broad similarities is twofold. The framework within which Malthus discusses these problems is quite different from that of Keynes, and Malthus is not very precise about the time period that his analysis is meant to cover.

Malthus retains a distinction between the manufacture of goods, which is 'productive', and the rendering of services, which is 'unproductive'. He thus has a more restricted notion of what constitutes national production than does modern national accounting methodology. He is not operating with the national accounting identity between national production, income, and expenditure, or with a system composed of households, firms, the government, and the rest of the world. His division of the economy is between agriculture, capitalist manufacturing, an unproductive service sector, the government, and the rest of the world. His general glut is a general glut of goods, which always threatens. He derives this threat from the proposition that the capitalist sector can never consume all the goods that it produces. So its profits, and hence its continued activity, depend on there being a 'considerable class of persons who have both the will and the power to consume more material wealth than they produce' (Malthus, *Works*: vi. 319). Because of shocks to consumption that occur in the non-capitalist sectors, particularly the government sector, capitalist saving and investment plans can prove to be over-ambitious, and expectations of sales and profits then have to be revised downwards.

Malthus's imprecision about time is even more important than these divergences from Keynes's framework of analysis. Keynes was evidently dealing with the short period, which means between nine and eighteen months. Malthus seems to be refer-ring to a longer period than this. It is an important feature of *The General Theory* that investment expenditure adds to aggregate demand, but that the goods and services that the investment generates do not add to aggregate supply during the period of analysis, that is, during the short period. In the next period, when the results of the investment do add to aggregate supply, national income has increased via the multiplier effect of the investment spending, creating the additional effective demand that validates the extra supply. This process can continue as long as the economy continues to have spare capacity and involuntary unemployment. In a recession, Keynes saw the problem as one of radical uncertainty that deterred private investors from invest-ing. He never argued that, if they had done so, their investment spending would not have revived the economy, or that their accumulation efforts would have been self-defeating. Rather, he claimed that when private investors are incorrigibly shy, additional government expenditure could revive the economy just as well.

Malthus makes a quite different claim. It is that when there is an excess supply of goods, additional investment expenditure cannot revive the economy. His position is stated clearly and at length:

> The remaining capitalists would be in no respect benefited by events which had diminished demand in still greater proportion than they had diminished the supply. Commodities would everywhere be cheap. Capital would be seeking employment, but would not easily find it; and the profits of stock would be low. There would be no pressing and immediate demand for capital, because there would be no pressing and immediate demand for commodities; and, under these circumstances, the saving from revenue to add to capital, instead of affording the remedy required, would only aggravate the distresses of the capitalists, and fill the stream of capital that was flowing out of the country. The distresses of the capitalists would be aggravated, just upon the same principle as the distresses of the labouring classes would be aggravated if they were encouraged to marry and increase, after a considerable destruction of people, although accompanied by a still greater destruction of capital which had kept the wages of labour very low. (ibid. 331)

Malthus was quite emphatic that the capitalist sector could not invest its way out of a general glut. Nor did he recommend increased government expenditure as a policy to escape from depression, although he did say that 'if the country had been subjected to the long continuance of excessive [government] expenditure, it must surely be against all analogy and all general principles, to look for the immediate remedy of it in a great and sudden contraction of consumption' (ibid. 347). For him, government expenditure was like a violent stimulant that produces subsequent exhaustion. One would never recommend its use, but, if used perforce, the best policy was to wean the economy off it slowly. This is clearly at a considerable distance from

Keynes's view that government spending should be used in a depression for pump-priming purposes.

As has been argued in Chapter 1, Malthus held the view that economic growth would be limited in the long run because of diminishing returns in agriculture. However, he also thought that growth could falter long before that limit was reached. Crises of disproportion could occur, generating adverse effects that lasted between eight and ten years. He writes of 'the main doctrine inculcated in the latter part' of his *Political Economy* as 'the progress of wealth depends upon proportions' (ibid. 344). If this was his intention, it suggests that he was a precursor, not so much of Keynes, as of medium-term development planning. Here one finds the same concern with the need for the proportional growth of sectors of the economy. Here one finds stated the need for the industrial sector to grow at a certain rate, relative to the agricultural and service sectors, in order to avoid either the deflation or the inflation of the price of goods, and inadequate or excessive consumption (see, for example, Lewis, 1966: 153–5, 167–71).

If Malthus had substantially anticipated Keynes's short-period model, it is improbable that Keynes would not have seen it. So what did he himself say? In the 1933 version of the essay, Malthus is given credit because 'time after time in these letters [he] is talking plain sense', even when he is 'met by a mind so completely closed that Ricardo does not even see what [he] is saying' (*CW*, x. 98). I take this to mean that while Malthus persistently pointed to economic realities, Ricardo failed to engage with them because his theory told him that they were impossible. However, Keynes then distinguishes between seeing the truth and comprehending completely why something is true, and says that Malthus was defective in the latter respect (*CW*, x. 102). This same distinction is carried forward more clearly into *The General Theory*. The quotation is well known:

For, since Malthus was unable to explain clearly (apart from an appeal to the facts of common observation) how and why effective demand could be deficient or excessive, he failed to furnish an alternative construction; and Ricardo conquered England as completely as the Holy Inquisition captured Spain. (*CW*, vii. 32)

Malthus was thus given a place in Keynes's 'brave army of heretics', along with Mandeville, Gesell, and Hobson. This group was described as people who, 'following their intuitions, have preferred to see the truth obscurely and imperfectly rather than to maintain error, reached indeed with clearness and consistency and by easy logic but on hypotheses inappropriate to the facts' (*CW*, vii. 377).

Keynes's evaluation of Malthus the economist was itself admirably clear and consistent. Malthus was right that there were general gluts, that saving too much was prejudicial to a country, and that sticky wages played a part in the process of adjustment. At the same time, he had no alternative intellectual construction that could link all these intuitions together in a logically satisfactory theory. If Keynes thought that Malthus was not an analytical precursor except in some partial and fragmentary ways, what was the nature of the inspiration that Keynes received from Malthus? It is manifest that the Malthus–Ricardo correspondence gave Keynes a whole new dimension to his appreciation of Malthus. He identified intensely with the intellectual impasse that the correspondence depicted, with Malthus's sense of being seized of the facts of common economic observation and yet opposed by minds that were impenetrable, because dominated by inappropriate abstractions. He felt increased sympathy and admiration for Malthus, because he projected on to him all the pent-up frustrations that he felt with his own similar position, and with the vexation generated by his long struggle to escape from the grip of logically elegant but unrealistic theories.

It had all happened before. Malthus was the *first* Cambridge economist to whom it had happened. He should have built an alternative construction, something that would have provided him and others with a complete comprehension of why the economic truth was, after all, true. He had failed, and his failure had set back economics for a hundred years. Keynes knew that he had to succeed, to stop truth being set back for another hundred years. He needed arguments, he was writing those arguments, and his essay on Malthus afforded some sweet relief from the writing of those arguments. But, for the most part, his arguments were different from Malthus's arguments.

NOTES

1. Beveridge was supported without reservation by Lionel Robbins on the methodological issue. In a footnote to his 1927 essay on 'The Optimum Theory of Population', he wrote: 'Considerations of space prevent here a discussion of Mr Keynes' attempt to devise a short-cut to the ascertainment of the position of such optima by the examination of changes in the purchasing power of units of manufactured products in terms of agricultural commodities. But it would be a pity to add one word to Sir William Beveridge's comment on this method' (Robbins, 1927: 131 n. 1).
2. For a summary statement of C. V. Drysdale's position, see Drysdale (1933).
3. A good recent account can be found in Soloway (1982).
4. King's College,
Cambridge
23.5.29

Dear Dr Stopes,

I am trying to make it a rule not to sign circular letters—except on matters with which I have a very close personal connection. So I must ask you kindly to excuse me.

Yours very truly,
[*signed*] J. M. Keynes
(BM Add. MS 58705, Fo. 101)

46 Gordon Square,
Bloomsbury
3rd April, 1930

Dear Dr Stopes,

It is rather difficult to know whom to suggest as a Chairman for your Cambridge meeting. I shall not be in Cambridge on that day myself. No doubt you are in touch with the local Birth Control organisation. Probably you would find someone amongst their Vice-Presidents or Committee who would help you.

Yours very truly,
[*signed*] J. M. Keynes

(BM Add. MS 58707, Fo. 73 (hand-written))

5. It is instructive to compare this quotation from Keynes with the opening sentences of Beveridge's 1923 Address criticizing Keynes's Malthusianism, viz. 'The impression that the civilised world is already threatened with over-population is very common today. Many, perhaps most, educated people are troubled by the fear that the limits of population . . . have been reached . . . I propose to begin by raising some doubts as to the validity of these arguments' (1923: 447).

6

England's Incredible Shrinking Population

I. KEYNES'S 1937 GALTON LECTURE

It was highly ironical, in the light of his total recantation of Malthusianism in 1928–30, that Keynes should have begun his last major intellectual encounter with the population problem by claiming that

perhaps, the most outstanding example of a case where we in fact have a considerable power of seeing into the future is the prospective trend of population.

Indeed, it was doubly ironical, because what his foresight told him was that

in the place of the steady and indeed steeply rising level of population which we have experienced for a great number of decades, we shall be faced in a very short time with a stationary or declining level.

Admittedly, the rate of decline was doubtful, but the extent of the changeover from rise to decline would be substantial (*CW*, xiv. 125).

Keynes cited no analysis of demographic statistics to back this claim. As early as 1895, Cannan had predicted the cessation of population growth in England and Wales some time before 1991, by assuming a continuation of changes in natality that had occurred since 1871:

During the last twenty years most of us have not succeeded in detecting any considerable change in the manners and customs and practices which affect natality, and yet it only requires a continuance of the change which has undoubtedly been going on to bring about a state of things which would cause the possibility of a decline of population, instead of the possibility of over-population, to be the bugbear of alarmists. (Cannan, 1895: 514)

And Dennis Robertson had spoken in the early 1920s of an imminent decline in population growth. From one point of view, perhaps, one could say that Keynes was belatedly acknowledging what others had been saying for a very long time.

In fact, it was more than that. By the 1930s, the use of birth control had become more widespread, leading to an acceleration in the fall of the crude birth rate. New population projections had been made that responded to the greater diffusion of birth control by advancing dramatically the date at which population growth would cease. In 1934 the Committee on Economic Information published G. C. Leybourne's projections, showing Great Britain's population starting to fall in 1946 and coming down to 33 million by 1976. This was a body with which Keynes was closely associated (Howson and Winch, 1977: 297–301). Dr Enid Charles produced even more dramatic figures of population decline. Her projections were made on three different assumptions. One was that fertility and mortality rates would remain as they were in 1933. The second assumption was that both mortality rates and fertility rates would in future decline along recent trends. The third assumption was that fertility would recover to the 1931 level. It was her second projection that was most generally seized on. This showed the population of England and Wales dropping from 40.5 million in the mid-1930s to a mere 17.5 million by the year 2000, by which time it would contain more people over than under the age of 60. This projection, published in 1935 as Special Memorandum No. 40 of the London and Cambridge Economic Service, would certainly have been accessible to Keynes, and was much discussed by contemporary demographers (e.g. Glass, 1936: 12–15; Kuczynski, 1936: 47–8; Titmuss, 1938).

It was this 'latest intelligence' on population that Keynes had in mind as the setting for his Galton Lecture in February 1937. To treat any of these projections as forecasts of the future size of the English population was, however, a fundamental error. Naturally, it is easier to see this with the benefit of hindsight. We know now that it took a further forty years for the UK to reach zero population growth. As a forecaster, Cannan turned out to be nearer to the truth than Leybourne or Charles. The latter two were over-impressed with the fact that in the early 1930s the net reproduction rate of the population had fallen below 1, and fertility had fallen below replacement levels. Projecting continuing declines from this base would necessarily indicate a rapid end to population growth, followed by absolute contraction (leaving aside the effects of net migration). Even without hindsight, it seems surprising that no one entertained the thought that the fertility situation of the early 1930s might be highly unusual. After all, the country was experiencing a most profound economic depression, and the prospects of another world war were never very far away. If fertility had fallen to historically low levels in these circumstances, might it not be expected to rise again at a later date when the circumstances had changed, rather than to continue a relentless decline? In the event, as we now know, fertility levels did recover strongly in the 1950s. The period fertility rates of the early 1930s were evidently distorted by decisions to postpone births, and thus did not properly reflect changes in the underlying cohort fertility rates (Teitelbaum and Winter, 1985: 10).

In using the least favourable of these projections as if it were a forecast, Keynes was acting no differently from his contemporaries. He showed no more insight, and no less. In their common defence, it has been argued that 'there was no way that anyone in the 1930s could have known that a recovery in fertility would occur in the 1950s' (ibid. 9). That is surely right. The future is never ours to know. However, if demographic statistics are relatively more knowable in advance compared with other social statistics, it is precisely because aggregate fertility, mortality, and migration do not alter dramatically, even over decades. To argue strongly for their predictability and then predict as a virtual certainty a 'substantial' changeover from growth to decline in 'a very short time' ought to have provoked in Keynes at least a little anxiety about self-contradiction. Even if one accepts as a plea in mitigation, as one should, the proposition that the extension of birth control was making future fertility behaviour less predictable, should not that very fact put one on one's guard against excessive faith in projections? Put the central question round the other way. How could anyone in the 1930s be so sure that a recovery in fertility would not occur in the 1950s?

Keynes's 1937 Galton Lecture took the second, and most dramatically downward-plunging, of the Charles population projections as a device to explore the relationship between population and other factors that determine economic growth, especially the demand for capital. The level of rigour with which Keynes handled the subject represents a distinct rise compared with that of his own previous work on this issue. *The General Theory* had been completed a year previously, and the intense discussions and writing down of arguments preceding and following its publication had strengthened his analytical sinews greatly. At the same time, that work had focused his mind on questions of equilibrium in the short term. This was a source of constant tension, seen repeatedly in his professional correspondence with Harrod, between Keynes's instinctive tendency to try to capture adequately the forces of short-term fluctuation and the need to achieve clarity about the conditions for steady-state growth. Harrod was much more single-mindedly taken up with the latter task.

Although he did not use the notation below, Keynes formulated the issue in terms of the following concepts:

K=the capital stock

n=rate of growth of population, taken as the rate of growth of the labour force

v=K/Y=the capital–output ratio (or 'the technique of capital')

$s^\star$=$(Y^\star-C^\star)/Y^\star$=the equilibrium saving rate (or the share of income not consumed, in equilibrium)

I=planned investment (or 'the demand for capital')

He then assumed that K was inherited from the past, that v was a reflection of 'the technique of capital' currently in use, and that n was given exogenously by demographic factors. The saving rate was determined by the distribution of wealth and the prevailing interest rate. Thus all of the basic concepts for exploring the conditions of steady-state growth were assembled.

On the basis of rough historical statistics for 1860–1913, Keynes estimated that about half of the real capital increase of this period had been absorbed merely to prevent the average capital endowment of the growing population from falling. Capital for that kind of capital-widening would obviously not be required for a population that was stationary. He deduced from this that saving at the current rate would be excessive, because autonomous adjustments in technique or consumption (C) would be small. The conclusion was that some policy intervention would be required either to depress the saving rate and/or to alter the capital–output ratio. If these interventions were not undertaken, and saving remained excessive, unemployment would result. It is in this analysis that one can hear an echo of Malthus on crises of disproportion.

Having now himself posed the problem of limits to steady-state growth, the question whether Keynes also solved it must be asked. Here we find another precursor claim, this time naming Keynes as the anticipator, not the anticipated. It has been argued that Keynes 'precisely anticipated' the dynamic theory of Harrod (Thirlwall, 1985: 20–1). However, it is more accurate to say that Keynes in 1937 posed the problem which Harrod's dynamic theory solved. Harrod submitted a draft of his article 'An Essay in Dynamic Theory' in August 1939 to Keynes, as editor of the *Economic Journal*. A strenuous tussle of minds ensued over the contents of successive drafts (*CW*, xiv. 321–50). Keynes found it very difficult to understand Harrod's dynamic equations, although he responded warmly to the new concept of the 'warranted' rate of growth. After a correspondence that occupies thirty pages of the *Collected Writings*, Keynes summed up his attitude to the final version in a letter to Pigou:

I do not think there has ever been an article about which I have corresponded with the author at such enormous length in the effort to make him clear up doubtful and obscure points and reduce its length. I produced a little effect, but perhaps not very much in proportion to the effort. In the final result, I do not find myself in agreement, but I do think that he has got hold of a very interesting point which, subject to the necessary qualifications, is of real importance. (*CW*, xiv. 320)

This is not the comment of a man who had himself precisely anticipated Harrod's dynamic theory.

Keynes had ended up by paying final homage to Malthus. By 1937, homage was due both to Malthus the population expert and to Malthus the political economist who had deplored the prejudicial effects of 'saving too much'. In these two roles, Malthus had provided two devils, not one—the threat of overpopulation and the threat of unemployment. Now that the former was chained up, the latter was on the loose. Malthus, like Cardinal Morton, seemed to have invented a fork such that the more society escaped from one prong, the more it impaled itself on the other. So it was that Keynes, after renouncing neo-Malthusianism, managed to maintain his affinity with Malthus. The odyssey of Keynes's beliefs about population and the instability of capitalism was mirrored in the vicissitudes of his twenty-year effort to write his essay on Malthus. In the 1937 Galton Lecture, he could offer a neat summary of his final position.

II. KEYNES'S CAMPAIGN FOR
FAMILY ALLOWANCES

Those who still believe in the essential constancy of Keynes's vision might be inclined to point to the fact that he proclaimed his allegiance to eugenics right up to his premature death. At the 1946 Galton Lecture, he described Galton as 'the founder of the most important, significant and, I would add *genuine* branch of sociology that exists, namely eugenics' (quoted in Freeden, 1979: 671; emphasis Keynes's).

Eugenics, however, as has been seen in Chapter 4, encompassed many policy positions. Keynes had moved almost unnoticed from the neo-Malthusian position to the promotion-of-motherhood position. No doubt, Keynes's reputation as a neo-Malthusian was still remembered in the early 1940s. His former pupil Hugh Dalton noted in his wartime diary for 27 August 1942 that 'Keynes (Jeremiah Malthus, as we used to call him)—now a Baron on the Board of the Bank—comes to talk to me' (Dalton, 1986/1940–5: 484). By this time, the old nickname had already become a relic of the past. In the circumstances of the Second World War, Keynes finally became an ardent advocate of the Family Endowment Society scheme of family allowances. That, too, had a eugenic justification, both positive and negative. On the one hand, it would produce births among child-loving couples who, without the allowance, could not afford the expense of parenthood. On the other hand, improved financial circumstances would encourage the use of contraception among those who wanted to limit their families to small numbers of children. As ever, the invocation of eugenics was no guarantee of doctrinal constancy.

It is, perhaps, hardly surprising that general expectations (however ill founded) of a sudden dramatic decrease in the size of the British population, coinciding with the outbreak of another world war, should have provoked a mighty resurgence of pro-natalist sentiment. Given the enlarged role of the government in wartime planning and resource allocation, it is no more surprising that the pro-natalists should have looked to the government to produce the measures that would bring about the higher levels of fertility that they desired. What is of greater significance for this account of Keynes and population is that Keynes finally allowed himself to be won over by the strand of pro-natalism that celebrated motherhood.

It was in the context of devising effective methods of war finance that Keynes found himself lending the pro-natalists a helping hand. In the autumn of 1939, he formulated his initial proposals for a scheme of wartime compulsory saving. He realized from the start that a major campaign of public and private persuasion would be needed if his scheme were to be accepted. His proposals were first published in *The Times* in mid-November, attracting great interest and comment. He corresponded in December with a number of those who commented on his *Times* articles. These included Eva Hubback and his critic of 1924, Eleanor Rathbone. Thereafter, he revised his original scheme in a number of ways to increase its political appeal. One of these revisions was to include in his package of proposals the payment of family allowances at a rate of five shillings per week for each child. This was criticized as excessively generous by John Hicks, but Keynes stuck to his guns (*CW*, xxii. 91–108).

Keynes's motives for including family allowances among his proposals for *How to Pay for the War* are not wholly clear. They seem to reflect an initial calculation that it would strengthen the political support for his war finance proposals if he could swing the women's movement of the day behind them. However, Keynes knew that he needed most of all to succeed in wooing the Labour Movement. He initially believed that the incorporation of family allowances would be very attractive to Labour, as it would improve the financial impact of his scheme on working-class families. To his disappointment, he discovered that trades unions, including Bevin's Transport and General Workers'

Union, were traditionally suspicious of family allowances, on the grounds that employers would take them as an excuse for lowering wages. In fact, he failed to gain the support of the Labour leaders, especially that of Attlee and Bevin. However, trade union opposition to family allowances was not the main reason for Labour's rejection of the plan. The great obstacle was simply the element of compulsion in compulsory saving. Attlee and Bevin were entirely unmoved when told by Keynes that the alternative to agreeing to compulsory savings was the attrition of real wages by an uncontrollable inflation. To put it charitably, perhaps they thought that this was too sophisticated an argument for their memberships. *How to Pay for the War* was able to be implemented only after the Chamberlain government fell, Churchill's National Government was formed, and Keynes was brought back inside the Treasury, where he had direct access to the new Chancellor of the Exchequer (Toye, 1999).

Keynes's own justification for the incorporation of family allowances in his war finance proposals was hardly very clear or convincing:

For some years past the weight of opinion has been growing in favour of family allowances. In time of war it is natural that we should be more concerned than usual with the standard of living; and as soon as there is a threat of a rising cost of living and a demand for higher wages to meet it, the question of family allowances must come to the front. For the burden of the rising cost of living depends very largely on the size of a man's family. At first sight it is paradoxical to propose in time of war an expensive social reform which we have not thought ourselves able to afford in time of peace. But in truth the need for this reform is so much greater in such times that it may provide the most appropriate occasion for it. (*CW*, ix. 394–5)

Harrod's explanation is that Keynes became convinced by his own rhetoric that compulsory saving would provide an opportunity for social amelioration.

There may have been an element of his coming to believe his

own radical propaganda. However, in addition to this, Keynes consistently adopted a high degree of flexibility in accommodating the suggestions of critics. In notes that he made for a speech which he gave to the Fabian Society on 2 February 1940, he made a virtue of this flexibility:

I am a highly teachable person. I learn from criticism and before now have laid myself open to the reproof that my second thoughts are often better than my first thoughts—which is an indication, some people think, of a dangerous instability of character.

Well it has happened again. I have played a low trick on my critics. I have improved my plan and have thus slipt out of their net. (HP/2/88–99)

Thus self-induced enthusiasm for social reform was certainly accompanied by a characteristically robust defence of the volatility of his opinions.

Keynes did not give explicit consideration to the population implications of the introduction of family allowances. He can hardly have been unaware that he was advocating the adoption at a national level of the nearest thing to the Speenhamland system that Britain had had since Malthus had denounced it a century and a half previously. Presumably, he would have justified such a move by reference to the oversimple forecasts of a dramatic population decline that Enid Charles and others had popularized. Those who, like Mrs Hubback, were also alarmed by the prospect of population decline, must have been mightily pleased at having helped to recruit such a powerful new supporter of motherhood.

III. THE 1940s: BRITISH PRO-NATALISM RESURGENT

One difficulty that the pro-natalists of the 1940s had to negotiate was that the campaign for the legalization of birth control had been won on the grounds of improved marital harmony, improved maternal and child health, and the freedom of parents to choose the number of their children. It had not been won on the ground of the excessive size of the population, the banner of the neo-Malthusians and Keynes in his pre-1930 mode. Thus the 1940s case for boosting the population size had to avoid encroaching too much on the valued contributions of birth control to the happiness of family life.

This problem set the tone of many of the contributions to the pro-natalist literature of the 1940s. The strategy of Titmuss and Titmuss (1942), for example, was to argue that the 1930s decline in fertility represented a silent strike by parents against the dehumanizing character of the acquisitive society that was capitalism. On this analysis, birth control had been adopted because it could be an instrument of social protest. The message, then, was that it would be impossible to stabilize the size of the population until the British people had democratically chosen a new type of economic system that would allow their natural instincts for procreation to be properly fulfilled. There was an element of truth in this argument. At least it recognized that the low fertility of the early 1930s was a distress phenomenon, and that there was a possibility of reversal if circumstances changed. Less plausible was the idea of low fertility as active protest aimed at a change in the entire economic system. If that had indeed been the case, the reversal that did come later would not have taken place.

Beveridge had been convinced of the merit of family allowances since the middle of the 1920s, as soon as he had read Eleanor Rathbone's *The Disinherited Family*. He did not look at the issue primarily as one of the welfare of the poor. The allowance was to be universal. He believed that it would bring eugenic advantages, raising the quality of the population in various ways. He maintained this position when he gave the Galton Lecture in 1943. Harrod was more concerned with the quantity of the population. On the one hand, he took it for granted that the danger of depopulation was a serious one. On the other, he did not believe with the Titmusses that the entire economic system would have to be changed before the danger could be averted. His 1944 proposal put to the Royal Commission on Population for an insurance-financed child endowment scheme was designed to be 'not inconsistent with the main features of our economic structure' (Harrod, 1952: 3). At the same time, he tried to make child endowment generous enough to encourage a move to an average of four or five children per family. Harrod argued that changes in the general standard of living did not affect reproductive behaviour, but that a redistribution of income in favour of parents, and progressively in favour of those with more children, would be effective in promoting reproduction by economic incentives. He also argued that such transfers would be seen as putting right a major source of social injustice. His specific proposal was for an allowance of eight shillings per week for every child after the first, the same amount as in the Beveridge Plan. He would have preferred a higher endowment of ten shillings a week, but thought that the public finances would not stand it. In fact, the Family Allowances Act of 1945 provided for even less generous child allowances of five shillings per week for every dependent child after the first.

In her own tract on the population problem published in 1947, Eva Hubback used later and less dramatically declining population projections than those of Enid Charles. Nevertheless, all of them showed a population in 1999 of somewhere between 28 and 36 million. Her aim was less ambitious than Harrod's: she was looking for the average number of children per family to rise from two to three. Her recommended policies were different again from those of both the Titmusses and Harrod. Accepting the existing economic system, she recommended not merely improved financial incentives for parents, but also widespread public education about child-rearing and improvements in the status of women (Hubback, 1947: 277–84). This is because she thought that women's psychology and the state of public opinion, as well as laws and economic incentives, influenced the falling birth rate.

Apart from the need to negotiate the obstacle that the small-family pattern had been freely chosen by fertile couples, the pro-natalists had to address another question that was implicit in the contemporary definition of the population problem. Beveridge, in his unpublished memoir on Keynes written between 1946 and 1949, provides a convenient statement of it:

We all realise now that even as the magnificent episode of the Nine-teenth Century in Britain neared its end with its apparently unlimited expansion the turn had been taken to something quite different. A threatened contraction of population is a new problem on which a Royal Commission is now engaged. The population problem today is different from what it seemed only twenty years ago; it is an entirely different problem in different parts of the world. Of excessive growth in India, of insufficient growing or declining elsewhere. (BEV ix (a), 52)

The task of the pro-natalists then was to explain why, in a world in which global population was rapidly growing, it was vital to reverse the depopulation of Britain by increasing fertility in Britain, rather than by encouraging migration from over-populated to depopulating countries. As we have seen, Mill and Marshall had been happy enough to encourage outmigration from Britain as a solution to her overpopulation. Applying the same logic in reverse, why not encourage inmigration as a solu-tion to her fertility decline?

Beatrice Webb, in her preface to the Titmusses' book, announced her answer boldly enough. The fall of the British birth rate was 'threatening the survival of the white race' (Titmuss and Titmuss, 1942: 10). Inmigration of assorted for-eigners could be no solution to *that* problem. Harrod did not put it like that. He suggested that narrow nationalist prejudice was not to be altogether despised, but that it would be better to develop an 'argument to meet even those who refuse to be impressed with the importance of the mere maintenance of

British stock and independence' (Harrod, 1952: 8). The argument was that Britain was an upholder of a free democratic system and that her loss of population would threaten the continuance of free democracies if undemocratic societies were able to achieve population growth.

Hubback took a similar, explicitly non-racial, line. She proposed that 'the British nation with its mixture of races and the influence it exerts on world affairs is abundantly worth conserving'. This was because 'these democratic ideals of freedom, of kindness, of justice, of reason and of the rule of law are needed more than ever in a world in which many countries have not yet discovered how to combine freedom with order' (Hubback, 1947: 114–16). She then deployed this argument from the superiority of British political culture against a policy of encouraging immigration, the obvious solution to a decline in population. If immigration from Eastern Europe and Asia were allowed,

we should then inevitably find ourselves involved in many difficult problems involved in efforts to assimilate a large number of people with different attitudes to life from our own; and we should end up as a people with a very different ethnic make-up and national characteristics from those we have today. It is questionable whether this would constitute an improvement. (ibid. 117)

The Royal Commission on Population finally reported in 1949. Its report took some of the wind out of the sails of the pro-natalists. It pointed out that a net reproduction rate of less than 1, the statistic that had set off the depopulationist alarm bells in the 1930s, did not bear the weight of interpretation that had been put on it. The net reproduction rate takes no account of the extent to which marriages which do eventually take place, and the births of children who do eventually get born, are either accelerated or postponed by external circumstances. In the 1930s, the circumstances of depression followed by the prospect of the outbreak of war evidently favoured postponement. When the statistics of the average size of completed families were examined, it turned out that it was only 6 per cent short of the figure of 2.34 required to keep the population at replacement level. Since the fertility of the 1940s was somewhat higher than that of the 1930s, the need for pro-natalist campaigns turned out to have been the result of a statistical mirage. Given that the British population was stationary, and not declining, there was no great political difficulty in establishing very tight immigration controls, particularly on immigration from Asia. These satisfied the democratic anxieties expressed by Harrod and Hubback, as well as the more materialistic concerns expressed by economists like Dennis Robertson, who believed that immigrants would make heavy demands on imported food and social services (1963: 302).

IV. CAMBRIDGE ON TERMS OF TRADE IMPROVEMENT AS POPULATION DECLINES

The threat of an imminent decline in the British population did more than convert Keynes to a belief in the desirability of family allowances, and revive British pro-natalist sentiment. It also led Cambridge economists to a small gleam of optimism in connection with the very difficult British foreign trading position. The nineteenth-century anxiety, revived by Keynes, that population increase would inevitably increase the country's reliance on manufacturing industry and on the export of manufactures, resulting in declining terms of trade, had its obverse. If population size was in fact shrinking, reliance on manufacturing production and export would be decreasing, and *ceteris paribus* the country's terms of trade would improve. This other, brighter face of the Cambridge doctrine was much appealed to during the war and the immediate post-war years of the 1940s. Between them, Brian Reddaway, Joan Robinson, and James Meade give a fair reflection of Cambridge opinion on the relation between movements in the terms of trade and population decline.[1]

(a) Brian Reddaway

Keynes's pupil Brian Reddaway shared his former supervisor's misplaced confidence in the population projections of Enid Charles. His response to the prediction of a rapidly declining population in Britain was to set out his own view of the economic consequences (Reddaway, 1939). It was his own view, and not a repetition of Keynes's. He nowhere refers to Keynes's 1937 Galton Lecture, and he seems not to have read it before producing his own work. His important departure from Keynes's approach, which treated the problem of population decline in terms of a closed economy, was to explore the implications of population decline for Britain's international trade. It is here that we find his position on the manufacturing and agricultural terms of trade.

Reddaway pointed out that if the British population did fail to increase, Britain's demand for imports would be smaller absolutely than it would otherwise have become, and that the country's total gain from the existence of foreign trade would also be smaller than it would otherwise be. But, at the same time, this cessation of population growth

does not mean that we shall be in a worse position to conduct our trade on a basis advantageous to ourselves; far from it. Our position will be stronger on account of our smaller numbers . . . the very fact that our need for imports would be smaller improves our chances of getting them on advantageous terms. To put it crudely, the more mouths we have to feed, the more outlets for our exports we must find and the stronger the presumption that we shall have to lower the prices we charge. (ibid. 218)

Having shown that a standstill in population would prevent the deterioration in the manufacturing terms of trade that a population increase would have caused, Reddaway puts this point ('perhaps the most important in our whole study of international trade') into its broader context, as follows:

The reason why this conclusion is of such great importance is that we might otherwise encounter very real difficulties in finding outlets for an adequate quantity of exports on terms even approximately as favourable as those we now enjoy. The population factor is not likely to put us in a better position than we are now; it will rather be required as an offset to the forces which are tending to make that position worse. Even with its aid we must, I think, expect some deterioration. (ibid. 219)

The major economic force that Reddaway identifies as a cause of the deteriorating terms of trade of Englishmen considered as 'belonging to one specialised group who produce certain manu-factured goods' (ibid. 219) was the growing efficiency of low-wage economies in producing many of the manufactured goods which Britain exported. It was the vulnerability of manufactur-ing to foreign competition as other countries develop that was the lynchpin of Reddaway's argument, just as it had been for Malthus. For the sake of the logical completeness of his argu-ment, Reddaway had to deny that Britain could keep one step ahead in export-product innovation. He should also have denied that the low-wage economies which were improving efficiency in their manufacturing sector were experiencing any technical progress in their production of food. These are the necessary assumptions of the doctrine of the declining terms of trade of manufactures.

(b) *Joan Robinson*

Joan Robinson also wrote an essay on the consequences of a decline in the population of Great Britain, which she said 'was written during the war', when 'a decline in the population of Great Britain was expected in the near future'. She had read Keynes's 1937 Galton Lecture, but was less alarmed than he was about the possibility that a population decline would reduce the demand for investment, and thence employment. Wartime damage and the build-up of large arrears in investment meant that there would be no immediate threat to full employment in the post-war period, while the clearing of the investment backlog would eventually require a 'far-sighted employment policy'. Her conclusions were that a population decline would raise the standard of living and would not be likely to result in any sub-optimality of economic production.

Like Reddaway, Robinson also considered the probable long-run impact of a declining population on Britain's international trade. She agreed with him that the basic impact would be favourable:

Now that Britain's industry shares world markets with powerful rivals, while a special and acute problem is presented by the abrupt fall in net invisible exports due to the war, her large population is a source of weakness to this country. Any decline in numbers which may now set in will relieve the situation, but is unlikely to be large enough to make a substantial contribution to solving it. (Robinson, 1978/1951: 131)

When she turns to the question of the probable future global long-run trend in the terms of trade of manufactures against agricultural goods, she is not absolutely firmly wedded to the Cambridge doctrine that population growth will deteriorate the terms of trade of manufactures. She certainly sees as possible a strongly unfavourable trend. At the same time, she acknowledges that technical progress in agriculture could be a countervailing force:

From a long-run point of view the outlook is extremely speculative. In the '30s rapid technical progress in agriculture, combined with a world-wide collapse of effective demand, created a glut of foodstuffs. Even a moderate improvement of the average of world prosperity, combined with the immense population growth which is going on outside the western world, would create a huge demand for food, and it would be optimistic to rely upon technical progress keeping pace with it. We must therefore reckon with a strong unfavourable trend in the terms of trade between manufactures and foodstuffs. On the other hand, it may happen that the gloomy forecasts will be belied by the spread of improvements in agricultural technique and the release of acreage for foodstuffs by the development of synthetic substitutes for agricultural raw materials. (ibid. 132)

The gloomy forecasts of which Joan Robinson wrote were to become gloomier in the immediate post-war years. The war years had intensified the resolve of many countries that had concentrated on producing agricultural exports to industrialize their economies in order to substitute home production for imports of manufactures. The depression of the 1930s had created exceptionally unfavourable terms of trade for exporters who relied on agricultural products and raw materials. They saw their future economic security in terms of industrialization, while the experience of the war had raised their confidence that an industrialization drive, particularly if organized by the government, could succeed. In addition, Folke Hilgerdt of the League of Nations had shown a statistical correlation between a high percentage of the labour force engaged in agriculture and low average incomes, and between a high share of labour in agriculture and low yields per acre (Hilgerdt, 1945: 38). The conclusion was usually drawn from such statistics that investment in industry would be more remunerative than investment in agriculture. Moreover, if population growth were accelerating in low-income areas, as was often the case, 'a quick forward advance' in industrialization seemed to be the most promising approach towards higher real incomes (Buchanan, 1946: 548).

(c) James Meade

This enthusiasm for the industrialization of 'backward areas', as they were called at the time, set off alarm bells among those economists concerned about the fragility of Britain's balance of payments. In 1938, Britain was still one of the three countries (along with the US and Germany) that accounted for half of the world's output of manufactures. This seemed to imply that she must be one of the major losers from a rapid diversification of the sources of that output. When Kurt Mandelbaum (later Martin) and others at the Oxford Institute of Statistics developed a model of how backward areas might industrialize, the immediate reaction was to recognize the existence of an acute dilemma for British policy. It was expressed in a review of Mandelbaum's work in the *Economic Journal*:

The proposition is widely accepted that there is no moral or economic justification for permanently retarding the industrial progress of the many millions of people now inhabiting the backward areas of the world; but neither is it compatible with human progress to develop industries in all these countries in such a way that the remnants of the nineteenth century division of labour are destroyed without an attempt to re-establish an improved system of an international division of labour. (Rahmer, 1946: 662)

One of the assumptions that underlay this anxiety is the belief that not only would generalized industrialization reduce the export volumes of the traditional exporters of manufactures, but also the purchasing power of a unit of manufactures in terms of primary products would decline.

James Meade clearly thought so when he discussed whether the then-new IMF and IBRD, together with the proposed ITO, between them constituted an improved system of an international division of labour, compared with a system of discriminatory state trading. Meade argued fervently for the former, as the only one suited to countries in Britain's trading position. In making this argument, however, he revealed how weak he thought that position was:

We import essential raw materials which we cannot to any great extent replace with home production but without which we could not maintain our industrial production and employment. We import foodstuffs which we should find it most difficult to replace with home production, but without which we should starve. We export manufactured goods, *many of which are not essential to the importing countries, being of a luxury or semi-luxury character* and many of which can, without too much difficulty or economic loss, be produced in other countries. In fact, we maintain a large population at a high standard of living . . . by relying on the international division of labour . . . Anyone familiar with the present compelling desires of underdeveloped primary producing countries to industrialize will realize the special dangers which now confront the balance of payments of a country in our position. (Meade, 1948: 110–11; emphasis added)

Malthus's worst nightmare of 1803 had become the reality of the late 1940s. Among the retrograde movements or, in Meade's words, 'special dangers' which Britain should consequently expect, declining terms of trade would have been one.

Even so, Meade did not set his face wholly against the primary producing countries' compelling desires. He pointed out that economically sound development projects could raise their incomes and create demand for higher-quality manufactured imports. Since he thought that part of the motivation of industrialization drives was not economic, but created by fashion and politics, he argued for joint consideration by developed and developing countries of the criteria of truly economic development projects. He believed that it was 'in fact, an improvement in agricultural techniques and equipment which is the first essential from their own point of view'. He also opposed international commodity agreements that artificially raised the price of primary products and thereby Britain's import costs (ibid. 111–13).

V. HANS SINGER AND THE END OF THE CAMBRIDGE DOCTRINE

In 1949, the UN published *Relative Prices of Exports and Imports of Under-developed Countries*, which was written by Hans Singer while he was at the Department of Economic and Social Affairs. The study was done under the general direction of Folke Hilgerdt, then the Director of the Statistical Office. *Relative Prices* was remarkable for at least two reasons. First, it was a sustained attempt to see what *historical* statistics indicated about the long-term trend in the agriculture versus manufactures terms of trade, although its origin lay in developing countries' concern with future price relativities as industrialization drives gathered pace. Second, it announced an empirical finding flatly contrary to the one that had pervaded much economic opinion since Malthus, and the one that Keynes, in particular, had striven so hard to establish empirically. A. J. Brown, who reviewed the study for the *Economic Journal*, perceptively described its findings as 'exceedingly interesting and not a little surprising'.

The most dramatic finding was this:

The general trend [in the prices of primary commodities in relation to those of finished products] from the 1870's to the last pre-war year, 1938, notwithstanding marked fluctuations, was unmistakably downwards. In other words, average prices of primary commodities relative to manufactured goods have been declining over a period of more than half a century. (United Nations, 1949: 23)

The statistical evidence for this downward trend was given in table 5 (ibid. 22), from which the figures in Table 3 below are extracted. To avoid confusion, note that these ratios are ratios of an import price index to an export price index, so that a declining ratio is beneficial to the UK, while a rising ratio is unfavourable.

The marked fluctuations in this downward trend have their own interest for our story. For the UK, the index of its import values relative to its export values fell by 36 per cent between 1876 and 1913, and by 1921 was somewhat below its 1938 level. From 1921 to 1938, the fluctuations were much smaller. So Marshall was right to see the effect of diminishing returns in agriculture being dominated by productivity improvements in cultivation and transport of primary produce. And Keynes, on the other hand, was quite wrong to imagine any turning point in the 1890s or 1900s in the downward trend. Something very dramatic hap-

Table 3. Ratios of UK Imports to Exports, 1876–1948 (1938 = 100)

Period (or year)	Current year weights	Board of Trade index
1876–80	163	
1881–5	167	
1886–90	157	
1891–5	147	
1896–1900	142	
1901–5	138	
1906–10	140	
1913	137	143
1921	93	101
1933	98	96
1938	100	100
1946		108
1948		117

pened during and just after the First World War, which perhaps has to be construed as a structural break in the series.

The upward turning point in the UN series occurs in 1933. Perhaps this is not entirely surprising, given the bold economic recovery programmes of the New Deal in the US and the impetus of rearmament and stockpiling in Europe. After the war, rehabilitation and reconstruction while normal supply routes were still disrupted would have worked in the same direction. Thus, it would be wrong to regard Reddaway, Robinson, and Meade merely as prisoners of an ancient Cambridge doctrine. In fact, the doctrine became empirically relevant to Britain in their day in a way that it never had been in the era of Marshall or the young Keynes. Ironically, the Cambridge doctrine was eventually challenged at the very moment that, under the pressures of war and the drive of the underdeveloped countries for industrialization, it had become relevant to Britain's economic situation for the first time since the Napoleonic Wars. As Hans Singer reported in a passage written in 1960:

The terms of trade of underdeveloped countries ... presented a rather mixed picture during the postwar period. The more pessimistic assumptions of a steady long-term deterioration in the terms of trade were not borne out; the terms of trade of underdeveloped countries throughout the postwar period have been more favourable than during the 1930s ... [but] commodity prices did show a weakening tendency from their Korean boom level throughout the 1950s. Thus it was possible for both sides to claim some confirmation for their views ... (Singer, 1975: 15–16)

This may have been one reason why the critique of the Cambridge doctrine remained controversial for so long, and has taken nearly fifty years to be assimilated by mainstream economists (Sapsford and Singer, 1998).

It was clear that the old framework of thought, inherited from Malthus, was no longer adequate. The long-familiar story of diminishing returns in agriculture and increasing returns in industry could not accommodate comfortably the new observations. In fact, F. D. Graham had already challenged the underlying logic of that story in 1923 (Raffer, 1994: 75–87). Graham had written that

It may well be disadvantageous for a nation to concentrate in production of commodities of increasing cost despite a comparative advantage in those lines; it will the more probably be disadvantageous to do so if the world demand for goods produced at decreasing costs is growing in volume more rapidly than that for goods produced at increasing costs, while at the same time competition in the supply of the former grows relatively less intense as compared with competition in the supply of the latter. For in this case the operation of the law of reciprocal demand will throw the terms of exchange of commodities more and more to the disadvantage of the country producing the goods of increasing costs. (Graham, 1923: 213–14)

The Cambridge doctrine rested too easily on the assumption that the demand for manufactures would weaken with every extension of the marketing of manufactured exports. Meade referred to such exports as being 'not essential to the importing country'

and of 'a semi-luxury or luxury character', implying that therefore the demand for them would be weak. However, the demand
for manufactured luxuries, particularly if they are consumption
novelties to the importing country, can be strong. The Cambridge doctrine also failed to notice sufficiently that manufacturing's falling unit costs could act as a deterrent to competition,
while agriculture's rising unit costs could conversely act as an
incentive to competition. The gap between average industrial and
average agricultural prices could thereby widen, turning the
terms of trade in industry's favour. Thus there cannot be any presumption that declining productivity of land will be compen-
sated automatically by improvements in the agricultural terms of
trade.

Independently of Graham, Hans Singer summarily dismissed
the argument that the terms of trade are governed merely by
relative changes in productivity, since productivity had evidently
increased faster in industrial production. He proposed an asym-
metry in the modes of distribution of the gains of technical
progress, in which for industrial products they accrued as
increases in producers' incomes, and for agricultural products
accrued as price reductions to consumers. The theory of the
asymmetric distribution of the fruits of technical progress was a
rationalization of the statistical trend which he had discovered
(Singer, 1975 / 1950: 48–52). Simultaneously and independently,
Raúl Prebisch (1950), then at UN ECLA, put forward a new set of
institutionally based distinctions between primary products and
manufactures, quite similar to those of Graham, as a series of
possible explanations.

Both Singer and Prebisch had to face the same line of critical
attack as Beveridge had unleashed on Keynes with such devastating success, that the empirical result they rationalized was
a mere statistical artefact. Unlike Keynes, they have been supported, particularly in the 1980s and 1990s, by the findings of
numerous highly skilled statisticians. These statisticians have
established that a small but cumulative fall (perhaps somewhere

between 0.5 and 1.0 per cent per annum) has been occurring for most of the twentieth century in the terms of trade of primary products (Sapsford and Singer, 1998: 1654). Singer and Prebisch between them have thus left the underlying theory on a broader base. The notion that positive impacts on the terms of trade of manufactures can and do occur because of systematically differ-ent institutional features of product and factor markets, such as cost-plus pricing and the unionization of labour in industry, is now widely entertained. The positive influence of technical progress, not only from the asymmetric distribution of its fruits, but also from its asymmetric impact on future demand, being favourable to that of industry while unfavourable to that of agri-culture, is now in wide currency.

Moreover, Hans Singer gave his own ingenious solution to the problem, which had exercised all the adherents of the Cambridge doctrine, including Keynes, of whether food imports from America to Europe and migration from Europe to America acted as safety-valves for excessive population growth in Europe. His solution was that

the supplies of food and raw materials pouring into Europe as a result of the investment-*cum*-trade system and the favourable terms of trade engendered by this system enabled Europe to feed, clothe, educate, train and equip large numbers of emigrants sent overseas . . . Thus the benefits to the investing countries of Europe arising out of the system described above were in turn passed on . . . and were the main founda-tion of the enormous capital formation the result of which is now to be observed in North America. (Singer, 1975/1950: 55)

This solution allowed him to maintain his sceptical argument that benefits of foreign investment accrue mainly to the foreign investor rather than to the country where the investment is made. Only when migration from the investing country is also taking place are all of the benefits captured by the receiving country. Moreover, the investment-cum-trade system was *not* self-defeating, because the enormous capital formation in

America would *not* erode the favourable terms of trade. Thus was a hundred and fifty years of Cambridge doctrine on the terms of trade overthrown by Singer and Prebisch, notwithstanding Keynes's own best efforts to keep it alive.

I shall not attempt to follow matters further, because to do so would be to engage with much of the corpus of modern development studies, and the politically inspired intellectual fashions to which it is subject. An appropriate concluding point might be the mid-1970s, when Singer I was replaced by Singer II. Revisiting his 1950 analysis, Singer himself became convinced not just that the Cambridge doctrine was incomplete and its empirical prediction was therefore wrong, but that the whole focus on the terms of trade was misleading. It was not the distinct characteristics of particular categories of commodity (manufactures versus raw materials) that were important in understanding why some countries developed while others did not. The essence of that understanding was seen to lie in the distinct characteristics of different types of country, so that the terms of trade of country B's exports of commodities of type X can continuously deteriorate against country A's exports of goods of type X. The concentration of technology generation within already developed countries and the role of multinational companies in organizing the global division of labour were the keys to solving the puzzle of persistent economic backwardness. In this way, Singer II moved the debate forward towards our contemporary concern with the welfare impact of the process of globalization.

Specialization and the division of intellectual labour within development studies have ensured that there has been no successor to the old Cambridge doctrine. Those who were still concerned about the Law of Diminishing Returns sought out new reasons why economic growth will prove to be unsustainable. New limits to growth have been proposed under the rubric of conservation of the environment. Here is a modern echo of Marshall's insight that the truly fixed factors are not the attributes of land, as they had been traditionally understood, but clean air and clean water, and that in the end it will be their availability that will determine the optimum size of population.

Today we are habituated to intellectual fragmentation. So it is difficult for us to remember that there ever was a single basic framework for analysing development, and that it was one that integrated, albeit in a simple analysis, agriculture, industry, international trade, migration, growth and technical progress, and distribution and poverty. It is within such an archaic framework that Keynes's writings on economic development have to be construed.

VI. SUMMING UP: 'THE LEAST FELICITOUS OF ALL HIS EFFORTS'?

Even when Keynes's contributions to the population debate have been noticed at all, which is rarely, there has been hesitation in evaluating them. For example, Skidelsky characterizes the 1937 Galton Lecture as follows: 'According to taste, this authoritatively gloomy conclusion, based on a series of audacious guesses, may be considered Keynes at his best or his worst' (1992: 632). Which is it to be? What should now be concluded, not only about the 1937 Galton Lecture, but about the whole range of Keynes's efforts to understand the relationships between population growth, capital accumulation, technical change, and the terms of trade, as we have laid them out here?

Keynes changed his position not once, but twice in the course of the evolution of his ideas. In 1919, the population devil was on the loose, and the terms of trade for manufactures were deteriorating, or about to deteriorate. By 1930, such pessimism was wildly mistaken, because there was a solution to the economic problem. By 1937, the population devil had been exorcised so thoroughly that it was the exorcism that was likely to cause a problem of excess intended saving. It was left to Keynes's junior Cambridge colleagues to point out the brighter side of the situation, the likely improvement in manufacturing's terms of trade.

During all of this period, it may be noted that the actual rate of population growth in England and Wales was much less unstable than Keynes's opinions about both it and its consequences. Changing one's mind is not itself a ground for criticism, as Keynes himself famously pointed out: 'When I see that I am wrong, I change my mind: what do you do?' That Keynes eventually recanted his youthful neo-Malthusianism, in the wake of the bruising debate with Beveridge, could be seen as a late response to superior logic and facts. The ground for criticism must be the unreasonable persistence in his neo-Malthusianism, and the failure to acknowledge publicly and to explain honestly the reasons for his change of mind.

The secondary nature of Keynes's interest in population questions might excuse the rather sketchy basis in research of some of his grander pronouncements on the topic. His failure to look carefully at the relevant demographic data, and to think carefully about the assumptions on which others made their demographic projections, might also be excused by the fact that demography was not his area of specialization. As we have seen, the 1920s and 1930s were, in terms of population growth, somewhat more volatile than the period 1870–1914, during which Keynes had grown to maturity. This may explain both Keynes's sensitivity to population matters, and the abrupt switches in his perceptions of what was happening. The real problem was that he too hastily interpreted each sudden blip as the start of a new long-run trend. Having made these allowances, one is nevertheless bound to recall that it was to the resources side of the Malthusian equation that he devoted most of his effort, and it was there that his analyses were also found wanting. His attempts to document empirically the decline in the terms of trade of manufactures were desultory and unconvincing.

There is a strong contrast between the coded advocacy of birth control in his professional writings and his vigorous public campaigning for it.[2] These partly hidden social concerns hindered rather than helped the quality of his analysis. The contribution of his support for birth control to his persistence in neo-Malthusian views has already been noted. He believed that birth control safeguarded the economic standard of living, but his concerns went wider than that. Keynes felt keenly that overpopulation could undermine the social psychology of Moorean moral idealism. He was speaking from the heart when he asked Beveridge rhetorically:

What is the use or the purpose of all our strivings if they are to be neutralised or defeated by the mere growth of numbers? Malthus' Devil . . . is a terrible devil because he undermines our faith in the real value of our social purposes, just as much now as when Malthus loosed him against the amiable dreams of Godwin. (*CW*, xix. 122)

Whatever one thinks of Keynes's social purposes, and in many ways they were admirable, one cannot help wishing that they were not so firmly in the driving seat of his population analyses. In this area of his work, and especially in the pre-1937 phases, instant prescription could have been traded off against analytical coherence with real advantage.

Despite the swings both in Keynes's understanding of the demographic facts, and the way in which he related these different understandings to capital accumulation (and sometimes also to technical change), there is one consistent thread in his thinking that can be identified. At all stages, he is concerned with the precariousness of steady growth. At first, it is the precariousness of the psychology of accumulation that threatens disaster. Then, rampant technical innovation, abruptly introduced to avert disaster, reopens the prospect of reaching the stationary state, but only if we can live with the 'disgusting morbidity' of the money motive for another hundred years and cope with technological unemployment. Finally, it is population decline that constitutes the source of upset, unless the capital–output ratio can be raised or saving depressed. Although the source of the threat varies, the prospect of economic breakdown in one form or another is Keynes's constant preoccupation. Keynes was deeply aware of the problem of uncertainty. As he put it in 'Population', 'there is hardly a feature of our economic life the long continuance of which we are justified in anticipating' (Fo. 23). In this, he was a true successor to Malthus, whose concern about the unsustainability of long-run growth he perpetuated.

In his obituary of Keynes, Schumpeter was scornful of the latter's early neo-Malthusian views. Referring to the controversy with Beveridge, Schumpeter describes it as an attempt by Keynes 'to conjure Malthus's ghost to defend (at the threshold of the period of unsaleable masses of food and raw materials) the thesis that, since somewhere about 1906 nature had begun to respond less generously to human effort and that over-population was the great problem, or one of the great problems of our time . . .' (Schumpeter, 1946). In the same vein, Schumpeter had previously remarked that 'in the second half of the nineteenth century it should have been clear to anyone that the valuable things about Malthus's law of population are its qualifications. The first decade of this century definitely showed that it was a bogey. But no less an authority than Mr Keynes attempted to revitalise it in the post-war period! . . . Will economics never come of age?' (Schumpeter, 1987/1943: 115 n. 6).

Schumpeter's criticism, fuelled as it was by professional jealousy, is no doubt too harsh. Keynes had after all dropped neo-Malthusianism before the early 1930s, which were the true years of unsaleable surpluses of food and raw materials. More telling perhaps were his criticisms of Keynes's post-recantation population work, although these were by implication rather than direct. In 1943, he considered the same problem that Keynes had discussed in his 1937 Galton Lecture—the problem of 'the vanishing of investment opportunity'. He, too, was aware of the Enid Charles projections of future population. He, too, saw that a considerable absolute decline in population would raise additional problems, because of its effect on the demand for investment.

Unlike Keynes, however, his response was to ignore such problems. He did so 'because this cannot be expected to occur during the space of time under consideration' (Schumpeter, 1987/1943: 113 n. 3). He did not feel the need to resolve the potential policy problems of every startling new population projection that came upon the scene.

On the issue of population at least, Schumpeter now seems a rather more reliable guide than Keynes. Schumpeter's obituary judgement on Keynes's population work has also stood the test of time. Compared with his writings on other long-run issues— such as the role of agriculture in development, the organization of the Soviet economy, the short-run monetary topics which were his central interest and achievement—his output on population surely does rank as 'the least felicitous of all his efforts'. To me at least, the 'element of recklessness in his makeup' seems, on the evidence surveyed here, very hard to deny. This recklessness characterizes more than simply his behaviour in the debate with Beveridge. It was already there in his Nietzschean approach to our duties to others in general, and to social policy towards colonial populations in particular. It was there after the Beveridge debate, in his unacknowledged recantation of neo-Malthusianism. His taking of population projections as forecasts of rapid and extreme shrinkage of population, and his switch to campaigning for family allowances, do not indicate a studied approach or a steady course. That Keynes was guided throughout his professional life by a single unifying vision is not a conclusion that one would draw naturally and easily after reading Keynes on population.

Does this volatility of opinion also apply to his racial views? Keynes never articulated any precise theories of race, or of racial inequality. Nevertheless, he was strongly influenced by popular attempts to apply Darwinian ideas of natural selection to human societies. He believed in an imminent competitive struggle between different 'races' of mankind. He believed that white or European 'stock' was superior in quality to all others. He believed that it was important to the highest degree that Europeans should triumph in the coming global struggle of 'races'. For him, this imperative was not an issue of morality. Indeed, it could not be so because, according to Keynes, a universal morality was an impossibility. Moreover, the conventional European morality of the day, Christianity, would, as Nietzsche had persuaded him, actively handicap those of European stock in achieving their victory.

In reality, this widespread discourse of global racial struggle was a prelude to an intra-European war of unprecedented ferocity and bloodiness. Keynes entered the world stage in its immediate aftermath, as an idealistic advocate of rational peace-making and intra-European reconciliation. It was his passionate advocacy in this cause that drew the admiration of a younger generation, some of whom had much broader global sympathies than did Keynes himself. This divergence was masked by the general contraction of the horizon of public debate in the inter-war years. Europe, and peripherally the United States and Russia, were the almost universal focus of interest. It was their unemployment, their depression, their recovery, their rearmament that mattered. The immediate dangers of Europe's situation were perhaps warrant enough for this. However, one of its results was that little evidence was generated that would throw light on the older Keynes's perspective on the world as a whole, to the point where some scholars seem to believe that he never had one. He certainly did as a young man, and it is a safe supposition that, although rarely expressed in later years, it remained much the same. Keynes himself argued that we acquire few new ideas after the age of thirty.

The lack of definition and articulation in Keynes's racial views hardly made them harmless. On the contrary, the very vagueness and looseness of racial discourse can be damaging, because of the scope this affords to irrationalism. What was evident in the inter-war years was Keynes's generalized anti-Semitism, recorded in his criticism of the 'impure Jews' in Germany. Prejudice and the habit of stereotyping were with him still, although in any scientific sense Jews are not a 'race' but a European cultural group. Keynes reassured himself contradictorily. He thought that his anti-Semitism was universal, but that others were too inhibited to admit it. At the same time, he stretched out his hand to some of the most talented of this persecuted group.

All of this leads one to see an abiding irony in Keynes's admiration for Malthus, and in his dedicated effort over twenty years to frame it on paper. It was wholly misguided in terms of his own intellectual commitments. He praised the population doctrines that Malthus was accused of by his opponents, but which Malthus persistently rejected. That is to say, in his neo-Malthusian period, he urged the need to reduce the number of people in order to raise economic welfare, he urged the beneficence of plague and famine in conditions of overpopulation, and he urged the desirability of artificial methods of limiting births. Thus what neither Malthus nor his critics were prepared to countenance in the early nineteenth century became the object of veneration to Keynes a century later.

At the level of personality, this irony speaks to Keynes's lack of familiarity with the history of economic doctrine. Despite his assiduous collection of first editions of the classic works, he was quite capable of innocently reinventing ideas that were already two centuries old. In the case of Malthus, his antiquarian approach to the history of ideas allowed him to attribute to Malthus ideas that were much more recent, and much more dubious in their origin.

At the level of ideology, this irony speaks to the immense cultural shift that the Darwinian revolution in biology had wrought on the social sciences, including economics. Many people, and not just Keynes, had come to assume that the workings of human societies could be understood through the prism of the new biology. To them, there was nothing illegitimate in interpreting the work of Malthus in this way, because Darwin himself had acknowledged it as his own inspiration. What was stripped away in this reinterpretation was the original framework of Christian religious thought, something that Keynes for his own part had already discarded. Without that, the modernized and secularized version of Malthus that Keynes propagated had no moral anchor. This imaginary Malthus had none of the intellectual subtlety or rational human sympathy of the original, and yet this was the lodestone that Keynes followed for so long.

To propose that Keynes was afflicted by a considerable coarseness of sensibility is no doubt controversial and will provoke objections from those who are interested in Keynes as a towering contemporary cultural icon. Is it not sacrilege, they will doubtless ask, to aim such criticism at a member of the cultural pantheon? This charge is groundless. It deserves not only to be rejected in the name of free enquiry, but also to be turned back on those who make it. If the question of sacrilege were to be raised, I would contend that it was committed fifty years ago. Those who successfully established Keynes as a secular saint committed it. Those who wrongly attributed to Keynes an all-embracing love of humanity committed it. Those who raised him from the status of a mere wise man to the rank of a Prophet of the Age committed it. That was the impiety. That was the hubris. That was the error that must now be redressed.

NOTES

1. I have excluded Colin Clark from my selection of representative Cambridge figures. This is not because he did not share the view that the terms of trade of manufactures were likely to decline. He did share it, forecasting that the decline would be substantial by 1960 (Clark, 1942). But this forecast was not derived from what I call here the 'Cambridge doctrine'. Clark had no time for economic doctrines. His approach was to look at the numbers, find statistical relationships between variables and then get his forecast, a procedure in which, as he later acknowledged, 'much went wrong' (Clark, 1984:

72–3). Austin Robinson's exasperated review has this to say about Clark and his research methods: 'I . . . see myself again with my head around Mr Clark's door in the Marshall Library at Cambridge, trying to get him to explain what exactly he has been doing, and being fobbed off with some quite unintelligible answer while he waits with hand poised to rattle out the next calculation on the machine' (1943: 239).

Austin Robinson was also quite clear that the violent change in the terms of trade which Clark wrongly predicted derived from his peculiar assumptions, e.g. that the USSR would become a massive importer of foodstuffs between 1945 and 1960 (ibid.: 241–2). See also the comments of Rostow (1960/1953: 189–92).

2. For details of Keynes's public work for birth control, see Sect. IV of Ch. 5 above ('Mr Keynes and Dr Stopes').

References

Ambirajan, S. (1976), 'Malthusian Population Theory and Indian Famine Policy', *Population Studies*, 30: 5–14.

Balassa, B. (1959), 'John Stuart Mill and the Law of Markets', *Quarterly Journal of Economics*, 73: 263–74.

Beveridge, W. H. (1923), 'Population and Unemployment', *Economic Journal*, 33: 447–75.

——(1924), 'Mr Keynes' Evidence for Over-population', *Economica*, 4: 1–20.

——(1943), *The Pillars of Security and Other War-time Essays and Addresses*, New York: The Macmillan Company.

——(1953), *Power and Influence: An Autobiography*, London: Hodder and Stoughton.

Bhatia, B. M. (1991/1963), *Famines in India*, Delhi: Konark Publishers Pvt Ltd.

Black, R. D. C. (1967), 'Parson Malthus, the General and the Captain', *Economic Journal*, 77: 59–74.

Bonar, J. (1966/1885), *Malthus and his Work*, London: Frank Cass.

Bowler, P. J. (1980), *Charles Darwin: The Man and his Influence*, Cambridge: Cambridge University Press.

Bowley, A. L. (1903), 'The Price of Imports and Exports of the United Kingdom and Germany', *Economic Journal*, 12: 628–32.

Brentano, L. (1910), 'The Doctrine of Malthus and the Increase of Population during the Last Decades', *Economic Journal*, 20: 371–93.

Brown, A. J. (1950), 'Problems of Under-developed Countries', *Economic Journal*, 60: 631–3.

Browne, J. (1995), *Charles Darwin: Voyaging*, London: Pimlico.

Buchanan, N. S. (1946), 'Deliberate Industrialisation for Higher Incomes', *Economic Journal*, 56: 533–53.

Budge, Seigfried (1913), 'Zum Malthus-Problem: Eine Anti-kritik', *Archiv für Sozialwissenschaft und Sozialpolitik*, 37: 930–41.

Cannan, E. (1895), 'The Probability of a Cessation of the Growth of Population in England and Wales during the Next Century', *Economic Journal*, 5: 505–15.

References

Cannan, E. (1924/1893), *A History of the Theories of Production and Distribution in English Political Economy from 1776 to 1848*, 3rd edn., London: P. S. King and Son Ltd.

Carey, J. (1992), *The Intellectuals and the Masses: Pride and Prejudice among the Literary Intelligentsia 1880–1939*, London: Faber and Faber.

Carlebach, J. (1978), *Karl Marx and the Radical Critique of Judaism*, London: Routledge and Kegan Paul.

Carpenter, S. C. (1949), *Winnington-Ingram*, London: Hodder and Stoughton.

Catanach, I. J. (1988), 'Plague and the Tensions of Empire: India, 1896–1918', in D. Arnold (ed.), *Imperial Medicine and Indigenous Societies*, Manchester: Manchester University Press.

Catephores, G. (1991), 'Keynes as a Bourgeois Marxist', UCL Discussion Paper in Economics, No. 91-23, London: University College.

Chadwick, O. (1990/1975), *The Secularization of the European Mind in the Nineteenth Century*, Cambridge: Cambridge University Press.

Chandavarkar, A. G. (1989), *Keynes and India: A Study in Economics and Biography*, Basingstoke: Macmillan.

Chandavarkar, R. (1992), 'Plague Panic and Epidemic Politics in India, 1896–1914', in T. Ranger and P. Slack (eds.), *Epidemics and Ideas: Essays on the Historical Perception of Pestilence*, Cambridge: Cambridge University Press.

Claeys, G. (1987), *Machinery, Money and the Millennium: From Moral Economy to Socialism, 1815–1860*, Cambridge: Polity Press.

Clark, C. (1942), *The Economics of 1960*, London: Macmillan.

——(1984), 'Development Economics: The Early Years', in G. M. Meier and D. Seers (eds.), *Pioneers in Development*, New York: Oxford University Press.

Cohn, G. (1912), 'The Increase of Population in Germany', *Economic Journal*, 22: 34–45.

Condorcet, A. N. de (1955/1795), *Sketch for a Historical Picture of the Human Mind*, tr. June Barraclough, London: Weidenfeld and Nicolson.

Coren, M. (1993), *The Invisible Man: The Life and Liberties of H. G. Wells*, Toronto: Random House of Canada.

Corry, B. A. (1959), 'Malthus and Keynes—A Reconsideration', *Economic Journal*, 69.

References

Cox, J. (1995), 'Keynes: An Archivist's View', *History of Political Economy*, 27 (suppl.): 163–75.

CW, The Collected Writings of John Maynard Keynes, 30 vols., Basingstoke: Macmillan, 1971–89.

Dalton, H. (1923), 'Two More Books on Population', *Economica*, 3: 224–8.

—— *The Second World War Diary of Hugh Dalton 1940–45*, ed. B. Pimlott, London: Jonathan Cape.

Danilov, V. P. (1988), *Rural Russia under the New Regime*, London: Hutchinson.

Darwin, C. (1981/1871), *The Descent of Man*, Princeton, NJ: Princeton University Press.

Darwin, F. (1995/1892), *The Life of Charles Darwin*, London: Studio Editions Ltd.

Dean, R. (1995), 'Owenism and the Malthusian Population Question, 1815–1835', *History of Political Economy*, 27: 579–97.

Desmond, A., and Moore, J. (1991), *Darwin*, London: Penguin Books.

Drysdale, C. V. (1933), 'Bradlaugh and Neo-Malthusianism', in J. P. Gilmour (gen. ed.), *Champion of Liberty: Charles Bradlaugh (Centenary Volume)*, London: C. Watts and Co.

Eltis, W. (1984), *The Classical Theory of Economic Growth*, London: Macmillan.

Evans, H. D. (1989), *Comparative Advantage and Growth: Trade and Development in Theory and Practice*, Hemel Hempstead: Harvester Wheatsheaf.

Field, J. A. (1911a), 'The Early Propagandist Movement in English Population Theory', *Bulletin of the American Economics Association*, 4th ser., 1: 207–36.

—— (1911b), 'The Progress of Eugenics', *Quarterly Journal of Economics*, 26: 1–67.

Fitzgibbons, A. (1988), *Keynes's Vision: A New Political Economy*, Oxford: Clarendon Press.

Foot, M. (1996), *H. G.: The History of Mr Wells*, London: Black Swan Books.

Freeden, M. (1979), 'Eugenics and Progressive Thought: A Study in Ideological Affinity', *Historical Journal*, 22: 645–71.

Galton, F. (1907), 'Probability: The Foundation of Eugenics', in *Essays in Eugenics*, London: Eugenics Education Society.

References

Glass, D. V. (1936), *The Struggle for Population*, Oxford: Clarendon Press.

Giffen, R. (1904), *Economic Inquiries and Studies*, 2 vols., London: George Bell and Sons.

Graham, F. D. (1923), 'Some Aspects of Protection Further Considered', *Quarterly Journal of Economics*, 37: 199–227.

Groenewegen, P. (1995), *A Soaring Eagle: Alfred Marshall 1842–1924*, Cheltenham: Edward Elgar.

Gunning, H. (1854), *Reminiscences of the University, Town and County of Cambridge from 1780*, 2 vols., London: George Bell.

Hahn, F. (1996), 'Keynes' Economics and his Present-day Critics', mimeo.

Halevy, E. (1960/1928), *The Growth of Philosophic Radicalism*, Boston: Beacon Press.

Hall, R. (1977), *Marie Stopes: A Biography*, London: André Deutsch.

Hall-Matthews, D. (1998), 'The Historical Roots of Famine Relief Paradigms', in O'Neill and Toye (1998).

Harris, J. (1977), *William Beveridge: A Biography*, Oxford: Clarendon Press.

Harrison, M. (1994), *Public Health in British India: Anglo-Indian Preventive Medicine 1859–1914*, Cambridge: Cambridge University Press.

Harrod, R. F. (1952), *Economic Essays*, London: Macmillan.

—— (1972/1951), *The Life of John Maynard Keynes*, Harmondsworth: Penguin.

Hilgerdt, F. (1945), *Industrialisation and Foreign Trade*, Geneva: League of Nations.

Hill, P., and Keynes, R. (1989) (eds.), *Lydia and Maynard: The Letters of Lydia Lopokova and John Maynard Keynes*, London: André Deutsch.

Himes, N. E. (1928), 'The Place of John Stuart Mill and of Robert Owen in the History of English Neo-Malthusianism', *Quarterly Journal of Economics*, 42: 627–40.

Himmelfarb, G. (1992), *Poverty and Compassion*, New York: Vintage Books.

Hirsch, F. (1977), *Social Limits to Growth*, London: Routledge and Kegan Paul.

Hodgson, G. M. (1993), 'The Mecca of Alfred Marshall', *Economic Journal*, 103: 406–15.

Hollander, S. (1985), *The Economics of John Stuart Mill*, 2 vols., Oxford: Basil Blackwell.

References

——(1997), *The Economics of Thomas Robert Malthus*, Toronto: Toronto University Press.

Hollingsworth, T. H. (1972) (ed.), *T. R. Malthus: An Essay on the Principle of Population*, Everyman Library, London: Dent.

Hoppen, K. T. (1998), *The Mid-Victorian Generation 1846–86*, Oxford: Oxford University Press.

Howson, S., and Winch, D. (1977), *The Economic Advisory Council 1930–1939*, Cambridge: Cambridge University Press.

Hubback, E. M. (1947), *The Population of Britain*, London: Penguin Books.

Jevons, W. S. (1965/1906), *The Coal Question*, 3rd edn., ed. A. W. Flux, New York: Augustus M. Kelley.

Johnson, E. S., and Johnson, H. G. (1978), *The Shadow of Keynes: Understanding Keynes, Cambridge and Keynesian Economics*, Oxford: Blackwell.

Kevles, D. J. (1995), *In the Name of Eugenics: Genetics and the Uses of Human Heredity*, Cambridge, Mass.: Harvard University Press.

Keynes, G. (1981), *The Gates of Memory*, Oxford: Oxford University Press.

Keynes, M. (1975) (ed.) *Essays on John Maynard Keynes*, Cambridge: Cambridge University Press.

Kingsland, S. (1989), 'Evolution and Debates over Human Progress from Darwin to Sociobiology', in Teitelbaum and Winter (1989).

Korn, E. (1998), 'Crotch and Crotchets and All', *Guardian Weekly*, 19 July.

Kuczynski, R. R. (1936), *Population Movements*, Oxford: Clarendon Press.

Lewis, A. (1966), *Development Planning: The Essentials of Economic Policy*, London: George Allen and Unwin Ltd.

List, F. (1977/1885), *The National System of Political Economy*, Fairfield, NJ: Augustus M. Kelley.

Lloyd, E. M. H. (1924), *Experiments in State Control at the War Office and the Ministry of Food*, Oxford: Clarendon Press.

Malthus, T. R. (1989/1803), *An Essay on the Principle of Population*, ed. P. James, 2 vols., Cambridge: Cambridge University Press.

——(*Works*), *The Works of Thomas Robert Malthus*, ed. E. A. Wrigley and D. Souden, 8 vols., London: William Pickering, 1986.

Mandeville, B. (1970/1714), *The Fable of the Bees*, ed. Philip Harth, Harmondsworth: Penguin.

References

Marburg, Jessie (1912), 'Die sozialökonomischen Grundlagen der englischen Armenpolitik im ersten Drittel des 19. Jahrhunderts', Ph. D. thesis, University of Karlsruhe.

Marshall, A. (1920/1890), *Principles of Economics*, 8th edn., London: Macmillan.

——(1975/1867–90), *The Early Economic Writings of Alfred Marshall 1867–1890*, ed. J. A. Whitaker, 2 vols., London: Macmillan, for the Royal Economic Society.

——(*Corr.*), *The Correspondence of Alfred Marshall, Economist*, ed. J. A. Whitaker, 3 vols., Cambridge: Cambridge University Press, 1996.

Marshall, P. H. (1984), *William Godwin*, New Haven, Conn.: Yale University Press.

Meade, J. (1948), *Planning and the Price Mechanism*, London: George Allen and Unwin.

Mill, J. S. (1904/1848), *The Principles of Political Economy*, London: Longmans, Green and Co.

——(1924/1873), *Autobiography*, Oxford: Oxford University Press.

Mitchison, N. (1979), *You May Well Ask: A Memoir 1920–1940*, London: Victor Gollancz Ltd.

Moggridge, D. E. (1992), *Maynard Keynes: An Economist's Biography*, London and New York: Routledge.

——(1993), *Keynes*, 3rd edn., Toronto: University of Toronto Press.

Munby, A. N. L. (1975), 'The Book Collector', in Keynes (1975).

Nietzsche, F. (1968/1901), *The Will to Power*, ed. Walter Kaufmann, London: Weidenfeld.

——(1994/1887), *On the Genealogy of Morality*, ed. Keith Ansell-Pearson, Cambridge: Cambridge University Press.

O'Brien, D. P. (1997), 'Marshall and his Correspondence', *Economic Journal*, 107: 1859–85.

O'Donnell, R. (1992), 'The Unwritten Books and Papers of J. M. Keynes', *History of Political Economy*, 24: 767–817.

O'Neill, H., and Toye, J. (1998) (eds.), *A World without Famine? New Approaches to Aid and Development*, London: Macmillan.

Paley, W. (1799), *The Principles of Moral and Political Philosophy*, 12th edn., 2 vols., London: R. Faulder.

Parrinder, P. (1993), 'Flying Mud', *London Review of Books*, 8 Apr., 17–18.

Petersen, W. (1964), *The Politics of Population*, London: Victor Gollancz Ltd.

References

Pigou, A. C. (1925) (ed.), *Memorials of Alfred Marshall*, London: Macmillan.
——(1962/1920), *The Economics of Welfare*, London: Macmillan.

Prebisch, R. (1950), *The Economic Development of Latin America and its Principal Problems*, New York: United Nations.

Prendergast, R. (1998), 'A Representative Man', *Cambridge Journal of Economics*, 22: 91–102.

Raffer, K. (1994), 'Disadvantaging Comparative Advantages: The Problem of Decreasing Returns', in R. Prendergast and F. Stewart (eds.), *Market Forces and World Development*, London: Macmillan.

Rahmer, B. A. (1946), 'Note on the Industrialisation of Backward Areas', *Economic Journal*, 56: 657–62.

Rathbone, E. F. (1924), *The Disinherited Family: A Plea for the Endowment of the Family*, London: Edward Arnold & Co.

Raverat, G. (1952), *Period Piece: A Cambridge Childhood*, London, Faber and Faber.

Reddaway, W. B. (1939), *The Economics of a Declining Population*, London, George Allen and Unwin.

Ricardo (*Works*), *The Works and Correspondence of David Ricardo*, ed. P. Sraffa, 11 vols., Cambridge: Cambridge University Press, 1951–73.

Robbins, L. (1927), 'The Optimum Theory of Population', in T. E. Gregory and H. Dalton (eds.), *London Essays in Economics: in Honour of Edwin Cannan*, London: George Routledge and Sons Ltd.

Robbins, L. (1978), *The Theory of Economic Policy in English Classical Political Economy*, Second Edition, Basingstoke, Macmillan.

Robertson, D. H. (1923), 'A Word for the Devil', *Economica*, 3: 203–8.
——(1963), *Lectures on Economic Principles*, London: Collins Fontana Library.

Robinson, E. A. G. (1943), review of Clark (1942), *Economic Journal*, 52: 238–42.

Robinson, J. (1978), *Collected Economic Papers*, vol. 1, Oxford: Basil Blackwell.

Ronsin, F. (1980), *La Grève des ventres*, Paris: Éditions Aubier Montaigne.

Rose, J. (1992), *Marie Stopes and the Sexual Revolution*, London: Faber and Faber.

Rostow, W. W. (1960/1953), *The Process of Economic Growth*, 2nd edn., Oxford: Clarendon Press.

Said, E. W. (1978), *Orientalism*, London: Routledge.

Sapsford, D., and Singer, H. (1998), 'The IMF, the World Bank and Commodity Prices: A Case of Shifting Sands?', *World Development*, 26: 1653–60.

Schumpeter, J. A. (1946), 'John Maynard Keynes 1883–1946', *American Economic Review*, 36: 495–518.

——(1987/1943), *Capitalism, Socialism and Democracy*, London: Unwin Paperbacks.

Singer, H. W. (1975), *The Strategy of International Development: Essays in the Economics of Backwardness*, London: Macmillan.

Skidelsky, R. (1983), *John Maynard Keynes. Hopes Betrayed, 1883–1920*, New York: Viking Penguin.

——(1992), *John Maynard Keynes. The Economist as Saviour, 1920–1937*, London: Macmillan.

Smith, Adam (1976/1776), *An Inquiry into the Nature and Causes of the Wealth of Nations*, ed. R. H. Campbell, A. S. Skinner, and W. B. Todd, 2 vols., Oxford: Clarendon Press.

——(1976/1759), *The Theory of Moral Sentiments*, ed. D. D. Raphael and A. L. Macfie, Oxford: Clarendon Press.

Soloway, R. A. (1982), *Birth Control and the Population Question in England, 1877–1930*, Chapel Hill, NC.: University of North Carolina Press.

Teitelbaum, M. S., and Winter, J. M. (1985), *The Fear of Population Decline*, Orlando, Fla.: Academic Press.

————(1989) (eds.), *Population and Resources in Western Intellectual Traditions*, Cambridge: Cambridge University Press.

Thirlwall, A. P. (1987) (ed.), *Keynes and Economic Development*, Basingstoke: Macmillan.

Titmuss, R. M. (1938), *Poverty and Population: A Factual Study in Contemporary Social Waste*, London: Macmillan.

——and Titmuss, K. (1942), *Parents Revolt: A Study of the Declining Birth Rate in Acquisitive Societies*, London: Secker and Warburg.

Townsend, J. (1971/1786), *A Dissertation on the Poor Laws by a Well-wisher to Mankind*, Berkeley: University of California Press.

Toye, J. (1993), *Dilemmas of Development*, 2nd edn., Oxford: Blackwell.

——(1997), 'Keynes on Population and Economic Growth', *Cambridge Journal of Economics*, 21: 1–26.

Toye, R. (1999), 'Keynes, the Labour Movement and 'How to Pay for the War'', *Twentieth Century British History*, 10: 255–81.

United Nations (1949), *Relative Prices of Exports and Imports of Underdeveloped Countries*, London: HMSO.

References

Ussher, R. (1897), *Neo-Malthusianism: An Enquiry into that System with regard to its Economy and Morality*, London: Methuen and Co.

von Tunzelmann, G. N. (1986), 'Malthus's "Total Population System": A Dynamic Reinterpretation', in D. Coleman and R. Schofield (eds.), *The State of Population Theory: Forward from Malthus*, Oxford: Basil Blackwell.

——(1991), 'Malthus' Evolutionary Model, Expectations and Innovation', *Journal of Evolutionary Economics*, 1: 273–91.

Waksman, S. A. (1964), *The Brilliant and Tragic Life of W. M. W. Haffkine*, New Brunswick, NJ: Rutgers University Press.

Wallace, R. (1969/1761), *Various Prospects of Mankind, Nature and Providence*, New York: Augustus M. Kelley.

Waterman, A. M. C. (1996), 'Why William Paley was "the First of the Cambridge Economists"', *Cambridge Journal of Economics*, 20: 673–86.

——(1998), 'Reappraisal of "Malthus the Economist", 1933–1997', *History of Political Economy*, 30: 293–334.

Weeks, J. (1989/1981), *Sex, Politics and Society: The Regulation of Sexuality since 1800*, London: Longman.

Weiner, M. (1991), *The Child and the State in India*, Princeton, NJ: Princeton University Press.

Wells, H. G. (1902), *Anticipations of the Reaction of Mechanical and Scientific Progress upon Human Life and Thought*, London: Chapman and Hall.

——(1905), *A Modern Utopia*, London: Thomas Nelson & Sons.

Williams, R. (1976), *Keywords: A Vocabulary of Culture and Society*, London: Fontana Press.

Winch, D. (1987), *Malthus*, Oxford: Oxford University Press.

——(1996), *Riches and Poverty: An Intellectual History of Political Economy in Britain, 1750–1834*, Cambridge: Cambridge University Press.

Wood, J. C. (1983a), *British Economists and the Empire*, London and Canberra: Croom Helm.

——(1983b) (ed.), *John Maynard Keynes: Critical Assessments*, vol. 1, London and Canberra: Croom Helm.

Woods, R. I. (1987), 'Approaches to the Fertility Transition in Victorian England', *Population Studies*, 41: 283–311.

Wright, H. (1923), *Population*, Cambridge: Cambridge University Press.

Wrigley, E. A. (1988), 'The Limits to Growth: Malthus and the Classical Economists', *Population and Development Review*, 14(suppl.): 30–48.

Index

Notes: Most references are to Keynes, who is therefore omitted as a qualifier in most entries. Page references in *italics* refer to quotations from works by Keynes. Those in **bold** indicate chapters

abstinence and chastity *37, 77,* 94,
    108, 169
acquired characteristics inherited 131,
    132, 134, 159
Africa 14, 41, 88, 162
age at marriage, *see* early *and* late
    under marriage
agnosticism 136
agriculture / manufacturing terms of
    trade 13–25, 33–5, 43, *63*, 225
    and capitalism and contraception
      (1919–36) 174, 176
    and decline of population in
      England 214–26 *passim*
    diminishing returns 14–22 *passim,*
      25, 35, 90, 91, 195, 220–2
    and 'Population' lecture *63, 109,*
      113
    see also food; terms of trade
altruism 131, 133
'America', *see* colonies; North
    America
Amos, Maurice 74
Anglicanism, *see under* Christianity
anti-semitism 159, 160
    of Keynes 139, 149–56, *154, 155,*
      231–2
    of Marshall 132, 133
Apostles, Cambridge 1
    paper to ('Egoism') 135–41,
      156
aristocracy 137
    age at marriage 39
    and contraception 49, 175

inherited wealth and
    primogeniture 124, 125
arithmetical, *see* geometrical
artificial population checks, *see*
    contraception
Attlee, Clement 207
Auriol, Vincent 78
Australia:
    birth rate decline 40
    immigration restricted 41
    marriage rate decline 39
    and terms of trade and population
      14, 23, 27, 36

'backward' areas, *see* development
Balassa, B. 191
barbarous and savage races:
    at lower end of evolution 125, 128
    Indians as 128, 146, 151
    and negative eugenics 119
    parasitic 132–3, 135
    reproduction: high rate of 145, 147,
      148, 150; low rate in future 150
    see also colonies; 'East'; race
Baring, Sir Evelyn 106
Barres, Maurice 78
Bateson, William 131, 153
Beale, Courtenay 183–4
Bedford, Bishop of 72
Bein, Alex 160
Bell, Clive 1
beneficent visitations, natural checks
    as *64,* 97–8
Bentham, Jeremy *58*

Index

Béranger, René 77
Bernstein, E. M. 156
Bertillon, Jacques 77
Besant, Annie 181
'best types':
  British as 26, 27, 133, 134
  dangers of reducing numbers of
    66
  increasing fertility, see positive
    eugenics
  less reproduction by 141–2
  marriage of 116–17
  middle class as 124–5
  white people as 26, 27, 133, 134, 148
Beveridge, William 72, 209, 210, 223,
  230
  Keynes's debate with 9, 19,
    172–80, 188, 198, 211, 227, 228,
    229
Bevin, Ernest 206–7
birth control, see contraception
birth rate, see decline; growth
bishops, Anglican, pro-natalism of
  60, 75–6, 112
Black, R. D. C. 192
Bloomsbury Group 1, 140
  see also Strachey
Blum, Léon 78
Board of Trade statistics 33–4,
  175–6
Bonar, James 81, 95–6
Bowley, A. L. 33–4, 175
Bradlaugh, Charles 181
Brentano, Lujo 30, 39, 40, 41
Briand, Aristide 78
British Columbia, see Canada
British Empire, see Empire
Brittain, Vera 184
Brooke, Rupert 149, 160
Brown, A. J. 220
Browne, Bishop George F. 76
Budge, Siegfried 80

Cadbury, George 72
Cambridge:

doctrine on terms of trade
  improvement with population
  decline 5, 9, 13, 35, 213–19; end
  of 219–26
Economic Handbooks 47, 167–8
Eugenic Society 141, 142
Keynes at 1, 2, 3
Political Economy Club 73, 170
see also Apostles
Canada 71
Cannan, Edwin:
  and decline of population in
    England 199–200, 201
  Keynes on 40, 59, 74
  and 'Population' lecture 81–2, 83,
    84, 86, 89, 112
  quotations copied by Keynes 59,
    60, 81–6
capital 228
  and diminishing returns 15
  and First World War 163, 165–6
  see also savings
capitalism and contraception
  (1919–36) **161–98**
  Beveridge, Keynes's debate with
    9, 19, 172–80, 188, 198, 227, 228,
    229
  neo-Malthusianism 8–9, 19, 161–6,
    172–80, 198, 227, 228, 229;
    recanted by Keynes 9, 187–90
  population issues (1919–23) 8–9,
    166–72
  see also Stopes
Carlisle, A. J. 72
Carpenter, Bishop William Boyd 75
categorical imperative 147
  see also Kant
Catephores, G. 190
CBC (Society for Constructive Birth
  Control and Racial Progress)
  182, 183, 184, 186–7
Chadwick, Owen 135, 152
Chamberlain, Neville 207
Chandavarkar, R. 103
changing mind, Keynes on 208, 227

development economics 5–6, 10,
217–22
devils:
  'going to the devil for the
    Universe' *138–9*
  Jews as *154*, 160
  Malthusian 8–9, 161–6
diminishing returns, law of 63, *109*,
162
  Beveridge on *177*
  raw materials *33*
  and terms of trade and population
    25–6, 28, *33*, 34, *37–8*;
    agriculture / manufacturing
    14–22 *passim*, 25, 35, 90, 91, 195,
    220–2
diseases and medical
    prevention / cure 15
  criticised 98–9, 112, 125, 128, 146
  and 'Population' lecture *64*, *65*, 99,
    100–1, 103–4
  see also plague
Drysdale, C. V. 180, 181–2, 197
dynamic theory 203, *204*

earnings of children 67, 68, 83, 108,
150
East India Company 107
'East' (*mainly* India, Egypt and
  China) 8, 10, *43*, 48, 88
  as barbarous 128, *146*, 151
  early marriage and numerous
    children 30, *39*, 49, *50*, *59*, 69
  emigration from 71
  famine and disease *64*, 99–107,
    128, 146, 157
  Keynes's lack of interest in 153
  orientalism 157
  overpopulation and population
    growth 49, *61*, *63–5*, 74, 91,
    99–108
  racial stereotypes 27, 132–3, 151
Economic Consequences of Peace, The
  (Keynes) 2–3, 8–9, 161–2, 166,
  187

and Beveridge 174, 176, 178–9, 188
Economic Handbooks, Cambridge
  47, 167–8
Economic Journal:
  Brentano article in 30
  Cohn article in 79
  Keynes as editor of 2, 79, 204
  Mandelbaum reviewed in 218
  Singer reviewed in 220
  on trade *33*, *109*, 113
'Economic Possibilities for our
  Grandchildren' (Keynes) 187
Economist's View of Population, A
  (Keynes) 76, 167, 168–9
Edgeworth, Francis Ysidro 80
education 26, 113
  of poor 10, 145, *145*
'Egoism' (Keynes) 135–41, 156
Egypt, *see* 'East'
Einstein, Albert *154*
Elderton, Ethel 29, 132
Eltis, W. 19
emigration 134, 147
  and 'Population' lecture (1914) 71,
    105, 107, 111
  restricted 29, *41*, 71, 111
  and terms of trade and population
    15, 18, 22–3, 24, 26–7, 34–5, 36
  to England 155, 211–12
  see also colonies *and under* North
    America
Empire 75–6
  see also colonies; India
Empson, Sir William *55*
'End of Laissez-Faire, The' (Keynes)
  181
environmental influence on children
  132, 134
Essay on Principle of Population, see
  Malthus
Essays in Biography (Keynes) 190
Essays on Economic Future of World
  (Keynes) proposed 166–7
Essays in Persuasion (Keynes) 154
Eugenic Societies 141, 142

Index

and rapid multiplication of unfit:
anti-semitism 149–56, 160, 231–2;
on Malthus on Darwin 119–23,
137; morality/ethics 135–41; *see
also* Greg
see also capitalism and
contraception; decline of
population; lectures; Malthus;
population; 'Population' lecture;
rapid multiplication; terms of
trade
Keynes, John Neville (JMK's father)
1, 52, 144, 159
Keynes, Lydia (JMK's wife) 46, 155,
183, 190
Kidd, Benjamin 131
Kitchener, Lord Horatio Herbert 65

labour 15, 163
Labour Movement and trade unions
178, 206–7
laissez-faire 116, 128, 130, 181
Lamarck, Jean/Lamarckianism 130,
131, 132, 134
Lambeth Conferences 76, 185
land, fixed supply of 13, 15
Lang, Archbishop Cosmo Gordon 76
Lannelongue, Professor 78
Layton, W. T. 72
lectures:
of 1912 by Keynes (on population)
7, 29–34, 50, 162–3; and Darwin
119–20; extracts from notes for
37–43; and Greg problem 144,
145; reformulated and expanded,
see 'Population' lecture (1914)
of 1914 by Keynes, *see* 'Population'
lecture
and Greg problem 129
see also Galton Lectures
Lewis, A. 195
Lewis, Wyndham 145
Leybourne, G. C. 200, 201
liberalism 119, 171
liberty and reproductive instinct 121

List, Friedrich 78–9
Liston, Glen 103
Locke, John 58
lower classes and reproduction:
decreasing, *see* negative eugenics
marriage rate 39
prevention/contraception 49–50,
69, 95, 118, 143–4, 146, 156
rapid 31, 41, 75, 145, 159, 178
and weak surviving 126
see also barbarous; feeble-minded;
race; rapid multiplication of
unfit; social support
Lucretius 72, 121
luxuries, love of (as population
check) 16, 85–6

Malthus, Daniel (father of Thomas)
48, 54, 56, 72
Malthus, Thomas Robert (and
Keynes):
and Corn Law support 16–17
and Darwin, *see under* Darwin,
Charles
and demand, lack of effective 8,
190–7, 195–6
and eugenics 29
final homage to 204
and geometrical and arithmetical
ratios 37, 60, 87, 89, 112
irony of Keynes's admiration for
232–3
and Jevons 24
Keynes's *Essay* on 8, 44–5, 48,
190–1, 197
life and family 53–5
and Marshall 26, 28
and Mill, J. S. 20, 22
muddled on economics, says
Harrod 191–2
and 'Population' lecture 57, 58,
88–99; contraception 94–5;
discarding principles 60, 89;
ignored 60, 80; published
version 44, 48; subsequent

Index

and Keynes 123, 135–41
relativism 123
and Social Darwinism 136
see also goodness
Morison, Sir Theodore 113
mortality, *see* death rate
Morton, Cardinal 204
Murray, Gilbert 72
My Early Beliefs (Keynes) 140

natalism, *see* pro-natalists
Nation / Nation and Athenaeum 153,
171, 177, 184–5
National Birth Control Council
186
nationalism, *see* patriotism
nationality and race confused 126,
151
natural checks on population:
as beneficent visitations 64, 97–8
and capitalism and contraception
(1919–36) 162, 169–70, *179*, *180*
diminished by social action, *see*
social support
and 'Population' lecture (1914) 101,
104–7
replacement of *169–70*; *see also*
contraception
see also disease; famine
natural selection 149
anxiety about weakening, *see*
Social Darwinism
failure in civilized nations, *see*
Greg problem
perverse operation of *30–1*, *41*, 49,
50
see also Darwin; struggle for
existence
Nazis 155
negative eugenics 116, 117–19, 156,
181, 205
coercive 118, 141–4
neo-Malthusians, *see under*
Malthusianism
'new countries', *see* colonies

New Generation League 182, 187
New Republic article 153–4
New Zealand 14, 23
Nietzsche, Friedrich 135–6, 137, 139,
159, 230, 231
North America (mainly United
States):
contraception in 47, 182
decline, population *40*
emigration to 22–3, 27, 41, 212,
224; restricted 41, 71, 111
food *63*; exports to Britain 17, 22,
27, 32, 43, 92, 162–3, 174–5
growth, population *38*, *41*, *67*, 112;
emigration to 22–3, 27, 41
and Keynes's anti-semitism 153–4,
155–6
loan from 4
manufacturing 217
marriage rate decline *39*
New Deal 221
post-war 231
race discourse: danger of USA
becoming black *41*; Keynes's
anti-semitism 153–4, 155–6, 160
standard of life 188
Norway 57

O'Brien, D. P. 134
obscenity, *see* pornography
O'Donnell, R. 9, 30, 166, 181
'old countries' 14, 15
see also Europe
optimum population, *see* ideal
orientalism 157
see also 'East'
Otter, Bishop William 54, *55*, 56, *58*, 74
Owen, Robert 68, 95–6, 112

Paley, Archdeacon William *55*, *58*, 60,
74, 81, 84
paradox, isolation 110–11
parasitic races 132–3, 135, 151–2, 154,
159
Paris Peace Conference 2–3, 161

Index

Parrinder, P. 160
patriotism and nationalism 49, 50, 151
  German 78
  and militarism 66, 70–1
  and procreation 60, 66, 109, 110
Pearson, Karl 29, 132, 141–2
Petersen, W. 7, 80, 167
philanthropy, democratic 60
Philosophical Radicals 95, 98
Pigou, A. C. 143, 204
  and sterilization 144, 156–7
Pitt, William, the Younger 55, 58, 59, 74, 81, 84
Place, Francis 96
plague 99, 100–1, 146
  prophylactic against 64, 101–4
Plato 118
policy, see public policy
political economy:
  classical 13–16, 59, 60
  Political Economy Clubs 53, 73, 170
poor, see lower classes
Poor Laws, see social support
population:
  Keynes on, see capitalism and contraception; decline of population; lectures; 'Population' lecture; rapid multiplication; terms of trade
  numbers, see decline; growth
  thinking before Malthus 80–8
'Population' lecture (1914) 2, 7–8, 10, **44–74**, 162–3, 180, 229
  on barbarous races 146
  and Darwin 119–20
  and Greg problem 129
  and racial wars 140
  reader's guide 50–1
  rewritten in 1930s 190, 191, 197
  summary of argument 48–50
  on terms of trade 63, 109, 113
  text 53–72; found years later 46, 190

  see also commentary on 'Population' text
pornogaphy / obscenity, contraception information as 68, 77–8, 182–3
positive checks, see natural checks
positive eugenics 116–17, 133, 205
Prebisch, Raúl 223–4, 225
predation and survival of fittest 121
predictions, see projections
prejudice:
  against 'unfit', see rapid multiplication of unfit
  anti-semitism 149–56
  see also race
Price, Richard 86
prices, export and import 33, 34, 219–20
probability 141
progressive evolution 134
projections / future:
  population 175, 199, 200–3, 210
  subsistence increase 61, 91
pro-natalism 49, 50, 206
  in 1940s 9, 208–13
  family allowance as 210
  motherhood promoted 171–2
  opposed, see contraception
  patriotic, see procreation *under* patriotism and nationalism
  and 'Population' text 60, 75–80, 81–6, 112
prosperity:
  as exceptional Victorian episode 163, 164, 168, 187, 188–9
  increase and fertility decline 30, 31–2, 39–40, 42, 82
  level 42
providence, divine 94, 97–9
public policy and Greg problem
  of coercive negative eugenics 141–4
  remedy at home and abroad 144–8
Punjab 64, 99–101, 102

Index

Index